〜

Alone with
Michelangelo

Alone with
Michelangelo

A Woman Follows Her Dreams to Italy

Marlene Hill

Paintings by Deanna Hunt

Frank Amato Publications, Inc.

P.O. Box 82112, Portland, Oregon 97282

503·653·8108 • www.amatobooks.com

Watercolors by Deanna Hunt

Map by Kathy Johnson

Book & Cover Design: Kathy Johnson

Cover painting: La Piazza (Piazza Navona) by Deanna Hunt

Printed in Hong Kong

Hardbound ISBN: 1-57188-237-5   UPC: 0-66066-00491-8

1 3 5 7 9 10 8 6 4 2

Dedication

To George, always.

~

Thanks

I want to thank my editor Kim Koch
at Frank Amato Publications for her excellent help,
and to Kathy Johnson, also at Frank Amato
Publications for her delightful design of this book and
her upbeat patience every step of the way.
To Giuseppe Spagnolo of Florence, Italy,
my warm gratitude—"*sempre*"—for helping me
polish my inelegant Italian.
To Thorn and Ursula Bacon for
their persistent encouragement along with
Thorn's assistance with the book proposal way back when.
To my first critique group around the long table
at the library in Salem, Oregon who gave me
invaluable insights when I began, and to
my current critique group in Portland, Oregon,
who have been my cheerleaders
all the while reminding me when
my sentences were in a muddle.
Thanks to my sons Mike, Bill and Jim—"grown men"
scattered across the country—
who watched from afar giving me their support
even though it may have been
"just one more crazy thing Mom was doing."
And last but not least,
thanks to my girlfriends—
also scattered across the country and
around the world—
who never doubted me for a moment.

THANKS EVERYBODY

Milan

Verona

Vicenza

Po River

Padua

Venice

Bologna

Pisa

Florence

N

W

E

S

Arno River

ENLARGED AREA

Siena

Arezzo

Milan

Venice

Chiusi

Pisa

Florence

Orvieto

Tiber River

ROME

Viterbo

Naples

Tarquinia

Cerveteri

ROME

Table of Contents

Map · page 6

PART III:

Siena's Horse Race and Orvieto's Tombs

PART IV:

Roma!
page 206

An inviting doorway in the Tuscan countryside.

PART I:
Starting Out

CHAPTER ONE

A fine Italian malady: a fever that won't go away.
The first time in Rome.
A glance at Padua. Italians make art of everything.
The Passeggiata.

I'VE BEEN IN ITALY MANY TIMES, THE LAST WAS 2001, BUT
on my first visit, a romantic fever struck me and it has never left.
By the time my Italian sickness was diagnosed, it was too late for
a cure. Although I die a little every day I'm away, the truth is I
don't want to get well. One way to bring the fever down is to go
back to Italy, but the relief lasts only a short while. From the first,
I knew I wanted to stay. The attraction was so strong that later I
wondered if I had belonged to that soil in another time. Certainly
W. Somerset Maugham understood these feelings of nostalgia
when he wrote in *The Moon and Sixpence*, "Sometimes a man hits
upon a place to which he mysteriously feels that he belongs. Here
is the home he sought, and he will settle amid scenes that he has
never seen before, among men he has never known, as though they
were familiar to him from his birth. Here at last he finds rest."

My first visit to Italy was more than thirty years ago when my
former husband and I traveled there in a sweltering August for his
first international physics conference. He was nervous about presenting his work at such a prestigious meeting. Nuclear physicists
from many countries, including those from the Union of Soviet
Socialist Republics, gathered at the venerable University of Padua,
but our trip began in Rome.

As the bus from the airport carried us into the torrid city, the
first thing I noticed was Roman women walking bare legged without girdles. They looked good; they looked real, jiggles and all.
After being pinched into a 1960s-style panty girdle for the

fourteen hours it took us to reach the Eternal City, their openness was a seductive contrast to the tightness back home.

Our fashion mavens dictated that even the young, slim women in the States should present unnatural, compact posteriors to the world. And we believed them! What would people think if we walked down the street with our natural female hip movements showing?

When World War II was over in 1945, women, who had worked in all capacities while the men were away, were herded back into their homes. Women's magazines, radio and burgeoning television shows all told them that *now* their important role was to serve their husbands, produce babies and delicious hot meals. And, of course, to dress appropriately. When I married in 1950, I too had suc-cumbed wholeheartedly to the propaganda that total happiness was in being a "wife." My own goals had been forgotten; instead, those energies were directed toward my husband's career. There were times, however, when dark broodings came over me, but I never shared them with other young mothers, my own Mother, or anyone. They stirred my very soul. I feared that my real self was gone. Sometimes I felt as if my life was over, that I would always be stuck in the role of household drudge, of perpetual Mommy, or of being the proper helpmate who entertained with a smile and patiently listened to bores at departmental parties, always ready to play seductress when my mate remembered I was there.

After watching those Italian women, their bare feet shod in open-toed sandals, dazzling with colored glass "gems" across the instep and with tiny, curved heels, who managed to walk graceful-ly over uneven pavements and cobbled streets, my head was turned one hundred eighty degrees before my own feet ever touched the Roman streets. I was enthralled, and while in Rome I did as the Romans did, I wore dazzling sandals and jiggled.

How free and accepting they were about their bodies. Later, along the coast road north from Rome, I saw all sizes and shapes of bikinis parading beside the sea, not just the Playboy-magazine types. Hardly anyone at home was wearing a bikini. I knew no one with a bikini, it was too risqué except for those in Hollywood, but for ordinary women, the bikini had not arrived. Like many Americans abroad for the first time, travel to a European country generated thoughts of what it meant to be an American, in my case, one from the reactionary, insular plains state of Nebraska. Growing up with parents who knew almost nothing about their roots and didn't care, I was envious of these Italians and their long histories. If someone took me for an Italian, I was flattered and secretly wished for some long-lost connection.

I'll never know exactly why it was love at first sight, but my passion for Italy may have been kindled at the outset because our first few days were spent in old-world luxury. Ignorance on the part of our travel agent and ourselves had resulted in our being booked into a room with a private bath at The Villa Hassler which crowned the Spanish Steps.

Our window offered a choice view of the city looking out over the rooftops of Rome. In the golden light of a summer evening, which lasted until ten or eleven, each dome and spire and chimney pot was etched against the glowing sky. In the cool mornings, from their window boxes and patio tubs, bright red and pink geraniums splashed their colors against the earthy tones of peeling stuccoed buildings. Late into the night, while my husband slept, I stood looking from our window down onto the top tier of the Spanish Steps where clusters of young people were talking, laughing and jabbing at each other. Over in a shadowy corner a boy in a white, long-sleeved shirt curled his arms around his girl and held her close. They sat astride the stone banister facing each other, her bare legs wrapped around his black-trousered ones, and one white, high-heeled sandal looked like the point at the bottom of a question mark. As I watched, there was no question that they were entwined in a delicious embrace; I was envious and couldn't leave that window until dawn.

The bathtub was seven feet long and three feet deep, the towels were thick, plushy royal robes as big as bed sheets; the bedspreads were of heavy satin; and the window had two sets of shutters forming an alcove four feet deep keeping the room quiet and cool. All this for $30 a night. Later, when we found we could have booked into a small pensione with shared baths for $5, we fretted that we had used the wrong travel agent.

How much would that room cost today? On a visit in 1990, I decided to find out. In wrinkled red blouse and black cotton slacks and black cork-lined sandals on my feet, I entered the polished interior of the Villa Hassler. A gorgeous young woman with sleek, dark hair swept back from her smooth, olive skin, wearing gold on her ears, throat, arms and fingers, said with a purr, *"La camera che dà sulle scale costa 427,500 lire, signora."* As I pushed the gleaming brass handle on the polished wooden door leading back to the top of the stairs, *le scale*, I realized that our room overlooking the steps would now rent for $285 a night.

On that earlier 1962 trip, I was thrilled again and again by meeting one more fountain in one more piazza around one more corner. Surprising juxtapositions of the ancient and the modern enchanted me, and we meandered through Rome for too few days before heading north for the conference. We drove up the western coast in a little Fiat 600 that wheezed a bit but never once sputtered or coughed to a stop. We turned inland toward Pisa to see its famous bell tower. In the 1960s, people were allowed to walk around and around on the seven-hundred-year-old marble steps to its top. Our moments spent at that magnificent complex of white, white buildings on green, green grass were a pleasant muddle because we had to hurry on to Padua skipping past Florence entirely.

For years afterward, Padua too, hung around the edges of my memory as a mysterious muddle. It had an eastern flavor with domed churches and confusing alleys that curved around brooding university buildings. Especially mysterious was a strange park-like area called The Prato near our room in a student dormitory. *Il Prato della Valle*, The Meadow of the Valley, was an enormous elliptical-shaped green area with a thick forest of tall, dark pines hovering over white statues that seemed to be guarding its circumference. If we got ourselves lost late at night, when we saw the ghostly statues looming ahead, we knew we were almost home. In the mornings, we must have exited in a different direction because I kept forgetting to find out who those odd figures represented. Later, I learned The Prato had been a racetrack for community festivals, possibly similar to the famous bareback race still held in Siena. When the city fathers decided to forego the races, these statues were erected to memorialize outstanding men of Padua, probably some of whom were those same decision makers.

Maybe the confusion was because we were both in a state of anxiety for much of our stay in Padua. He was nervous about his first big presentation which never happened after all because he was one of several younger participants from the West who were bumped from the agenda by a group of Russian scientists who came in unannounced—never having submitted their proposals to the organizing committee—but who insisted on giving their papers. Naturally, he was disappointed.

We had a tantalizing glimpse of the ancient little city. Memories of golden-domed churches and dark streets lined with endless arcades were fused somehow with those ghostly figures encircling The Prato. All were stored away for another time.

Maybe my infatuation for all things Italian was because Italians seem to know how to make art out of everything they do. They know how to savor small things and live in the moment. On a train that summer, two gentlemen sat across the aisle. One with olive skin and sparse brown hair was stuffed into a shiny, brown suit much too tight and much too worn. He had a large, bulbous nose and full lips which, in profile, reminded me of one of the marble busts from ancient Rome we'd seen in the Museo Borghese. The other was thin with a long, narrow nose and chin and ebony eyes set back under heavy black brows in a chalky white face. He had long, slender hands and long, pointed black shoes matching his once-elegant black suit. The slender one gently drew a perfect, golden pear from his bag, and using the foldout tray just below his window for stability, he carefully peeled the pear. Taking off the thinnest amount of skin possible; he sliced it into fragrant strips which looked like petals of a flower. He offered the first petal to his companion and slowly they consumed every single glistening bite. Never have I enjoyed a pear as much as I did watching them eat theirs.

~

Could my passion for Italy have been sparked by the evening *passeggiata*? People don't stroll much in the States anymore, but in every city, town and village in Italy, along about five or six in the afternoon, the streets reawaken from siesta. Shops open, people come out from behind quiet doors, and by seven the main streets are packed with people walking up and down, up and down. Families with toddlers and baby carriages window shop together. Youths walk in groups; girls flirt with boys as they pass each other again and again, often joining together in the middle of the piazza in noisy banter. The boys ogle the girls in rather naive ways—a bit too loud, a bit too silly. Young lovers walk arm in arm or cuddle in corners of the grand old buildings, all under the accepting eyes of everyone else. Old folks chat and greet each other like long-lost friends. A few years later in Volterra, one of the tiny hill towns of Tuscany, I noticed the same people greeting each other eagerly every night. Sometimes last-minute shoppers dashed out before the evening meal, but the main purpose was to socialize, to touch hands and shoulders in brief hugs, for about a half hour, and then move on.

In larger towns where people are more sophisticated, it's like a huge cocktail party. In Rome, Via del Corso closes to vehicles each evening. During the day, Corso flows in fits and starts with many honking horns and drivers shouting insults and waving their arms at each other, but for these few hours, people walk to and fro as if they too were back in a small village. Even in their largest city, Italians insist on perpetuating that strong sense of community developed in their city-states centuries before. After all, those city-states were not united into one Italy until 1870.

The open sharing and physical contact between the old and the young, men and women, women and women, and even between men and men was something I enjoyed vicariously. I desperately wanted that closeness and intimacy for myself. Yet, back home it was out of the question; there I had grown up with a different example—my husband too. I had to sort out my joys and sorrows behind closed doors and keep all personal affairs walled up inside the house, inside the psyche, and even walled from other members of the family.

~

When our time was up, the days and nights had blurred. I felt rushed, confused and filled with a kind of gloom. We had pictures and mementos to carry back with us, but a heavy melancholy settled around my shoulders something like Grandma's horsehair blanket which she wrapped around me to sweat out the croup. Something had happened to me in Italy that was not rational. Those germs couldn't be sweated out because a part of me knew I had come "home."

~

CHAPTER TWO

Grandma, why Italy again? It's my spiritual home.
Why all alone? To reinvent myself.

THOSE GERMS LAY DORMANT FOR YEARS WHILE MY children grew up, my marriage broke apart, and a new life began. During those years, I had a chance to travel other places enough to realize my passion for Italy was not because I hadn't been anywhere else, it was because Italy had taken me hostage from the very first. It seemed my nose was always stuck in books about Rome's history and art, or Etruscan history and art, or Florence's history and art. I even preferred novels and mysteries set in Italy. Like most avid readers, I had several books going at the same time and they lay all about the house or in the car. For some reason this irritated my Mother.

"You're always reading about Italy, what's so great about Italy?"

Nevertheless, a travel system was taking shape, and I made notes and lists, and revised lists, to remind me of where to go and what to take. Whenever the subject came up, my parents whined, "You've been there, why do you need to go again?"

For a time, my line of defense was that if there were an emergency, I could be back in a day.

Sometimes, I slipped into a whine myself. Still, they didn't understand. It became a touchy subject; until finally I said, "You may as well get used to it, I'm going back as often as I can, and as long as I'm able."

They got it, but never quite admitted to it, and their complaints continued.

One afternoon my grandson, Frankie, asked, "Hey Grandma, what's so great about Italy?"

How does one explain one's passion for an old place with old buildings filled with old art to someone whose idea of heaven would be to leap speed bumps on his daredevil bike forever? I had tried giving rational answers to adults. I had talked about the wealth of art, the glorious history, and the magnificent architecture. To others, I'd tried romantic answers about the warmth of the people, their respect for art and music, food and wine, but it's only other adventurers with their own passions who truly understand.

There are no blood ties, no "acceptable" connections that pull me back. Certainly passion has never been acceptable for anyone reared in the WASP tradition where even a belly laugh was suspect. But, spiritually, Italy is where I feel grounded. In the end, I have no proof nor legitimacy for feeling connected; it is a simple knowing.

Chloe, a granddaughter who would read the dictionary if nothing else were available, asked, "Why do you travel all alone, Grandma?" Her question was easier to answer.

If I am alone, I notice more. I read local signboards posted around a city and pick up a feel for what the place is about. I get more practice speaking the language. I get to figure out the money system or the bus and train systems, all the practical things that help me feel involved.

When traveling with a companion, the relationship takes precedence and absorbs a huge amount of my energy. Conversing in our own language has a way of wrapping us in a comfortable cocoon. But when I immerse myself in a different culture, my parameters for thinking change. Old notions and judgments come with me, of course, but if alone, I'm more likely to speculate about different ways I could live my own life. Every so often an amazing insight opens a brand new door. Sometimes an insight closes an old door.

It may seem frivolous but taking off that girdle made an impact on my psyche. I admit to squeezing into it again when I got home, but the notion that other shackles in my life might be more illusion than reality was like a seed that took root. Through the years, it grew bit by bit.

Finishing a meal with salad rather than starting with one seemed like an affectation to friends who came to dinner parties after I'd been to Italy. Salads are more refreshing at the end of a meal and easier on the digestion, I argued. Soon they accepted it as one of those crazy Italian ideas I'd brought back with me. The salad thing was a paltry start, yet it was a first step which helped move me toward a significant change in the way I looked at everything.

"Chloe," I said, "I think I travel alone for selfish reasons."

When in Italy, I'm like a kid in a candy store with one quarter to spend. There is so much from which to choose. The question is always, what to do first? What to save till last? My time there is like that precious quarter burning a hole in my pocket. It will stretch just so far, and I don't want to waste a moment shopping for someone else's Aunt Grace rather than looking at the powerful knee of Michelangelo's *Moses*.

Alone I can tramp until I drop or laze at a coffee bar for hours. I can walk or take the bus, go to bed early or read half the night. I can drop into a museum or a restaurant, take one look around and if it doesn't suit, drop right out again—with no negotiation required.

Perhaps most of all, I relish walking into an anonymous place, closing the door behind me knowing I have no predetermined responsibilities. The physical and mental challenges of traveling alone stimulate some forgotten energy. Tackling those challenges regenerates my self esteem. Maybe I go to reinvent myself.

⌢

CHAPTER THREE

I stay in small hotels as the Europeans do.
Six travel rules.

IT WAS A HAPPY MISTAKE TO BOOK INTO THAT ELEGANT hotel all those years ago, but it's much more interesting to do as the Europeans do. They avoid the luxury hotels to save money, of course, but also to feel closer to the real Italy. Europeans stay in small, family-owned hotels without private bathrooms or classy amenities, and no one cares how they dress or whether they're properly escorted. The staff in small hotels are usually more enthusiastic about their establishment and city than those in luxury hotels or American franchises. In a plush hotel, I feel isolated from the very culture I've come to see.

Except for a small number of men who think a single woman, no matter her age, is there solely for them, the truth is, tourists bore most Italians. Even lone women are not an interesting fact or in their lives. And, how do they know for sure whether I am alone? My companion could be off in another direction or meeting me later on. Only my concierge knows for sure and she hasn't batted an eye at travelers' eccentricities for years—maybe centuries.

Some say that European inner cities are safer for lone female travelers than inner cities in the States because middle-class Europeans haven't fled to the suburbs. The rich, historic centers in Italy are not deserted at night. People live there. They are out and about. Italians may be frugal with lighting inside their homes, and certainly most small hotels use low-wattage bulbs in their rooms, but they all believe in lighting up their streets and alleyways. Of course, I don't go to questionable areas in Italy any more than I would at home, but I've walked back to my room from a concert as late as midnight in Rome. It might not be a lazy stroll at that hour, but it isn't with a pounding heart either.

One way to increase one's safety as well as be able to melt into the background to observe how things work is to be inconspicuous. I dress in loose-fitting clothes, carry no purse, and wear no noticeable jewelry, although a wedding ring may help avoid unwanted attention from men. By becoming almost invisible, I feel comfortable watching instead of worrying about being watched. It also helps to act as if I know where I'm going. I may, however, stop to consult a map; tourists with maps are as ubiquitous in Italy as the Roman spigots left running in small squares and alleys. I don't notice them until I want a drink, and people with maps aren't noticed unless they seek help.

In such a popular tourist country, seldom does anyone come running to help me decipher my outspread map; that's fine with me. It's more fun to figure it out. If I do ask directions, I'll find a willing guide. In a city, it may only be a gesture in the right direction. In a village, I may have a guide all the way to the corner or to my destination.

When I'm alone, I'm more apt to pay attention to the business of being safe fiscally. No matter how often I travel, I'm always a bit "green." The moment I'm distracted by the complexities of a bus system or come upon something stupendous is the very moment I am most vulnerable to predators. I think I've worked out a good travel system. It gives me peace of mind and frees me to just be there. If anyone would ask, my advice would be to set up a system that works for the individual, then keep it simple, and stick to it. My system has six rules that work for me:

1. Carry money in a belt under my clothes.
2. Take only what I can carry myself.
3. Take one good guide book.
4. Check bags at station before finding a hotel.
5. Use the toilet every time I pay for food or drink.
6. Assume nothing. Ask, ask, and ask again.

Money. Money stays around my waist *under* my clothes except in the shower or in bed. What's to keep someone from cutting the belt of a fanny pack and vanishing into the crowd? A soft, cloth money belt holds it all: my return tickets, passport, travelers' checks, extra cash, and credit cards. This way, I become my own walking safe deposit box and the control and freedom I feel is priceless. A pouch hanging from a string around the neck works too, but it's not easily accessed in public. With a waist belt, I can melt into the woodwork and reach under my blouse or sweater to retrieve what I need. At a bank or money exchange, I've learned to wait until I step up to the counter to reach for my passport and travelers' checks. The bank counter or desk seems to be sacred; it is the one place where Italians stand back and give me space. After the transaction, I stay right there until everything is snugly back in its place. No one complains. In spite of the received information that Italians are happy go lucky and carefree, they are frugal, practical folks and respect others who take care of business.

I use quiet, casual movements which don't draw attention to myself, and I never work with the belt out on the street. One can always tell just where other tourists keep their money because they invariably pat the pocket to make sure. Sometimes I forget I'm wearing the belt, but I needn't pat myself, instead I press my elbows to my waist for reassurance. My walking-around money goes into deep, front pockets of skirt or slacks, one for bills, the other for coins. I'm trusting that pickpockets can't reach into my front pockets without my knowing it. I don't even think about using a rear pocket or an inside jacket pocket.

When I pull a bunch of lire notes out of my front pocket, however, they sometimes look like last year's bird nest, partly because they vary in size and color according to worth and partly because the paper is thin and crumply. A small wallet will bulge and bang against my thigh when I walk, and I've tried using a money clip or even a jumbo paper clip. The paper clip slips off and the money clip fits too tightly. And, I can hear my Grandpa talking about uppity folks with fancy money clips. My solution is five-by-three-inch note cards. I fold a couple cards around the bills for stability without bulge; an added advantage is that I can write phone numbers or do a fast bit of arithmetic on them.

After my first train trip, I have an even better tool because most train tickets are of card stock about the same size as lire notes. A sturdy rubber band holds it all together. Grandpa would approve. When I pull off the rubber band and slip it over my wrist in order to pay for something, no one is shocked. Maybe the Italian shopkeepers are too polite to comment, but who cares what they say after I've gone on my way?

In the hotel, the money belt goes down the hall with me to the toilet or shower—always. In bed it gets shoved down to my feet, not under the pillow. I sleep soundly, but my theory is that clever thieves couldn't get it from between the sheets without waking me.

Baggage. There's no exception to this rule, I take only what I and I alone can manage. That's it. One carry-on bag and a large, sturdy knapsack which can serve for extras or for side trips when I've settled in one place for a few days. Color coding my clothing simplifies matters. For me, it's black. Black silk turtleneck shirt as a first layer, black v-neck or pullover sweater with a cardigan to serve as a light jacket or a bed jacket. Two or three colored scarves to "accessorize," and maybe a bright shirt or sweater helps break the monotony for myself—who else would care? Italy offers a wide selection of clothing and a sweater or scarf bought there is the best souvenir because I will use it over and over.

If you go to shop, my rules won't work for you. It takes discipline to not accumulate too much for the return trip. I've often been tempted to ship excess purchases home, but so far have managed to avoid that hassle. Italian postal regulations are complex and laden with bureaucratic nuances. Once I did buy too many books. I boxed them in a Mexican beer carton found outside a store early before the trash man arrived. It tickled me to tote books bought in the Old World in a box originated in the New one. By taping it securely and fashioning a handle out of heavy twine, I managed to lug it to the airport and check it through. Years later, in Florence, I discovered a shop designed for wrapping packages to conform to postal regulations. They do a good job for a small fee. The postal charges are another story.

On the flight, I wear either black slacks or a black skirt—both with deep front pockets. I take a black blazer and a raincoat with wool liner which don't need to be packed. I wear the jacket and lash the coat to my suitcase with a bungee cord. Long silk underwear serves as pajamas and as an extra layer for bitter weather. Silk dries quickly and takes little room in the suitcase.

It's incredible how quickly the lightest bag picks up tonnage. After trying several variations for a couple of years, I eventually followed the lead of flight attendants and invested in a bag with the wheels built in. Now, they're everywhere and for good reason. You can forget all about taking an inexpensive, down-to-earth trip in small, charming hotels if you bring more than you can carry. They have no porters and few elevators. You can also forget about traveling on Italy's convenient train system if you insist on lots of luggage. It's too hard, too stressful and you're defeated before you begin.

Guidebook. By trial and error I've found that one choice guidebook is well worth its weight in my knapsack. One method I did try—but only once—was to take notes compiled from several sources so that when I left a location, I tossed the notes with abandon and lightened my load. The disadvantage of this method was having to shuffle a lot of separate papers, and invariably, I omitted critical information that hadn't seemed important when creating the notes back home.

There are a multitude of good guides available aimed at all pocketbooks and points of view, but a young woman in Verona introduced me to *Let's Go Italy* compiled by Harvard students with economy in mind. It's my favorite. It has the added enticement of being humorous without being cutesy, and it drops interesting tidbits that some of the more staid guides don't mention. One was a warning about a temperamental old woman of Cortona. She guarded two glorious works by Luca Signorelli. They were mounted back-to-back on a mechanized altarpiece in a sixteenth-century church too small to display both at the same time. Only she knew where the switch to operate the apparatus was and she savored her power.

Check Bags at Train Station Before Finding Hotel. If I do it, I won't make a poor choice of hotel simply because I can't manage my bags another step.

Toilet. This rule seems obvious but is often forgotten. If I pay for a coffee or a lunch, I use their toilet. This rule has everything to do with how pleasant each day will be; my feet and back may tire and there may be times when it's too warm or too cold, but with a full bladder my mind shuts down completely. In Italy, "attended" public facilities are clean, well-lighted places and cost a pittance, but they're few and far between. Large department stores offer good restrooms; most museums have pleasant restrooms which can sometimes be used without entering the museum proper, otherwise, if I pay, I get to pee.

Ask, And Ask Again. Even at home we need to ask how something works: Where to get off the bus? Where a repair shop is? Do I have to change trains? In Italy, things can change arbitrarily so I ask and then ask someone else the same question again. It's good to let those around me know what I need. When there's an announcement over the loud speaker that the track number has changed for the train to Roma, what to do if I don't understand the announcement? If I've already asked a bystander or two if this track is for Roma, I'll be okay. When I couldn't speak more than a few words of Italian, I could at least say, "Roma?" with a question on my face. Then, if there *were* an announcement, someone would rescue me because travelers help other travelers; they feel good because they've done a good deed, and I feel good because I've been rescued from hours of delay. The times I played it cool and didn't ask were the times I got to feel sorry for myself.

⟜

CHAPTER FOUR

Milan, a rough start. Already, two rules are broken.
Leonardo's Last Supper. *Caffè Americano.*
Rubber stamps, the soul of Italian bureaucracy.
In this cold, impersonal city, individuals offer warmth.

AFTER SO MANY YEARS AWAY FROM ITALY, I WONDERED IF
starting out in rugged Milan was a mistake. My ultimate goal for
that first trip alone was Rome, but my reasoning for touching
down in Milan was that Padua was not far away. Mysterious Padua
had haunted me through the years with its eastern domes and
shadowy arcades. But, landing in Milan, the powerhouse of Italy,
is like landing in New York City; one needs time to toughen up.
Most city dwellers have no patience with country bumpkins, and
like a typical yokel, instead of asking where the central train station was, I charged in and bought a bus ticket to *Il Centro*, the center of town. Train stations in Italy are usually in the center, but not
this time. Milan's city center was a thousand miles from the station, so I broke two rules: I didn't ask; and as a result, I couldn't
check bags at the station.

When I stepped off the bus near the *Duomo*, the cathedral, my
"lightweight" nylon bag slung across my shoulder got heavier with
each step. Soon, I was ready to forget my plans for a cheap room
and take anything, at any price, but there were no vacancies in that
part of town. None.

Where was Via Tunisia anyway? According to several guidebooks, numerous inexpensive hotels were on Via Tunisia close to
the station. Weariness and desperation were taking their toll and
the worst part for me was that I felt embarrassed by my personal
demons. I "should" have asked for the station, and with map in
hand I "should" have been able to sort myself out. Instead, I was

traveling in ever larger circles around that blessed Duomo with its millions of sharp spires jabbing at the cloudless sky.

Milan did not seem charming. The fabled Galleria with its glassed-over ceiling was dirty and uninteresting. And, where were all the elegant shops? Where were all the fashionable people? Hopefully an overnight stay would be enough to inspect the Duomo, take a tour of *La Scala*, and see Leonardo's *Last Supper* before setting out for Padua. Lugging my bag around the church that first hour did not endear it to me, yet, in spite of my frustration, I had to acknowledge that the thousands of carvings were intriguing. One sprightly marble fellow seemed to be mooning the crowd below, and another was dangling monkey-like upside down. Some long-ago artist must have enjoyed himself.

High above such antics, the feathery spires were lovely, but the piazza in front of the cathedral was unsightly and unkempt. Instead of tended grass or decorative paving stones, weeds sprouted among dirty bits of gravel, and trash blew around in the dry, dusty air. The dryness seemed unusual, I thought. Milan lies in the Po Valley, and according to books I'd been reading, it was normally humid or foggy. There was no coordinated design for the open space around the cathedral to set it off, certainly nothing with beauty or proportion in mind. It was large; that's all I could give it. They could have taken lessons from the Field of Miracles in Pisa or the cathedral complex in Florence or the Campo in Siena or from a hundred other beautiful spaces across the face of Italy.

In the end, I relented and took a cab. The cab driver was pleasant and didn't overcharge, but I was too busy berating myself to notice anything along the way. At the heroic Mussolini-style station, I checked my bag, read the departure schedules for Padua and finally set out unencumbered to find Via Tunisia. Upon finding it, I was comforted immediately because here was the typical Italian street I had remembered. Smells of fresh-ground coffee came from some of the small shops on the street level with their hotels and apartments above.

After hearing *completo*, no vacancy, six or seven times, I was feeling discouraged until a gracious landlady on the fourth floor of one of those buildings put her arm around me and led me into one of her cool, quiet rooms. She obviously felt sorry for the frazzled woman wilting on her doorstep. It was her last available room and it cost 42,000 lire ($28 in 1990, the rate being about 1500 lire to the dollar) more than I'd planned on, but I promised myself to make up the cost elsewhere.

In spite of my meager ability to speak Italian, the best part of that long day's struggle from Portland, Oregon to Milan, Italy, was that I was communicating. If I use as much Italian as I can, drop in an English word when necessary, keep the rhythm flowing—and smile a lot—the meaning gets across. And even better, I was understanding a bit.

The stern guard at the main entrance to La Scala, the most famous opera house in the world, was not helpful. He scowled as I approached him.

"No! No! No entry, go around to the side."

If only I had the courage to persist, but I hadn't toughened enough. That was my first mistake. Joining a long line beside the building was my second. Evidently, the young man standing in front of me didn't catch my word for "tour" and picked up on the word "tickets" and said, "Si, si," when I asked if this was the line to buy tour tickets.

I could see ahead that a doorman was allowing only a few to pass in at a time, and "al Italiano," occasionally someone would crash in ahead for some special reason. Finally, it was time for my group to step into the coolness of the building only to be herded down a flight of stairs into a room where four people were manning ticket windows called *sportelli*. They sat behind a forbidding counter topped with wrought-iron dividers and glass with a small circle cut in it through which people shouted back and forth at each other. Everyone crowded around the four windows. While I waited and watched, it dawned on me that I'd been standing in the hot sun for forty-five minutes to buy tickets for next week's concert.

Once again the need to ask, and ask again was crystal clear. It can be tricky to know when to ask again because sometimes it's too late when I realize that what I thought I understood I didn't. As I emerged from La Scala discouraged and disappointed, it was already late morning, and the church and convent complex of *Santa Maria della Grazie*, where Leonardo da Vinci's *Last Supper* clung to the wall, would probably close at noon. According to the map, it was about a mile away so I set out in a mad, sweaty rush. It cost 10,000 lire ($6.60) to enter the monastery's refectory to see the famous painting. Some churches charge nothing to see their treasures, but in truth, it was a small fee to stand in the very place where that incredible genius once stood.

At first glance, I felt disheartened because a large platform was in front of the painting—left from the ongoing restoration work—and yet another barrier stuck out in front of that. Since the painting was already high on the wall, no one could get comfortably close. It was disappointing.

What did I expect to see having already seen so many reproductions? Da Vinci had used pigments mixed with egg and oil on dry plaster, which is much less durable than true fresco painting done while the plaster is wet. His colors hadn't wedded into the wall, and Milan's humid air had done further damage. According to art historians, he had been trying out one of his infernal experiments with different media, and the paint began to wither within the first year of its completion. Experts have bemoaned the condition of his colors for centuries.

Even at midday the lighting was poor, yet, in spite of the flaking fuzziness of the colors, the drama of the moment when Christ announces his betrayal comes through with a jolt. Each of the agitated twelve leans or gestures in some singular way toward his calm center.

It's the little things that get me. Leonardo's masterpiece was in the shadows, but an elaborate display detailing the accomplishments of the restorers was brilliantly lit.

⌒

Weary, oh so weary, and the vision of a big cup of coffee began crowding out thoughts of paint, plaster and Leonardo's drama. I'd already had a smooth cappuccino in one of the bars along Via Tunisia, and although a tiny cup of espresso is lovely after a meal, what I wanted most of all was a full-sized cup of steaming coffee to revive my jet-lagged psyche.

I walked into one of the ever-present coffee bars of Italy, wondering how to ask for a large cup of coffee. There must be a particular name for it, I thought. I requested, *Un dopio espresso con acqua calda*, a double espresso with hot water. They understood! It was delicious. Already things looked better. A young boy served while the older man supervising him told me that next time I could ask for a *caffè Americano*. Just then an American couple came in and asked where they might find fabric stores. Since I'd noticed three on Via Tunisia near my room, I told them, and the boy gave them detailed directions. Less than one day in Milan and I was helping foreigners.

⌒

Back at my hotel, my bag was indeed securely locked inside the landlady's waiting room just as she had promised earlier that morning. She had seemed in a hurry to leave, but took time to explain about the luggage room and gave me a goodbye hug. Milan didn't have a lot of appeal, but in this big, impersonal city, her individuals had been genuinely warm. A cheery maid of about forty-five years with coal-black hair (probably dyed because Italians tend to gray early), deep-set brown eyes glowing from her fair-skinned, round face took me to the window where we both leaned out so she could point to the next Metro stop. Upon leaving the building, I looked up and there she was waving from the window. She was a pleasant reminder that in this life, it's the individual that counts. As soon as I was out of her sight, however, I ignored the Metro and continued to walk above ground for fear I'd hop on the wrong car and miss the train station altogether.

Endless porticoes shelter weary wanderers.

At the intersection where homey Via Tunisia met Via Pisani, the scene changed abruptly. A cold, drabness and sameness set the tone of this broad street. Pisani was lined with tasteless architecture all the way to the train station. The buildings were big, ugly chunks of concrete, but, at least these fascist-style buildings had retained the notion of arcades from earlier times. How comforting it was to walk in their shade even though the bag dragged on the muscles of my neck. The heat and jet lag dragged on me too, and I had some anxious moments when I feared two months in Italy would be too long. Subsequent trips have taught me to ignore those first-day blues.

The area in front of the glowering station was unsightly. Someone may have once intended it to be green and park like, but instead, stiff stubble, vinelike weeds and scattered trash greeted me.

"Oh no," I thought, "would Rome be like this? Has this happened to beautiful Siena and Florence too?"

The dark maw of the underground pedestrian entrance opened and seemed a cool inviting way to avoid the formidable tangle of cars and taxis dodging each other around the Central Station which was *not* in the center of town. I glanced at the map of Milan and noticed I'd seen only a tenth of the city, and I didn't care.

To activate a train pass, an official must stamp it twice with beginning and ending dates. The rubber stamp business in Italy must be lucrative because officials use them everywhere. Whenever I enter an Italian post office, I hear an underlying sound of rubber stamps thumping documents. They even stamp each piece of mail with its date of arrival—actually, a nice touch.

As I stood in line, I mused about bureaucracy. It is said that the elaborate overlay of bureaucracy comes from the meticulous systems set up when the peninsula was under Austrian influence, but don't forget that the old Romans had a way with organization too. One could say that bureaucracy has flourished in Italy for more than 2000 years. Systems are seldom simplified; each successive overlord or "manager" tweaks them if only to personally mark them, something like animals mark their territories.

It took twenty-five minutes in line for the stamping process. How practical was this train pass going to be, I wondered? Time would tell if it was the most economical way. I planned to keep track of normal second-class costs for every time I took the train with the pass to make a comparison. It was a good intention but since the beauty of having a pass is that I didn't have to stand in line to buy tickets, I admit I didn't do the calculations after all. In years to come, I grew more comfortable with the train system, my language improved a bit, and I tended to stay in one place for longer and longer periods so I never used a pass again.

I found a seat, stowed my baggage on the racks above, and settled in. The bumbly Italian train worked its magic on me, and I doubted two months would be long enough.

↶

CHAPTER FIVE

Fair Verona: Giulietta's balcony.
The Arena: a small version of the Colosseum.
Churches have the best buy in postcards.
Piazza dell'Erbe. I meet Patricia.

AH, FAIR VERONA. TRULY, A FANCIFUL SOMETHING IS IN the air. Giulietta's charming statue stands beneath her flower-decked balcony and her tomb lies behind a pretty wrought-iron gate in a crypt nearby. All fabrications of course, and everyone plays along, but the magic must have affected me because when the train slowed down, the good witch of Verona waved her wand and without thinking, I grabbed my things and hopped off.

What an advantage to have no reservations waiting for me in Padua—or anywhere. My trip goals had been purposefully vague, but even so I surprised myself. My plan was to start in Milan, stop at Padua for nostalgic reasons, maybe go on to Venice, then Florence, with a possible side trip to Siena, on to Orvieto for sure to see Etruscan tombs, and, finally, saving the best to last, to walk the streets of Rome again.

First impressions of a place are powerful and the young woman in the tourist bureau was kindness itself. Because of her, I will always remember Verona as a mellow, hospitable town. While I waited my turn, however, I felt anxious because I was low on cash. It was too late to go to a bank, the next day was Sunday, and if I were to find a cheap room, it would almost certainly require cash. Not only did she cash a small travelers' check and hand me a fistful of maps and information, she called ahead and booked a room at *Casa Della Giovane*. Seldom have information offices cashed travelers' checks for me. Some tourist information offices offer almost no support, and others, like this happy place, hire employees who truly understand why they are there.

The hostel's name means House of the Young Woman, and was managed by an association of the Catholic church which obviously was willing to ignore the age limitation. Perhaps October was not their busy season. The Casa was much more interesting than any Hilton and had a delightful assistant willing to answer endless questions. I shared a room with a gentle Italian woman and got to practice the language because she spoke no English—none. There were three beds to a room. The charge was only 15,000 lire for a bed no matter whether all three were occupied or not. This price, I thought, would definitely balance out the 42,000 lire paid in Milan. She may have chosen the best bed, but the two empties were equally saggy; they looked like hammocks *before* lying on them. Exhaustion, however, worked its spell.

Verona is a soft place with the River Adige shaping itself into a letter S through the oldest part of the city. It wasn't always soft. A powerful, often cruel family, The Scaligers, held sway here. When I climbed onto one of the parapets and peered through a notched opening high up on the Scaliger Bridge, not only did I see beautiful church domes, bell towers, battlements of ancient castles and the Arena spread out below in a pink glow, I also felt shivers because even fairy-tales have their terrifying episodes. The sun was brilliant in the autumn sky and the chilly wind lifted my hair, but ancient vibrations of vicious battles below this bridge and along this river resonated in my bones or was it a touch of vertigo?

The formidable bridge charges straight out of the courtyard of *Castelvecchio*, and the Old Castle looks exactly like a castle should with battlements, towers, merlons and crenels, and, in this case, its own bridge controlling a sizable river. In the thirteenth and fourteenth centuries, the Scaliger lords were a fierce bunch, at times, benevolent, possibly on the order of the Medicis of Florence. The major difference was that most of the Medicis stayed out of the limelight preferring to rule behind the scenes.

Patricia, a young California woman also staying at the Casa, had read about the difference in crenelation styles throughout Italy. If the notches along the top of a building were squarish, they symbolized the papacy; if they were in the shape of swallow tails (Vs), they symbolized the city state, which usually meant the most powerful family of each city. Verona's crenals were decidedly swallow tails, that is, the Scaligers ruled. I recognized the snob in me, because whenever I find one of these bits of trivia, I hug it to my chest and feel superior to other wanderers tramping about unaware.

Another old stone bridge called *Il Ponte Della Pietra*, The Bridge of Stone, is from Roman times, theoretically that is, because with Verona's position so near the strategic Brenner Pass, every one of the bridges across the Adige was blown up in World War II. The stones were taken up one by one from the river and reconstructed "in total faith with the original" according to an official publication. Totally faithful or not, it is beautiful and looks old indeed.

When I reached the other side, I climbed a steep, breath-snatching flight of steps winding up and up to Castel San Pietro. Lovers were sitting on the walls overlooking the city; it was indeed a fine spot for smooching and I wanted to call my own love back in Oregon. How different my present relationship was from the first one. I looked down at the water of the Adige flowing under the bridge and was reminded that it was good to have made that break from a relationship that had turned sour.

Musicians in tuxedos were walking along the curve of Piazza Bra just below the ancient colosseum, which in Verona likes to be called The Arena. Through the summer months, they perform lyric operas inside; how sweet it would be to attend one some time, but that would mean traveling during the hottest months among great numbers of jostling tourists. October or November suited me better; lodging is easier to find when the crowds are gone. It warmed my heart to see this magnificent place from the first century being actively used instead of set aside as a dusty relic for tour guides to hurry people through on the way to yet another monument or shopping spot before lunch.

The Arena is intact all the way around up to its two tall stories, and then above that, four proud arches stand up to another level. The rest was destroyed by earthquakes in the 1100s. During the day it has a soft, pinkish glow like so many buildings here because most local quarries carry that soft hue. Maybe the pink color is what Shakespeare had in mind when he opened his play *Romeo and Juliet* by saying, "In fair Verona, where we lay our scene." In her book *Serenissima*, about Venice, Erica Jong may be right when she speculates that William had traveled to Italy before writing his Italian plays.

In the evenings, they light the Arena both from within and without. The archways leading to the seats inside are illuminated and the soft lights reveal the intricate patterns of bricks and stones which form its ancient curves. A miniature, well-manicured park with a few comfortable benches lies near the Arena's walls. Maybe I couldn't go into the Arena, but I could buy a gelato and sit and look as long as it lasted—or longer.

Brek, a self-service chain restaurant across the way from the Arena, was much more than the usual steam-table affair. Crêpes were cooked to order, pastas were prepared on the spot and various salad fixings were available for mixing oneself. For me, the thick, hot vegetable soup, a glass of red wine, a hunk of bread and a salad topped with green, virgin olive oil were just right. It felt so right to be in Italy. All doubts had dissipated into the enchanted air. Or had I simply recovered from jet lag? The Veronesi take their passeggiata every night along the grand curve of Piazza Bra beneath the Arena, moving on to Via Mazzini, a quiet walking street of elegant shops which leads to the large, oblong market called *Piazza dell'Erbe*. The Piazza of the Herbs has a history going back to Roman times when it was the forum in this strategic Roman city.

Passing through the Piazza dell'Erbe on my way to the hostel every day, I often stopped into a basilica nearby called Sant'Anastasia. It was quiet and usually empty except for two or three old women. Two endearing stone hunchbacks on either side of the entrance held huge, red marble stoups of holy water on their bent backs. They have been holding them for about five hundred years, and I liked to pay them my respects.

~

The Basilica of San Zeno is probably the oldest in town. The abbey and church complex date back to the fifth century A.D., and the large bronze doors with their forty-eight biblical segments go back to the tenth and eleventh centuries. Some say these doors were the inspiration for the craze for bronze church doors all over Italy. What I hoped to see here was the triptych, *Enthroned Madonna and Child with Saints* by Andrea Mantegna. Fortunately, it was not covered in restoration cloths and was in its original position on the high altar; it was my first Mantegna 'in the flesh.'

There was an abundance of gilt on the pillars and frame as well as in the picture itself with the golden halos on the mother, child and angels. The madonna and child were believable; the baby seemed to be a real, pudgy infant, except for a wistful look on his face. His mother looked grief stricken as if she already knew what was coming for her son. Sad-faced madonnas are everywhere, but this mother and child seemed particularly moving. I counted nine haloed-angels singing or playing instruments all around her throne and the rich colors glowed especially when I fed the light meter. Many churches provide a meter connected to a spotlight focused on certain paintings. If someone inserts a coin, usually a 200 lire piece, the light comes on for one minute. Some churches had raised the price to 500. Because I was getting a feel for the cost of things, I began to grumble like a native, yet in 1990, 500 lire was all of thirty-three cents.

In later travels, I found the famous frescoes which Mantegna did for the Gonzaga family in Mantua to be more alive and interesting, but I am glad I took the trouble to find this triptych because it represented Mantegna's earlier work. After I left Verona, I learned there was another Mantegna in the museum of the Castlevecchio. I should have entered the museum before I went onto the Scaliger bridge, but that day when I stood in the castle

41

One of many comfortable bars found all over Italy.

courtyard, the soaring bridge drew me like a magnet and I forgot all about the museum.

San Zeno is one of those wonderful, old romanesque churches with a flat ceiling and a long nave supported by a forest of huge gray pillars. Some of the pillars have carvings and paintings built into them, and the upper walls they support hint at gray and white stripes. The lower walls are made of alternating stripes of pinkish bricks and limestone, a familiar style in Verona. Zeno is Verona's patron saint and an overwhelming, blocky statue of him sat on a throne. His robe was painted a shiny, bright red and he held a golden staff. His throne was crammed into a niche which seemed too small for it, but gradually I came to expect this sort of placement in Italian churches, they just have so much art. Faded frescoes on the wall behind him may have told his story.

At a sales table set up in the vestibule, I bought colorful postcards at an excellent price; since I had promised many people, I scooped them up. The cards depicted all aspects of Verona and were not confined to this one church or to religious scenes. To me, cards are a better way to remember art and monuments than my own awkward snapshots so I also bought some to keep.

The wines from the mountains around Verona are famous, including white Soave, red Valpolicella and Bardolino. Patricia invited me to join her and two young Australian women for a glass or two at a wine bar before moving on to a bargain trattoria. Patricia and I had literally bumped into each other in the hallway near our shared bathroom. She felt as fragile as a bird when we embraced in an awkward effort to keep our balance. Her delicate features, bright brown eyes, light brown hair and dusting of freckles across her nose reminded me of a little brown wren.

For at least an hour we were the only women in the small family restaurant. Evidently women didn't eat out unless with an escort or with family. The men were probably unmarried local laborers or workers who had to leave their families back in southern Italy where unemployment was high. The fixed-price menu offered a huge amount of food including pasta, meat, vegetables, salad and bread. The problem with a fixed price or "Menu Turistico" is that we eat too much. It's the law. None of us needed to worry about gaining weight though, not with our travel style of walking miles everyday up and down the steps of churches, bridges, museums as well as in our hostels with no elevators.

It was fun to chat in one's own language after stumbling along in Italian, but it seemed we were spending an inordinate amount of time putting men down. Well, the Italian men are good subjects to poke fun at because they take their manhood so seriously. They do preen in every shop window. In the barber shops, I could see just how serious they were as they checked the mirrors from front to back, took time for manicures, and had involved conversations about styles, sprays and lotions. When I passed by the open doors of these shops, their perfumes lay heavily in the air. There seemed to be four times as many barbershops as beauty shops; that's different from back home where men seem embarrassed to admit they have any interest in their appearance at all.

Walking home together, we giggled and compared notes. The consensus was that Italian men are much less inhibited about grabbing their crotch in public than American or Australian men are. Like tourists touching their wallet pockets for security, Italian men touch their male organs. It had been pleasant being with attractive, intelligent young women, but by the end of the evening, I wanted no more male bashing. Patricia agreed with me that being a feminist doesn't have to mean one hates half the population.

Although it would be breaking house rules to call as late as midnight, Graziella, the young office worker, had explained how I could get in to use the pay phone. Italy is nine hours ahead of Pacific Coast time so I could reach our office about three in the afternoon. Later we arranged that I would call about three in the afternoon and reach home at six in the morning since my love is an early riser anyway. Hoping I had understood Graziella's directions, around 11:30 p.m. I set out in the dark. The house lights in the old building were on timers; how strange I thought, but in later travels, I discovered this to be a normal practice because electricity is so expensive in Europe, but it was an uncomfortable novelty then. My room was on second level and the office was on third; the switch for the hall light was near my room and it stayed on just long enough to hurry up the stairs and slip into the office. But, once inside I couldn't find the office switch. Not to worry, I'd memorized my calling card number and thanks to Italians' belief in well-lighted streets, there was ample light coming in a window to see the dials.

My call home was overdue; I'd been putting it off because Italian operators gave me the telephone terrors, they usually spoke too fast and were invariably impatient. AT&T had set up a new system, however, and I wanted to try it. I had read and re-read the instructions on the miniature card furnished by the company. It should be easy I thought, but technical instructions and I don't always see things the same way so I was prepared for some trouble. When three cheery musical tones sounded followed by an encouraging American voice saying, "USA Direct, how may I help you?" It was like hearing an angel from heaven.

Electronically I was immediately in the U.S., and all this was terrific, except the domestic card number was needed and I'd memorized the international number! I didn't find the hall light switch outside the office, so back down the dark stairs I went feeling my way with hands on the wall, being especially careful around the angle at the landing where the width of the steps changed rapidly. As quietly as possible, I crept into my room to scrabble in the dark for the other number hoping not to disturb my roommate. She didn't stir; maybe she was exhausted from a hard day's work.

The second call reached a cranky American operator but when I finally got through, it didn't matter because I heard my husband's encouraging voice and all was well. It's funny how intimidation works; after the first success, I always wonder what all the fuss was about.

Unaware of how the USA Direct system worked, Graziella had suggested that I might need to use the S.I.P. phones. I'd seen S.I.P. phones at the train station and elsewhere, but again was shy about how to work them. S.I.P., the Italian phone company at that time, had been selling phone cards long before our phone companies offered them, and it was already a popular Italian system back in 1990. Until recently, many Italians haven't had private phones mainly because it took as long as two years for installation. That may be part of the reason why almost sixty percent of the population in Italy now own cell phones—that and their pathological need to chat.

One can buy a 5,000 or 10,000 lire phone card, slip it into the slot of most public phones and talk until the card runs out. A digital readout on the phone tells how much money is left on the card while one speaks. It works like a dream. Without a card, many, many coins are needed; a conversation can be cut off mid-sentence when the coins run out, and coins are hard to come by. At home my purse usually bulges with coins and I try to use them up, but in Italy, it's the exact opposite. I guard my coins warily. Either they don't mint enough or someone hoards them. Friends tell me that in the 1950s, vendors often gave hard candies instead of change.

In later years, I've noticed the shortage has gradually gotten better, but if I'm not careful to hide my *spiccioli*, shopkeepers still insist on having my last coin rather than making change. Sometimes they reach into my palm and choose what they need, assuming I don't understand their money system. They never cheat me but it's unnerving. Maybe it became a habit to avoid making change during those shortage years, but I suspect that avoidance just goes along with their idea of service.

One afternoon I sat at an outside table of a bar across the street from The Old Castle in Verona and nonchalantly ordered caffè Americano as I'd been taught in Milan. No one knew what I meant. So, back I went to ordering a double espresso with hot water if I wanted a large cup of coffee. That was Milan, this was Verona. History books tell us each city-state had its own fierce ways, but I thought that ended with the Middle Ages and the Renaissance. Not so, and it's what makes traveling around Italy so interesting; each area still maintains its own character.

Piazza dell'Erbe, *"L'Erbe"* as the locals call it, is delightful every morning with fresh produce and flowers, but their permanent booths hide the exquisite beauty of the buildings surrounding them. Not only do the buildings form a magnificent architectural space, but many of the Venetian-style structures have elaborate frescoes on their facades with the colors still in excellent condition. The sixteenth-century frescoes left on a few buildings in Rome can be seen only if one's imagination works overtime, but then, autos aren't allowed to drive through *L'Erbe*.

Madonna Verona, possibly a Roman statue which could have stood here in the ancient forum, stands on a pedestal above a fountain holding a battered bronze banner with a motto long ago faded away. Her fountain has been washing fruit, rinsing out buckets and tidying children's sticky fingers for several centuries.

⌐⌐

CHAPTER SIX

Vicenza, home of Palladio. Juicy golden cachi.
Olympic Theater's trick stage set.
La Rotonda, the model for Thomas Jefferson's Monticello.
A dilemma.

ANDREA PALLADIO DREW ME TO VICENZA (HALFWAY
between Verona and Padua) partly because his designs had influenced so much architecture in the United States, but mainly because of *La Villa Rotonda*. When I told Patricia that *La Rotonda* had been Thomas Jefferson's model for Monticello in Virginia, she was enthusiastic and eager to join me. For fifteen years I had escorted wives of my former husband's visiting colleagues through Monticello. Even though I often dreaded my escort duties, I grew to admire old "T.J.," as local citizens called him. Now was my chance to see the source of his inspiration.

Vicenza looked respectable and businesslike, and obviously wealthy folks lived there. For centuries, the city has produced gold jewellery, leather and textiles. In a country that leads the world's production of gold jewellery, about fifty percent of the gold imported into Italy is processed in Vicenza. It was a great place for window shopping, but people on the streets seemed cool; we felt like outsiders.

We visited the *Palazzo della Ragione* in the middle of town, also called *Basilica Palladiana*. In 1549 Palladio was given the job of redoing the old fourteenth-century city hall or basilica. He created a structure of loggias and roofed arcades all around the old building; tomes have been written about his revolutionary treatment using classical models and renaissance know-how. This commission was his main source of income for many years as he flitted to Rome to study, to Venice to accept church commissions, and to

whip out designs for private villas all along the Brenta canal leading from Padua to Venice. The Basilica wasn't finished until long
after his death; many of his projects were not finished until after
his death.

In the market in front of the Basilica, I tasted my first perfect,
ripe persimmon. There will never be another quite like that one.
Back home, they are either small, hard, and bitter or unpleasantly
overripe. I remembered seeing these golden fruits called *cachi*
hanging like plush ornaments on bare tree limbs in the backyards
as my train passed by. *Cachi* are messy, sticky and delicious; they're
almost like eating pudding with one's fingers. It's one of those
fruits I just know my digestive tract welcomes. Fortunately, a running spigot was tucked in a corner of the famous building; but, of
course, where there's a market, there's always running water.

One of the many prosperous shops in town had the most exquisite fabrics I had ever seen. Lying about were marvelous wools, silks
and linens, and also laces, brocades, satins, and velvets, each one
prettier and richer than the next. How Mom would have loved
touching them; she had been a fine seamstress before arthritis
crippled her hands. Would she enjoy being here with me, I wondered? Maybe for a little while.

Patricia was shopping for knit pants with stirrups, the kind
young women were wearing that year; they wore them as tight as
possible with long sweaters arranged to come just barely below
their derrières. They looked smashing, and tiny, slim Patricia
would too. For one brief, shining moment I even considered a pair
for myself. My legs would probably pass muster encased in dark
tights, but gravity does take its toll, and, it would be a bit of a dis-
sonance to see someone wearing youthful clothing with a grandma face. No, I would stick to my long black skirt or slacks in keeping with my aim to be inconspicuous. We parted and agreed to
meet at the Olympic Theater at two.

At 2:30, the theater opened and what a surprise it was. Obviously, I
hadn't read enough about Palladian buildings in Vicenza, because

this was indeed a strange place. The entire ceiling was painted light blue with fluffy clouds. Rather weird, I thought, for a theater. We took our seats on wooden benches forming a semi-circle facing the stage, and there, in front of us was an elaborate, permanent wall set back about ten feet or so from the edge of the stage—about where a curtain might normally be. It had pillars with Corinthian-style capitals and arches, tabernacles and reliefs. All across the length of the stage above, niches held sculptures of heroic-looking figures. These niches were on two separate levels with carved friezes at the third, top level. More heroes stood around the perimeter of the seating area, in fact, the entire theater seemed filled with cold, carved figures, all noble of course. Palladio designed the theater to mimic ancient Roman theaters, and it was intended for classical productions to suit polite society of the 1500s.

There were three openings in this odd stage wall which faced the audience; a center arched opening was the largest with one smaller arched opening to either side. Through these arches, I could look down the streets of a refined city. As I viewed the center street, both sides of it were lined with renaissance palaces, pillars and more statues built into more niches. The other two "lanes" showed only one side because they each veered off to stage right and stage left. My mind assumed that the other sides of the street were just as splendid. All the streets ended at far off points.

Incredible carving wasn't it? Not so. It's all a trick. The floor rises, the buildings grow smaller and except for the front wall, it's all painted. If a player were to step into one of these avenues, the street would come up and the rooftops would come down, and if she took a few more steps, her nose would come smack against the wall. What a fantastic deception. Performances here would be formal and dispassionate, but if given half a chance I'd be first in line.

We could have joined a group listening to an annoying guide who explained much more than anyone would want to know. The other groups left and then only the offensive fellow was left; he spoke louder and louder trying to drum up business from the few individuals scattered around the theater. It's tiresome when people assume I want to hear their golden words; he irked me more and more with each passing moment. Until he raised his voice, it had been pleasant sitting there absorbing the environment and speculating about how the plays would work on that unusual stage and just generally dreaming. With him, no such luck. He was an insufferable old man. He spoke four languages; I had to give him that.

As we left, the old fellow placed himself so that everyone had to pass right in front of him while he made ingratiating remarks. If he expected money from me, he was truly mistaken. He probably made a pretty penny as a pick-up guide because the least anyone would give him would be a one-thousand-lire note and about forty or fifty filed past him at that hour. They ran people through the auditorium at least two or three times a day, and during the busy season probably four times. He must have picked up at least $200 a day for being loud and obnoxious.

~

We almost missed seeing *Villa Capra* (nicknamed *La Rotonda*) because it sat a couple of kilometers south of town and didn't show up on the map given us at the station. Whenever we asked people directions, they couldn't seem to give us an idea of how to walk there; they either misunderstood or didn't believe we were serious about walking. As the day wore on, we were distracted by other sights; Patricia seemed tired and I hesitated to mention it again, but when I did, she surprised me by saying, "Let's do it!"

With some vague directions, we took a bus and hoped there would be people to ask along the way. Our bus driver stopped in a sparsely settled area. We hurried up the road in the direction he pointed and turned up a long flight of broad steps leading into some trees. Surely something special must be at the top. It was coming on dusk and the heavy trees on either side formed a darkish tunnel which seemed threatening; someone was approaching from the top of the steps. We felt uneasy until we realized it was a woman. Instantly we breathed a sigh of relief and commented how it was a shame that we had to be wary of half the world's population. The young woman with a paisley bandanna tied around her hair, worked at the villa above. No, it wasn't *La Rotonda*, but she urged us back down to her boyfriend waiting at his car. As we approached him, she pulled off her scarf and let her heavy, dark locks fall around her shoulders. He beamed at her loveliness, and then led us on to *La Rotonda* only a few more yards past our grand steps. He seemed pleased that we were so keen to see it. I eagerly explained that President Thomas Jefferson had built his home from this design. He was dutifully impressed and did not understand a word I said but smiled as they went on their way.

The ornate iron gate was closed, but just inside was a ticket area and we could see a sign showing that it was open only Tuesday and Thursday mornings. It was late Friday afternoon so we were doubly out of luck. We peeked through the grill and felt enchanted anyway as we looked at this famous building with its red-domed roof, its four porticoes of six white pillars each and wide steps opening out to four different directions—a perfectly balanced house. It looked like a temple. Maybe our view of it in the fading light was best after all. We'd never know whether the grounds were well kept or whether the stucco was freshly painted. It looked lovely and romantic in the dying light, and we were pleased with ourselves.

As we stared through the grillwork, I explained to Patricia that Jefferson had used dark, native red bricks with dazzling white pillars and trim. This style was copied throughout Charlottesville from the dingiest apartment houses to the local dairy also named Monticello except the dairy pronounced the "c" as an "s," whereas for his home, Jefferson insisted on the Italian pronunciation of the "c" as in cello. How different Palladio's original looked without the strong contrasts of dark and light; his subtle color scheme consisted of soft, fawn-colored stucco and pale red terra-cotta tiles on the roof. Although our line of sight afforded a view of just one portico, we could imagine the others. If we lived there, we could move from one area of the house to another according to whether we wanted to soak up the warming rays of a wintery sun or avoid the sweltering summer ones. Palladio's ideas were copied over and over in plantation mansions throughout the American Southland. I thought about Tara and Twelve Oaks.

The spell was gone and we anxiously retraced our steps to the bus stop; soon our bus came but whooshed right past even though we stood directly under the street light and waved. What to do? There were no shops open and the area seemed more and more desolate. We had a train to catch, supper to eat and a 10:30 curfew. It was dark and chilling down. It seemed silly to wait for another bus; they might have stopped running for the day. We giggled like nervous school girls and started hiking as fast as we could toward town. All in all it had been a satisfying day. Patricia had been a worthy companion and I could tell she appreciated my inspiration to visit Vicenza. Being a tourist is indeed hard work, but that day I wanted it to last forever.

Back in Verona, I spent a half hour alone the next morning in the spacious Piazza dei Signori where Dante Alighieri stands with a pigeon or two resting on his head and shoulders. In Florence, he was a political being and a member of the Guelph party which supported the pope, but when it later split into the blacks and whites he got into a pickle by supporting the wrong color—the whites. Knowing he'd be silenced by the blacks, he escaped, and for awhile the Scaligers of Verona gave him refuge, thus his memorial in this broad piazza. Eventually he fled to Ravenna where he remained in exile until his death. Poor Dante, he spent the rest of his life longing to be back in Florence all the while writing nasty things about his political enemies. Would I ever be able to read his works in Italian, I wondered? Giving Dante a final salute, I ambled on through the city.

The church of *San Fermo* where the old church lies below the new one, the new one built five hundred years ago, was not an "important" destination, rather it was one of those places that just draws me in. The smell of candles and incense was wondrously heavy. A service was in progress upstairs, but the lower level was empty. There, I could take my time with the faded eleventh century frescoes. There's a certain quiet pleasure found in inspecting these old buildings, especially when few people are around. I enjoy trying to fill in the missing pieces in the garbled brochures translated into English. With a notebook in my knapsack, I take notes to remind myself of what I feel at the moment or about the art I see. These notes jog my memory for further study back home. With only one formal art course—Art 101 at the University of Virginia—I had fallen in love with Italian Renaissance art. On that long ago trip with my former husband, I had carried voluminous class notes hoping to find some famous works, but time had been too short and was filled with too many compromises.

In the ancient church below street level, my thoughts strayed to a different compromise. I needed to think through the problem of whether to join Patricia in Florence, and especially in Rome, or to stick firmly to my plan of traveling on alone. If you add a partner, you lose your freedom, I thought. She had trepidations about Rome because of rumors of gypsies and pickpockets, and wanted to go with someone. I was handy. After listening to her fears, I had begun to worry too that it might not be good anymore.

Of course, there were pros and cons. Patricia seemed moody at times, but she was also a good sport and willing to try new things at the last moment. It would be cheaper to take hotel rooms together and pleasant to have a companion for evening meals. Our interests didn't mesh well though, and time was precious. If we did travel together, I had already voiced my desire to go my own way during the daytime. She had agreed. Maybe the situation would solve itself, I thought wistfully, as I rose to walk out of the old church.

No, no, I thought, and sat back down. I owed it to myself to be clear. Everything was in place. My best friend, who happened to be my husband, had agreed to take over some of my bookkeeping chores in our business, and even more important, to check on my elderly parents every day by phone and visit them at least once a week so that I could follow my dream. I had worked and planned too long for this venture of going it alone to change so abruptly.

From the upper church, I could hear music; I sighed and looked around at the old frescoes again. My mind was made up. After going to Padua alone, I might see her in Florence, but I simply had to have Rome to myself. The quiet time in old San Fermo was just what I needed.

On Friday, my roommate left for her home in Turin. The following Monday, she would move on to another city for another week. She demonstrated products in large department stores—a hard, lonely job. Each morning, she would settle at a little table staked out near the lone window in our room, and there she would eat cereal and fruit for her breakfast. No doubt she grabbed coffee on the run as do most Italians, probably adding two or three spoonfuls of sugar to a tiny cup of espresso or three or four if she chose a cappuccino. Chances are she ate better breakfasts than most who seem to run on sugared caffeine and a sweet brioche until siesta. Many Italian breakfast buns don't interest me. You might say that a *corneto* looks like a croissant, but you would be fooled because it is not flaky and crisp, it is soft and sticky sweet instead. Cappuccino is definitely a morning drink in Italy, and if you drink one after lunchtime you've announced loud and clear that you're not a native.

Patricia left for a side trip with a friend, and I was alone in Verona. She had recommended a bakery that sold whole-grained bread called *integrale*, so I was up and out early. Then I headed for the train station for departure information, but felt disoriented; nothing looked right. A slender young woman led me to a bus stop. At the last moment, I recognized the gate called *Porta Nuova* and knew it was just a short walk to the station. Do the natives think we tourists can't walk or did I look too old to her? It's easy to forget that I have a grandmother's face, especially when I'm having fun. Maybe Italians don't walk as much as I'd always thought. They must get their exercise somewhere because few are fat and absolutely none are obese. Once I did see an obese woman waddling ahead of me, but as I slipped around her, I heard a snatch of her conversation to her companion, "I'm ready for a good ol' cheeseburger."

Upon leaving the information window, I fretted about whether to walk to the station at dawn the next morning or take a city bus, or was there a later train for Padua? Clearly more information was needed. I went back to get in line again. Why didn't she tell me? Why didn't I ask? Information people can be infernally literal. They answer my specific question but offer no other alternatives and give the impression that I'm taking too much of their time. They are usually busy, yes, but doesn't my time count for anything? After warily waiting for my turn, all the while keeping an eye peeled for a possible line crasher, I find it hard to remember all the details in a hurry. I should ask about special schedules for weekends and holidays because they don't volunteer that information. Even if I had a train table in hand, and even if I could understood its complexities, there would always be exceptions and changes. The lesson here was to take more responsibility for myself and learn to stand up to the government officials—politely of course.

Remembering my aching neck and shoulder in Milan, I dreaded lugging my 'lightweight' nylon bag for the rest of the trip. A nun beside me on the city bus said I could buy *un carello*, a little cart, to hold my bag from a shop on the Piazza dell'Erbe. There were all kinds of shops along the periphery of the piazza but no luggage shop; had I misunderstood her? Just as I was giving up hope, there it was. Bless her. I chose the sturdiest carrello in the shop and rushed back up to my room to try it out. It would be perfect, and with its strong bungee cord I could fasten the bag firmly onto the cart and tuck my bulky, down jacket liner and umbrella under the cord. Then, I would pull it all behind me with style and grace. I was so thrilled, it was as if I had invented the contraption myself. Pulling my snazzy cart to the station, I headed for Padua.

◡〜

CHAPTER SEVEN

Memories and demons. Giotto re-visited.
Golden-domed Il Santo full of glitter and holiness.
Donatello was here. Etruscans too.
Galileo's University. The Prato demystified.
Lost in dreamy Padua again.

Nothing looked familiar. After almost thirty years, I desperately needed a map of Padua. According to my notes, the tourist office was near Largo Europa, so I hopped a bus in that direction, but I couldn't see the stops while standing on a crowded bus. When I stepped off, Largo Europa was already three blocks behind, and a pesky little demon hissed behind my shoulders that I wasn't doing it right.

Why didn't you ask the bus driver to tell you where to get off? Why didn't you look for the tourist office in the station? Why this and why that?

This venture alone must have been bothering me more than I had realized.

A kind man pushing a squeaky old bicycle led me to the proper address; he looked poor and uneducated but was genuine and helpful. He asked if I was from New York which seemed funny, but after all, an uneducated person in Portland, Oregon might ask an Italian if she were from Rome. Yes, it was the correct address but, no, it wasn't the information office. A woman suggested I ask the man at the newspaper stand. He was in no mood to help a bothersome tourist, but he told me the office had been moved back to the station. To make myself feel even worse, I bought a large, expensive map from him and got to scold myself further—a silly scold, as it turned out, because that map has been a pleasure to see on my wall for years.

At last I recognized areas of the city and began indulging in the nostalgia I came for, especially in the Scrovegni Chapel where Giotto's colorful frescoes cover every inch of the ceiling and walls. With the diagram of the chapel painted and labeled on a funny, paddle-shaped wooden board, I set out to identify each picture.

The first time here I'd been incredibly ignorant about Giotto di Bondone, understanding little about the tradition out of which he came. He had made a huge leap from the static Byzantine art to a more natural, humanistic style. He managed to give weight and feeling to his figures, especially the weight, I thought. To me, his solid figures looked stiff and stagey, but according to Bernard Berenson, a crusty, yet well-respected twentieth-century expert on Italian Renaissance art, Giotto's importance lies in "the power to stimulate our tactile imagination... essential in the art of painting."

I felt embarrassed to remember how I'd made fun of Giotto's works because they had looked childish to my untutored eyes. I'd been on a "ladies tour" which in itself had put me off because they seemed to be a bunch of silly, twittering women. Now, thirty years too late, I suspected they knew what they were seeing, and I might have learned from them had I been less judgmental.

A few steps from the chapel is a church connected with Saint Augustine's chain of convents called *Frati Eremitani*, the Hermit Brothers. It is a long building with the usual flat ceiling of a basilica, this one made of slender wooden lattices. The delicate pink and white horizontal stripes of the interior stone walls give the illusion of a much longer nave than it really is. In 1944, during an American bombing error, almost all of the frescoes by Andrea Mantegna were destroyed—*forever*. I strained to see what was left feeling angry and frustrated at all war mongers, no matter how "good" the wars were. The soft colors, faded paintings, and smell of wax worked on me, and soon I felt calm and forgot about the stupidities of war.

Peace settled on my shoulders as I relaxed across the street at an outside table set between two pillars, two out of the hundreds of Padua's characteristic arcades. Even if they did brand me as a foreigner, I drank two rich, foamy cappuccini, one after the other at two in the afternoon. The uninterrupted columns edged the narrow Street of the Hermits like a line of cowled monks who seemed to march away forever. Once again, Padua felt mysterious and inviting.

Il Santo, the Church of Saint Anthony, is a town favorite and kept in perfect repair. From a distance, it has an eastern look with its eight domes, and two thin bell towers that look suspiciously like minarets. Inside, I confronted total exuberance and show-stopping glitter, a mixture of Byzantine and Italian sensibilities. In spite of being overwhelming in its elaborate decorations, the total effect is not offensive.

We made fun of it back in the 60s especially because of its relics and preserved parts of saints' bodies. Again I felt ashamed. It seemed strange to enshrine finger bones or jaw bones, but now I understood a bit more about how it all worked. There was a time when the relics had a powerful meaning to worshipers, and it was important for each church and city to outdo each other with their religious grandeur, with their church size and with their relics. If these relics give comfort to believers, I thought, and if I'm made welcome to come look at them, then I will never ridicule them again.

A special chapel is set aside to hold reliquaries and treasures; it was constructed in the late 1600s by a student of Gianlorenzo Bernini. Filippo Parodi learned his lessons well. It must surely rank as the most ornate, florid, convoluted example of high baroque. People were lined up to walk through single file so I got in line too. An elegantly-dressed "gentleman," who behaved like a boor, shouldered his way in front of me. Why? He didn't seem to be in a hurry once he nudged me aside. Just needed to be first I guessed. It seems important for some Italians to be first; maybe it has to do with presenting the best face forward, or is it to save face? This rudeness is not strictly a male trait; females shove ahead too especially in shops for bread or cheese. They may find it just as irritating to see the English and Americans line up like sheep for everything.

In 1981 Saint Anthony's bones were found and verified by a papal committee. The interior of the church was then rearranged to place the sepulcher holding his seven-hundred-fifty-year-old skeleton so that now people can walk behind it. They place their hands on the side of his casket and pray. Who knows what each individual prayer might be? It's likely they ask for some kind of physical healing since pictures and silver offerings in the shapes of body parts are mounted near the casket. As I walked past, I too brushed my hand across his bier wishing good health for all our family; it couldn't hurt.

No matter how many times I enter *Il Santo*, I feel like a kid at a carnival.

"Come see these jewels, come see this sparkling casket over here, and lookee here and lookee there!"

The dome area at the high altar is spectacular with the bronzes, the gold leaf and the marble bas-reliefs by Donato di Niccolo di Betto Bardi, known as Donatello, that tell stories of Saint Anthony, and also with the carved figures of colored marble and stucco, the frescoed walls and arches, and above it all hundreds of stars on a dark blue background. Seven bronze figures by Donatello, are near the main altar, but they are not easy to see because of deep shadows. Travelers should carry huge flashlights into these dark churches. How did folks see these glorious works before electricity? They must have burned many huge candles. Yes, I remembered having seen four-foot candles about six inches in diameter glowing in front of large paintings in dark Roman churches. The smoke must have darkened many an artist's careful strokes.

Donatello's famous bronze crucifix was in clear view, mounted high above everything else. It is exquisite, but was there ever a figure by him that wasn't? His equestrian monument standing outside the church is impressive as well. It may have been the first of its kind during the Renaissance. In the spirit of the times, he looked to Rome and modeled it after Italy's most famous equestrian statue, Marcus Aurelius, now at the Capitol in Rome.

Donatello's figure astride the massive horse represents one of Venice's more successful *condottiere*, mercenary soldiers called Gattamelata, the honeyed cat. Padua is in the region called the Veneto and was long dominated by Venice. I was wishing I had time to visit Venice, but I felt an obligation to keep my appointment with Patricia in Florence.

The evening service was starting; the mellow organ played and the handsome, young priest (as only young Italian men can be) sang the service. The congregation sang back to him. Who couldn't be moved by a sense of awe at the idea of people joining in a tradition that has held them together for centuries? I felt a strong sense of history and continuity there. It's part of what draws me back to this country. And the beauty. And the architecture. And the art. And the food. And the humanity of people who know how to make art out of life.

Guariento! A new discovery for me. In Padua's art museum, his beguiling, golden-haired angels lead nasty little devils on golden leashes as if they were harmless poodles. His winsome angels, ravishing in their golden gowns, hold golden orbs on their laps, and seem to be saying, "Here's the world, catch it if you can!" To my mind, he's got it all over Giotto who wouldn't know animation if it raised up and bit him. Yet, Giotto is credited with changing the course of western art.

Guariento di Arpo studied under Giotto but clung to the more sumptuous Byzantine-Gothic manner probably because he'd been hired to paint in Venice. He must have understood that those splendor-loving Venetians would never appreciate Giotto's severity. On the other hand, Giotto must have known how to sell himself in Tuscany where the climate was right for monumental artistic changes. In his books *Lives of the Painters, Sculptors and Architects*, Giorgio Vasari wrote that Giotto was known to be an ugly little man yet he was an engaging jokester who charmed everyone around him.

Somehow I missed seeing Giorgione's *Leda and the Swan*, which was supposed to be in the museum, but found another treat more meaningful to me. Attached to the art museum was a small archeological museum. On general principles, I went in and was surprised to find an extensive Etruscan exhibit. Until then, all the sources I'd read indicated that the Etruscans had not been successful against the fierce "Veti" tribes—the ancient peoples of the Venetian area. I was unaware the Etruscans had achieved *any* sort of a foothold this far northeast, but this material found in recent tomb excavations of southeastern Padua told another story.

There were bronze pots with raised nobs which seemed to have been added as a whimsical afterthought. The pots were different from any I'd seen in books or museums, and the incising on a giant ceramic pot was unique too. There were charming little bronze figures used as votive offerings, and gorgeous red amber beads; they were large and polished to a high gloss. Obviously the Etruscans had traded with people from the Baltic area. What a happy find.

Back on the street, I watched a little girl and her Mamma walking hand in hand and wondered what it would be like growing up in Padua among these ancient, crumbling buildings. Would she see their beauty? Would she get a sense of proportion here in Padua or over in Vicenza where the master of proportion had reigned supreme? Would it seep into her bones and last beyond her teen years—those years when she would surely proclaim she hated everything old? Even crumbling, even faded, these storied places evoke a sense of grace and order. Men were re-working a street patiently laying cobblestones into handsome fan shapes. Their tap, tap, tap was a nice sound. Cobblestone streets are always beautiful but especially so when glistening in the rain. Sometimes the shapes of the buildings, their roof lines with chimney pots, their graceful proportions, or their crumbling plaster take my breath away. I so need to believe that one day that little girl will value her environment and participate as a grown woman in projects to preserve its beauty.

A university boy riding a bicycle with his girl sitting sideways on the crossbar close to him leaned over ever so gently and kissed the back of her neck. I missed *my* sweetheart at that moment. Such moments grab me unawares; they are sudden and powerful. Maybe it was because I was already feeling wistful about my surroundings, perhaps feeling sorry for the little girl of so long ago who had missed out on artistic beauty. I had not seen majestic buildings or entered an art museum until I went away to university. Whatever the reason, suddenly I felt lonesome for my love. I missed his physical strength and his emotional strength, and it came to me that he was my solid anchor. No matter how far away in miles I drifted, the force of his personality and the sound of his voice steadied me. Sure enough, a call home put everything right.

~

According to a brochure, the strange, long building in the center of town was built in 1218. Said to be the "largest hanging hall in the world," it had once been the city's ancient Court of Justice. The entire hall is frescoed with religious and astrological symbols; what an interesting juxtaposition, I thought. It's curious that they still prize an ugly wooden horse built for some sort of jousting ceremony back in 1466. Chances are no one knows what to do with it, and since it's been there so long, who would have the courage to chuck it out?

The building dominates an immense piazza with an outdoor fruit market on one side, a vegetable market on the other, and underneath it all, a lively maze of meat and cheese markets are all crowded together with jovial hawkers vying for custom. Smoky aromas of spicy sausages hanging from rafters mingled with the sharp smells of aged cheeses, and somewhere in the stalls, someone had just brewed a pot of coffee. Its heady elixir wafted over all. It was Saturday night and the market was buzzing, in fact, the whole town seemed to be out with their families. Young university men and women in groups or couples were strolling through the stalls looking, laughing, buying and eating. There were shops for candy, cakes and, of course, gelato in chocolaty or fruity flavors. Caught up in the gaiety of the market, I bought a large hunk of Parmigiano Reggiano. I carried it for days. Without doubt, it was the best cheese I've ever eaten before or since.

⌒⌒

Somewhere among the scattered, ancient university buildings was the one which contains the Anatomical Theater. In 1962, visiting scientists and wives had been taken there. We stood and looked down on the dissecting table which "they said" had a secret trap door through which the body being studied could be dropped in case someone from the church might come spying. The story sounds just that, a story, but it was a fascinating gallery with five concentric circles of wooden carved stalls where students stood to listen and watch the demonstrations being conducted in the center below. In another area of that same building was a wooden pulpit for lecturers called the Pulpit of Galileo who taught in Padua from 1592 to 1610.

⌒⌒

Il Prato della Valle had been transformed. My memory of The Meadow of the Valley was that of a dark, eerie place with two rings of strange figures guarding the moat encircling it. The Prato had been our landmark at night for finding our dormitory nearby. Centuries ago this was at the edge of town, but today, buildings completely enclose the oval-shaped park. Now, it was brightly lit with gaudy-colored lights strung among tawdry markets crowding onto the grass. The mystery was gone. Water was still in the miniature moat and several elfin stone bridges cross to Memmia's Island named after the person who designed this freakish place in 1775. Thirty years ago a thick forest of pines crowded behind the stone statues of illustrious men, but now scarcely a tree is left. Without those shadowy trees to give them a sense of importance, they looked plain silly.

Across the way, an Italian tour group was entering *Santa Guistina* so I tagged along. Even if I hadn't just spent time immersed in *Santo's* glitter, this church would seem exceedingly plain. Built over the oldest chapel in Padua, around 700 A.D., it is starkly severe in its simplicity. They went below to a well where Guistina had performed a miracle, I followed. From the back of the group, I thought the guide said that the bones of many

Copy of Michelangelo's David *stands in front of Palazzo Vecchio.
To his right is* Hercules and Cacus *by Bandinelli, sometimes
called a 'sack of potatos' by the Florentines.*

martyrs were also in the well. I wondered if they were mixed with
hers. There was no literature to explain and I didn't feel free to ask
since I wasn't technically part of their group. Beyond the well is
the original chapel made entirely of very white, very cold marble—even the carved benches. Everything was white, hard, and
cold. Does serenity need to be so chilled, I wondered. My warm
room beckoned me.

The city was lively with students, yet the sounds were muted,
probably by the miles of porticoes. I would leave the next day, and
in spite of demystifying the Prato, Padua, itself, still held an aura
of mystery for me. I knew it would pull me back. Everything
looked dreamlike with the soft lights mounted in the center of
each dome formed by the small arches covering the walks. Those
same enchanting arches, however, were worrisome because they
created loop after loop of dark shadows. I found it difficult to ori-
ent myself. The continuing curves and pillars prevented me from
seeing ahead to pick out landmarks, and I'd done it again. After
traipsing through museums and churches at opposite ends of the

city, I was thoroughly exhausted and chilled through, and to make matters worse, I couldn't find my hotel. A young college woman pointed me in the right direction. With relief, I realized I was almost there. My tiny room was warm. In no time at all, I was snug in bed excited about moving on to Florence the next morning.

Brunelleschi's famous dome in Florence.

PART II:
Florence,
A Renaissance Happening

CHAPTER EIGHT

Grumpy Florentines?
Piazza della Signoria and a copy of Michelangelo's David.
The Academy Gallery and the real thing.
An expensive gelato
The Duomo Museum:
Donatello and Luca della Robbia.
A Change of Heart about Florentines.

DANTE'S BONES HAVE BEEN LYING IN RAVENNA FOR MORE
than seven hundred years, but the Florentines still hold an empty
tomb for him in their sepulchral Church of Santa Croce.
Conveniently, of course, they have forgotten how they sent him
packing in 1302 because he supported the wrong political party.
At that time, two factions in Florence were fiercely battling one
another for control of their City-State: the Guelphs, supporters of
the popes; and the Ghibellines, supporters of the emperors. Dante
Alighieri was a member of the Guelphs.

At the beginning of 1300, Florence was in turmoil. The
Guelphs were in power but they split into two camps, *I Neri*, the
Blacks and *I Bianchi*, the Whites. Dante worked for the Whites.
Although both sides ostensibly supported the pope, the Whites
were the constitutional party. They supported the citizens' government. The Blacks, more aristocratic and more violent, relied on
the support of the populace. The pope favored the Blacks because
he mistrusted the democratic policies of the republic (supported
by the Whites) which strove for Florentine independence from *any*
outside power. Records reveal that in 1301 Dante was prominent
among the ruling Whites, but in June, he returned his famous
answer, *Nihil fiat,* roughly translated "Nothing doing!" to a proposal to grant soldiers to the pope. Soon after that, he was lost

sight of for a time. Various rumors abound regarding his activities, but we do know that on trumped up charges of hostility to the Church and other corrupt practices, in January, 1302, he was barred from ever holding office. In March, he was condemned to be burned to death if he ever came into power in the Commune again.

During the next few years, he sought refuge in various places, including Padua, Verona, Pisa and Bologna. After 1306, all clear traces of Dante were again lost for several years. Finally in 1317, Dante Alighieri settled in Ravenna where he completed his *Divine Comedy*, never to return to Florence. It was clear that he had to stay away, the opposition would have killed him had he hung around one day longer.

I can understand that; Florentines can be a hard-nosed bunch. Once at the end of the day, I wandered into a shoe shop. After looking around for a few moments, I found a pair of boots that looked appealing. I was the only customer, but the two clerks standing behind a counter ignored me. They were chatting with one another as if I were not there. Maybe I should have noticed that they were spreading cloths over some of the merchandise. Maybe I should have taken the hint that it was their closing time, but since I was already there I decided to ask if they had the boots in my size.

"Mi scusi, signorina, c'e' il mio numero di questi stivali?" Excuse me, miss, do you have these in my size? I asked, holding one up.

Obviously they wouldn't know my size, but I couldn't think of another way to ask. One of the women frowned and screwed up her face in disgust, probably at my accent as well as my question.

"No, no, signora, non abbiamo stivali per lei. *Siamo chiusi."* No, no, madam, we do not have boots for *you*. We are closed.

The hostile message was clear. My stumbling skills in the language usually improved with a friendly face; most Italians are encouraging and helpful when I try to speak their language, but in this situation, the language door in my brain slammed shut. I couldn't think of how to remind them that the shop door had been open, that they hadn't told me they were closed when I entered, and so on. I left in defeat and felt thoroughly put down. As I slumped away, however, I reminded myself to not take it personally even though my poor little psyche felt bruised.

Then the open-minded side of me that sees another point of view, sometimes to my own detriment, argued, "Those poor gals were probably weary from standing in the shop for hours dealing with so many tourists."

"Still," I said, as I stiffened my backbone, "that was no excuse for rudeness."

On another occasion in Florence, I went into a bar that had the telltale symbol of a telephone hanging outside indicating a public phone. When I pulled up a stool to sit at the telephone across the room from the counter, you'd think I had committed heresy. The sour barista standing behind the bar gave me a deadly look. His worst reaction came when I laughed heartily while joking with my love back home. Should I have giggled and simpered? The man grew more and more restless, all of which I pretended not to notice. After all, it was a public phone and his behavior seemed silly. Finally, he motioned angrily that someone else was waiting to use the phone. No one in the bar seemed anxious or interested, but I signed off anyway. To appease the barista, I bought a coffee I didn't want, but my custom wasn't wanted either. He threw the change onto the counter. I drank the bitter brew and left. This time when I walked away, I couldn't think of any benevolent excuse for his behavior except that I was a woman alone, a tourist, and was enjoying myself too much. Then again, maybe he was sour before I entered his bar.

This compact little city, however, shelters too many splendors to let that stop one from coming back again and again. And, they know it. A young woman from Seattle working in a scarf boutique near Palazzo Vecchio said when Florentines are criticized for their rudeness, they shrug and say, "As long as we have Michelangelo and the Ponte Vecchio we don't need to worry." Arrogant, yes, but I suppose we should spare some sympathy for these hard-working citizens because their beautiful little city is jammed with visitors from April through September. By mid October, the shopkeepers and museum attendants are exhausted. Gradually, over the years, my attitudes have changed, and now I admire the immense patience Florentines have with all of us.

But, that first time alone in1990, I wasn't so sure. The woman at the information office of the train station was pleasant enough and placed a call to American Express for me to find out if Patricia had left a message, but I was told that I must appear in person before they would look for it. When I said I'd never make it before closing and hoped the message would tell me where to meet a friend, the person on the phone reluctantly agreed to look, but then reported nothing.

It was pouring rain when I arrived from Padua and discovered my "waterproof" jacket wasn't. Papers in an inside pocket were sodden, one of which was the flimsy claim ticket for my bag which I had immediately checked at the station before I went looking for a hotel. Later, when I returned to the station, the attendant fussed because of the ticket's sorry condition. His greenish eyes frowned at me under thick sandy-colored brows. Even though I was surprised that he was angry, I remember thinking about those green eyes and sandy hair. Just goes to show you can't count on stereotypes, I thought. His ancestors must have come from one of the many conquerors from the North, barbarians the Italians called them in times past, whether from Germany, France or Austria. Or, maybe his forefathers were even Vikings who seemed to have been everywhere.

He growled something that sounded like, "Where have you been keeping this ticket...?"

Hunching my shoulders as close to my ears as possible, and opening my palms to heaven, I gave my best rendition of an Italian shrug and said, *"Piove! Piove!"* "It's raining, it's raining."

He grumped as he took the ticket from me in his large hand with thick reddish hairs on its back. He smoothed out the crumpled ticket beside his tally machine. Obviously the thin strip wouldn't fit into the machine until it was dry, and just as obviously, he needed to fuss. He said something humorous to a colleague and then fetched the bag for me almost smiling when he returned.

The charge for checking bags was nominal, 1500 lire, about $1 per bag in 1990, and well worth it. I discovered, however, that in Florence, there was an extra charge of 1500 lire for a coat or umbrella lashed to the suitcase. Anywhere else, such additions were no problem. After achieving an almost smile from him, it was a mistake to make the comparison and an even bigger mistake for me to mention Rome.

"Bah, Roma!" the attendant said, adding something I didn't quite catch, but the general tone was that nobody in Rome did anything right. Most Italians north of Rome seem to feel that way, mainly because Rome is a city of bureaucrats who tend to delay crucial documents indefinitely for whimsical reasons. At that point, I grabbed my bag, thanked him, and left.

The room I found in a hotel near the station was on a busy, noisy street called Via Nazionale. I didn't notice the name of the hotel; the door to the lobby was open and from outside it looked inviting. The cost for a single was 74,000 lire (about $49), almost five times what I'd paid in Verona, but it was pouring, the sky was darkening by the minute, and I crumbled. While registering and relinquishing my passport, I looked around to see that the lower area of the hotel was not attractive after all. The carpet was dirty, not because of the recent rain, it was ground-in, serious grunge, and several sleazy men were leaning against the back wall filling the lobby with their cigarette smoke. They were probably Italians, I had no way of knowing. They were speaking in a slurred manner but it seemed to be Italian, possibly one of hundreds of dialects used on this peninsula. "All Italian men are not suave and debonair," I counseled myself. I didn't want to face that lineup another evening, so I told the clerk my stay would be for one night only.

The upstairs was surprisingly clean and fresh and the toilet and bath rooms down the hall were spotless. In spite of my "firm" decision to travel on alone, I realized I had been looking forward to hearing about Patricia's adventures. Also, I was hoping she had found the hostel we'd heard about while in Verona. This experiment to journey solo was turning into a workshop in self knowledge, self esteem and certainly self reliance. When my friends (and family) told me I was brave (or foolish) as the case happened to be, I tended to belittle the courageousness on the one hand but strengthened my resolve to persist on the other. The truth was that I loved doing it all: finding the correct trains, handling the foreign money, locating lodging, shopping for unexpected necessities, and, of course, choosing the restaurant that appealed to me. Yet, the other side of that truth was that traveling alone is stressful, nerve-wracking and just plain exhausting.

It was a jolt to be back in a bustling, noisy city after the calmness of Padua, but I was dry and warm and feeling cozy as I listened to the rain pound on my window ledge. It was good to hunker down alone and recharge my energies.

The following morning I changed hotels. My next room at hotel Concordia overlooked a narrow street called *Via dell'Amorino*, Street of the Little Darling; "It would surely be quiet," I thought. The price was better, 39,000 lire plus an extra 2,000 for a shower, and it too was scrupulously clean. The owners were truly little darlings. La Signora was short and softly plump with wispy, faded blond hair twisted in a knot on top of her head. She had the smoothest, pink cheeks imaginable; maybe her complexion secret was why Il Signore adored the ground she walked on. They seemed to be doing what they most wanted to do in all of life. One cannot ask for more. He was a bit taller than she with a round belly encircled by a wide belt made of what appeared to be soft, hand-tooled leather and fastened with a silver buckle that had some sort of animal rampant, maybe a lion or a griffin. He spoke softly and knew a bit of English. With some English and some Italian, I understood they had bought the place when they came to Florence from Naples on their honeymoon thirty-six years ago. After a few minutes, he went on about his business, and she invited me into her kitchen for a cup of tea. She asked where I was from and if I had children. I was able to answer those few simple questions which, of course, I asked of her as well. We shared family pictures and smiled at each other a lot. I was tempted to stay put whether I found Patricia or not.

Later in the evening, though, I wondered just what kind of hotel I had chosen. A couple of men were sitting in the first floor lounge area, (in Europe, the first floor is one flight up from the ground floor). These two dark-bearded men looked as if they might be from the Middle East; they wore well-cut western business suits but had turbans on their heads. They were attractive in a dangerous sort of way. In the middle of the night when I went across the hall to the bathroom, a couple of lovely black women were sitting on a bench outside my room. If they had been speaking to each other, it must have been in whispers, because when I opened the door I was surprised to see them there so close to my room. Somehow I got the impression they "belonged" to the men and had to wait on that cramped, backless bench while the men smoked in the comfortable area just around the corner. I never found out who they were or how long the women sat outside my room.

When I located the American Express office, a message was waiting for me. I learned later from Patricia that it had been there the night before, but what can one do? Go away and write about the cruel Florentines as Dante had done in his *Divine Comedy*? In his most famous work of all Italian literature, he did just that. Written in three parts: *The Inferno, Purgatory,* and *Paradise* is an allegory of human life, in poetic form, told as a vision of the world beyond the grave. Full of literary and historical symbolism, it's complex, to say the least, and needs to be read with experts' exegeses close at hand. Certainly, Dante took the opportunity to denounce the corruption of the church and condemned many of the contemporary popes to various levels of hell described in his work. But, some of the people he assigned to the other layers of hell were easily recognizable as Florentine citizens of his time.

It is interesting that he longed for Florence and wrote of its beauty as well as its corruption. It's true, one can both love and hate a place, and in those early days in Florence, I experienced such mixed feelings. My sense of disenchantment may have had something to do, however, with my own struggles and self-proclaimed weaknesses with this venture.

For sure I would never have reached the American Express

office before closing that day of arrival because the office had moved across the Arno River. Let that be another lesson, I scolded. Always check the address on arrival. Mentally shaking a finger at myself, I decided to never again trust information from old guide books. It seemed as if I was forever jotting down reminders of what *not* to do, yet, on the whole, most of my "rules" were working.

⌒

Patricia's note directed me to La Mia Casa, Number 23 at Piazza Santa Maria Novella. The pensione was full, but between the lively housekeeper, who spoke some English, and the owner, Signor Something, grim and gray of face, it seemed that I might be able to move in the *next* day. My accommodation would be one of four in a room at a comfortable charge of 15,000 lire ($10) per night, and when I was shown the spaciousness of the mammoth room with a twenty-foot ceiling, I could see that four would not be crowded. Each person had a night stand beside her bed; all shared a large wardrobe for clothes. An oversized basin was against one wall and a solid table, about eight by four feet where everyone's toilet articles could be spread out, stood next to the basin. The entire establishment was unkempt and dingy, but since Patricia was already there, I decided to chance it. I left her a message to meet for supper.

Because of the uncertainty of where to settle, my anxiety level was high and my spirits were low. I just wanted to get on with being in Florence and again wished I hadn't agreed to meet Patricia. All of this shilly-shallying could have been avoided if I hadn't. After a call home, I was able to put things in perspective because George, my dear love, always asked the right questions to clear my head. I felt re-energized. With a lighter step, I headed for the Piazza della Signoria.

⌒

The Piazza della Signoria is that huge, popular space where cafes are expensive because it's the place to see and be seen. The *Palazzo Vecchio*, Old Palace, dominates the grand area with a strong, masculine force. The building is massive. It looks like a fortress with a battlemented gallery across the top from which a tower thrusts upward to ninety-five meters above the ground, about one hundred four yards. This mighty shaft, placed a bit to the right of center, has a small open balcony with a turret supported by four sturdy columns and more battlements before it reaches the final top. I felt overpowered by the brute force of the asymmetrical tower which commanded, no *demanded*, my attention the moment I stepped onto the square. And, I loved it!

The facade is rough with stones jutting unevenly, but there are some graceful, arched windows on the upper levels. At night, when beams of light are focused on the facade, the effect is softened somewhat, but, this place has been the roiling political center of Florence since Medieval Times—it's still the City Hall—and if one hears any echoes from ancient times, they tend to be those of strife rather than romance. Built around 1300, not long before Dante was forced to leave, it will surely stand another seven or eight hundred years.

Just in front of the Old Palace stands a copy of Michelangelo Buonarroti's most important sculpture, possibly the most famous sculpture in the western world. The original *David* stood here since 1504, when Michelangelo was twenty-nine, but fortunately in 1882 someone finally had the good sense to bring it in out of the pollution caused by exhaust from chimneys, combustion engines and, of course, wind and rain. The copy that replaced the original is so beautiful that I debated with myself about standing in line the next day at *La Galleria dell'Accademia*, The Academy Gallery.

What a mistake it would have been to settle for the copy. Only the original holds the sustained breath of divine inspiration that guided young Michele's hands. There seems to be an inner glow in the stone that gives the sculpture a sense of enduring life. He had polished the white carrara marble to a sheen leaving only a rough point on the top of *David's* head. That rough nob was left there on purpose to keep his creation connected with its original source in Carrara. The slab from which *David* sprang, had been given to him after someone else had tried and failed to make another figure, but most of his sculptures were made from stones he chose himself from the massive marble canyons of Carrara north of Pisa. He is reported to have spent days and even weeks walking among the white marble mountains he loved so much in order to choose the best raw material.

As I walked round and round the magnificent figure so strategically placed in the gallery, the temptation was strong, but, of course, I didn't actually touch the stone. I felt the pulse of genius in it just the same.

Also in The Academy are four unfinished sculptures sometimes called *Slaves* or *Captives* which had been planned for the grandiose tomb of Pope Julius II. These four sculptures and another one of Saint Matthew stand side by side along a wide hallway leading to the circular area where the *David* stands on a pedestal. *David* is, of course, the central focus of the small gallery, and you can see him all the while as you stroll past the other figures. Each time I visit the Gallery, I find myself looking at *David* and sort of holding myself back instead of racing forward to see him first. I tarry and gaze at the other figures, savoring the moment when I finally arrive to stand at his feet.

The unfinished figures are stupendous in their own right, and the year Michelangelo died, 1564, thank goodness his nephew, Leonardo Buonarroti, gave the four *Captives* to the Medici family. They too stood outside for many years in the Boboli Gardens across the Arno behind the Medici's home called Palazzo Pitti, but at least they were preserved, honored and kept together. Four additional unfinished *Captives* are in the Louvre in Paris.

The Academy four are all dramatic, twisting, rough-hewn figures struggling to emerge from even rougher stone which seems to struggle just as vigorously to hold them back. Popular names have been attached to them: "The Young Giant," whose left arm lifted across his face is pinned to his shoulder by a clump of rock unwilling to let go, or so one could imagine; "The Atlas," obviously named because this seated figure is holding a boulder on his shoulder which completely entraps his head and neck; "The Bearded Giant" is named, of course, for his full, rich beard. He is the most completely formed of all the others. His feet are not defined, but both arms are almost free, and his face is definitely emerging; and "The Awakening Giant" arches his back and stretches both trapped arms as he tries in vain to rest himself free of his bed of stone.

The most dramatic unfinished statue in the Academy, however, is that of *Saint Matthew*. Matthew is the only one of the twelve apostles commissioned by the Duomo Committee that Michelangelo ever actually began. He holds a book up in the crook that would be between his left elbow and his shoulder if we could see the entire shape of his arm. All we do see is his hand clasping the book; our imagination does the rest because the arm and shoulder are buried in uncut stone. In fact, the slab of marble from which Matthew seems to be struggling to free himself seems almost like an intentional backdrop. It suggests a rounded halo framing his head. With the book in his left arm, he looks back over his right shoulder—a beautifully, muscular upper arm and shoulder by the way. He appears to be leaning his head against the "halo." His face is chiseled in profile, and his eyes are open possibly looking for divine inspiration. His Gospel is a lengthy one and reports the story and mission of Jesus in more detail than the other three. One might believe he's feeling the heavy spiritual burden of his task. Matthew has some sort of loose, sleeveless tunic which parts enough to reveal the power in his limbs. With his left knee thrust forward, his body wants to come twisting out of the stone. That powerful left leg is just waiting to push off to free himself.

Except for the *David*, to me, *Saint Matthew* is the most fascinating sculpture in the Academy.

To modern eyes, accustomed to abstract art which often looks unfinished, it would be easy to substitute our own notions of who Michelangelo was. Certainly this dynamic genius, driven by his passion for artistic expression, was a man whose own nature must have been molded as he did his stones by the exalted hands of a Divine Spirit. At first sight of these *Captives*, many are tempted to view Michelangelo as an artist who left these figures unfinished in order to send a message. Perhaps their efforts to emerge from the stone were meant to call attention to the frustrations or disappointments he had dealing with the deceit and greed he felt all around him. Or, because they were intended for the tomb of Julius, maybe they represented the Holy Spirit struggling in different forms to come forth into mankind's hearts. Maybe they even represented different aspects of old Julius' spirit himself trying to shed his many sins in order to enter the heavenly kingdom. But, the information that comes to us refutes such ideas.

First of all, Michelangelo had a tremendous sense of pride, which may have brought on many of his troubles in dealing with other people, other artists and certainly his patrons. Maybe his pride drove him to bite off more than he could chew. One of the things he took pride in was to do a job from start to finish, and the emphasis was on finish. Much of his anguish was because he was often thwarted in being able to finish his projects. In his letters, he complained bitterly—with some paranoia—of his clashes with outside forces that kept him from working. In the five years just before Pope Julius II called him to Rome the first time, Michelangelo had been most productive. But, it seems, from that time on, he felt more and more frustrated by the very real obstacles that kept him from working on the tomb for Julius. The main obstacle, of course, was Julius himself with his irascible nature coupled with his tendency to put Michelangelo off, assign him the job of painting the Sistine Chapel, or simply to be unavailable. He was one of the most warlike popes and was often off campaigning to gain more lands and power for the papacy, or possibly more glory for himself.

The tomb for Julius seemed to have been Michelangelo's favorite project, but he felt frustrated at every turn. His letters to family and friends reveal his struggles with this endeavor and with other jobs particularly when the commissions came from popes, cardinals or nobility which they increasingly did. They were, of course, some of the most prestigious opportunities, and he was no doubt envied by many. Those VIPS, however, were the very ones who ignored his requests for decisions, changed their minds on a whim, or delayed payment for purchases he made for them out of his own pocket.

Here is a telling letter written from Florence in May, 1506:
Giulano da Sangallo, Florentine Architect to Pope Julius in Rome.

Giulano, I was informed by a letter of yours that the Pope was angry at my departure, and that His Holiness is ready to make the deposit and to do what we agreed upon; also, that he wants me to return and not to worry about anything.

About my departure, it is a fact that on Holy Saturday I heard the Pope say at the table, to a jeweler and to the master of ceremonies with whom he was conversing, that he did not want to spend another penny on stones, either large or small. This amazed me a great deal: just the same, before leaving, I asked him for part of the money I needed to continue the work. His Holiness answered me to return on Monday. I returned there on Monday, Tuesday, Wednesday and Thursday. At last on Friday morning I was turned out of doors, that is chased away. The man who sent me away said that he knew who I was, but that he had such orders. I was thrown in great despair. But this was not the only cause of my departure: suffice it to say that it made me think that if I remained in Rome, my tomb would be made before that of the Pope.

Now you write me on behalf of the Pope. Make His Holiness understand that I am as willing as ever to carry out the work, and if he wants by all means to make that tomb, he should not mind where I carry out my work, as long as within the five-year period we agreed upon, it is set up in the place of his choice in St. Peter's, and it is as beautiful as I promised it would be: for I am sure that if it is carried out, there will be nothing like it in the whole world.

Now, if His Holiness wants me to proceed, let him set up said deposit, and I will have the numerous blocks of marbles I ordered from Carrara and those I have in Rome sent here, even if this should be against my interest. After I finish each piece, I could send it along, so that His Holiness would derive the same pleasure from my work as if I were in Rome. As for the money for the work, I will make out a written obligation to suit His Holiness, and I will give him whatever guarantee he asks of me, and the whole city of Florence will be my witness. I will do it better here and with more devotion, because I will not have to think about so many things. Nothing more."

Michelangelo also worried about details at home with his father and brothers and their wives. Sometimes he begged them for patience with him for not being there to handle household or details and not being able to send them more money. Other times, he admonished his brothers for not being more diligent in their own efforts. He worried about their health and even more about his own. A pattern emerges that hints that he may have been a hypochondriac. Certainly he worried that he wouldn't live much longer. From the age of forty onward, in his letters he spoke often of himself as an old man, of how old and tired he was, and that he didn't expect to live much longer. Yet, he lived until age eighty-nine!

Here are a few excerpts from letters about health and family worries:

At age 38, to his brother, 1513.

...I do not think I will be able to come this September, for I am so hard-pressed that I do not have the time to eat. Just the same, as I promised you, I want to give you one thousand large gold ducats, so that, with the others you have, you begin to be on your own. I want no share of your earnings, but I want to be sure that at the end of ten years, if I am alive, and if I should want them, you will give me, in money or in goods, these thousand ducats...Concerning the four hundred ducats...

At age 43, to an agent of Pope Leo X, 1518.

...I beg you to let me know soon what you think I should do, ... If in my letters to you I should not write as correctly as one would expect, or if, sometimes, I leave out the main verb, please forgive me, for I have a bell ringing in my ears which does not let me think of anything I want."

At age 50, to an agent to Pope Clement, 1525.

...If, as I said, my pension is paid to me, I shall never stop working for Pope Clement with all the strength I have, which is not very much, since I am old. At the same time, ...these continuous irritations have prevented me from doing anything I wanted the last few months: for one cannot be busy at one thing with his hands, and at something else with his brain, especially when one works with marble. They say here that these annoyances are meant to spur me on; and I tell you that those are poor spurs which make a horse go backwards. I have not received my pension for over one year, and I have been struggling with poverty. I am left all alone to bear my troubles, and I have so many of them that they keep me busier than does my art; this is because I do not have the means to keep someone to manage my house.

Another reason why these *Captive* figures were probably never meant to be left unfinished is that he was a perfectionist. He never succeeded in establishing a typical artist's *bottega*, that is, a workshop in which apprentices were taught by watching and following a master. Typically these apprentices would be given some of the drudgery-type of work, even some of the final finishing and polishing. He tried to establish such a shop, but as a rule, few of his helpers satisfied him for long; he had difficulty delegating to students. No one seemed to do anything right. He set high standards for himself and expected the best from others as well. The reward we have for this trait is that when we look at a work attributed to Michelangelo, we can feel sure it was executed by his own hands.

Scholars and art students have gained insight into how Michelangelo worked when they study these unfinished pieces. Many are convinced that they reveal what Michelangelo meant in his poetry when he claimed the figures were already there inside the blocks of marble and all he did was remove the superfluous stone. With the bent leg thrusting forward, as if about to step right out of the marble, the unfinished *Saint Matthew* is a superb example of this marvelous belief.

> *The best of artists can only select*
> *the concept which the marble already contains*
> *within its excess. But there only attains*
> *the hand that obeys the intellect.*

. . .

> *Just as by cutting away, O Lady, one extracts*
> *from the hard alpine stone*
> *a living figure which alone*
> *grows the more, the more the stone diminishes.*
> *So all our acts*
> *and all good works for the soul*
> *trembling still for its divine goal*
> *are, in the excess of one's own flesh, hidden*
> *within the crude coarse encrusted skin.*
> *You, however, you alone*
> *can draw forth from me*
> *that which lies in my remotest extremity*
> *I have no other course*
> *for of myself and in myself there is neither will nor force.*

The second poem was probably written to Vittoria Colonna, a dear friend with whom Michelangelo had a long-standing platonic relationship.

My heart aches for Michelangelo. He was a kind of misfit from early childhood. His Mother died when he was about six. Michelangelo was sent to live with stonecutters for a time, in fact, he often said that because his wet nurse was the wife of a stonecutter, he took in marble dust with his milk. Although his ancestors came from wealth and nobility, most of the wealth had been dissipated by his grandfather, so that Ludovico Buonarroti, Michelangelo's father, had few financial resources to rely on and didn't seem capable of amassing any on his own. Ludovico hoped his sons would be successful in business to re-establish the family's wealth, and he was understandably not happy about

Michelangelo's 'foolishness' in drawing and chiseling stone. Later, however, when his son earned money through his artistic skills, he was willing to let him support him and the rest of the family. In fact, Michelangelo supported his father and brothers and their families for most of his life; even after his death they benefited from his efforts.

Fortunately, numerous letters from Michelangelo to family and associates were preserved, and from them, it seems to me that his father was a pompous fool who needed Michelangelo's guidance in matters of business as well as managing family affairs, yet, nowhere in any of those letters does he ever show anything but concern and respect for his father.

My heart goes out to Michelangelo because he was lonely and longed for intimacy. If rumors and innuendos are true, he was a homosexual and fought against that "sin" within his breast and with his God as well as with society's mores. Much of his poetry reveals artistic frustrations and struggles, but there are numerous love poems as well. He may have had a relationship with one apprentice, Francesco Urbino, who was with him for twenty-five years; there doesn't seem to be any proof, but I hope he found some happiness

Back at Piazza della Signoria, at a bar near the corner, a cappuccino cost 4,500 lire, not bad for table service at this prime location, but later what a shock I had when I discovered the gelato shop on the corner wanted 12,000 lire ($8) for a double dip cone. I was outraged! Why didn't I hand the cone back to the clerk? Why didn't I ask the cost before I ordered? Who would expect such a ridiculous price? It was an obvious slap in the tourist's face and another reason for me to be cross with the Florentines. I walked away grumbling mostly at myself for being so unaware. Still, that zingy scoop of lemon gelato on top of a scoop of dark, rich chocolate was a brief moment of paradise.

Not far away, the front of the Duomo sparkled. It had been cleaned recently and the scaffolding was gone. No doubt it is a continual process especially since they allow the worst kind of traffic to roar past the building within twenty feet of its precious marble facade. The large diesel city buses and tourist buses spew black clouds of soot into the air, regular autos pass by, of course, and the uncontrolled exhausts of the worst culprits of all are the motor scooters which pollute the sound waves as well.

The red, green and white colored marbles of the elaborate geometric designs were brilliant even on cloudy days. The Duomo's official name is *Santa Maria del Fiore*, Saint Mary of the Flowers, but to everyone it's the Duomo. It was built over a much older church, *Santa Reparata*, dating from the sixth or seventh century, and had been reconstructed many times over. One day, I will visit the excavations to see ancient foundations going back to Roman times. For now, I was thrilled to be walking on ground resplendent with ancient memories. They crowded in upon me and steeped me in feelings of belonging somehow. My bones knew that some long-ago time I belonged to this land. The cars, scooters, buses, bicycles and, of course, the thousands of feet crossing and re-crossing the street that circles the Duomo thrummed in my breast like a repeat performance of that long ago past. Maybe there wasn't the dreadful combustive damage to the air in times past, but there was certainly the same hubub created by energetic, resourceful people. It seems that the people of this peninsula have been more blessed with ideas of design and beauty than in any other lands. Since I feel a kinship with it all, maybe that is why I get angry and agitated when I see how the city leaders are allowing such wasteful destruction of their beautiful monuments. The Duomo is but one of many buildings suffering from the smoky assault, but because of the light colors, the black grime and filth show up within a few months of being cleaned. And, with each cleaning, a bit more of the precious marble is scoured away.

A duomo or cathedral isn't necessarily the largest or most beautiful church in a city; the term is an ecclesiastical one indicating that it's the resident bishop's church. There can be only one duomo in a city and only if the city has a bishop. Strange as it seems, Saint Peter's in Rome is not officially a cathedral. The

Pope's "seat," as bishop of Rome, is in Saint John in the Lateran, beyond the Colosseum. In the case of Florence, Saint Mary of the Flowers is the bishop's seat and indeed it is the biggest in the city. In fact, it is the third largest church in Christendom, with Saint Peter's first and Saint Paul's in London second.

Ostensibly, the Florentine Duomo was meant to be for the glory of God, but there may have been some reflected glory for the town fathers as well. Can't you just hear them as they gathered in the Palazzo Vecchio, devising ways to tax the people even more in order to build the biggest and best cathedral in all of Tuscany, always looking for ways to surpass their rivals in Pisa and Siena.

Some day, I thought, I would come back in January when the crowds are gone and spend a whole day identifying all the figures in all the niches, and over all the doors. I would wear a muffler and bring my binoculars to look at the *Porta della Mandorla,* The Door of the Almond, which dates from 1391. I would need the magnification to see the intricate carving above the doorway, partly because it might be blackened with smudge from the evil forces of pollution and partly because the arch is so high. The *Assumption of the Virgin,* carved by Nanni di Banco around 1420, is in an almond-shaped frame of the doorway's gable, thus the name *mandorla.* What interests me more is that two heads on the gable are said to have been done by a very young Donatello. There are, of course, other doorways and other carvings and this is but one monument in the city.

If it were cold, I could take a break for a steaming hot bowl of *pasta fagioli,* that wonderful winter combination of pasta and white beans fortified with garlic. When you eat a plate of pasta and beans in Italy, the pasta has been cooked *al dente,* it is never soft and mushy as it usually is in bowls of what American restaurants call 'minestrone.' Minestrone in Italy is a rich vegetable soup made from a beef stock with no pasta in it whatsoever. If it did have pasta, it would be firm or would be sent back to the kitchen immediately by Italian eaters. Known as 'bean eaters,' Florentines do know how to transform a simple plate of white beans into a savory delicacy using a luscious combination of green, extra virgin olive oil and a few well-chosen herbs.

Next, I might bring a detailed guidebook with me to undertake a study of the figures on Giotto's campanile begun in 1334. Even though most originals have been removed to the safety of the Duomo Museum, I prefer to get a feel for the artist's original intention. When the mood takes me, I've been known to plunge into a project and wallow in a sea of details. For example, it is a delight to decipher all the characters in the carved *Creation of Man* done by Andrea Pisano, or identify each of the different figures symbolizing the arts and industries. One more good reason to travel alone; because if I stand in one spot for an eternity, no one is waiting impatiently for me to move along. The campanile is faced with the same slabs of colored marble as the Duomo: the white from Carrara, the green from Prato and the red from The Maremma, an area in the southwestern part of Tuscany.

In the same grand plan, with fewer tourists around, I would be able to stand close enough and long enough in front of Lorenzo Ghiberti's famous east doors of the Baptistery to identify each story in each of those ten panels of which Michelangelo is said to have called, "The Gates of Paradise." My detailed guidebook would help me identify each story from the Old Testament.

There was a heated contest over who would be chosen to do these doors and Filippo Brunelleschi and Lorenzo Ghiberti were the two finalists, but Filippo lost out. He was bitter about it. He felt he had lost because Ghiberti had invited opinions and even incorporated some ideas from prominent citizens who just happened to be on the selection committee. Brunelleschi felt this was unethical; he, himself, had worked on his submission in private. But, Brunelleschi was not what we would call a 'people person,' and didn't know how to promote himself, obviously Ghiberti did. Ghiberti wrote one of the first autobiographies of the Renaissance, and it is fascinating to read how he viewed his own grandeur and read his version of the contest. Without question, Ghiberti's work is glorious; certainly Michelangelo was a person to recognize talent.

If you want to judge for yourself, you can see the two contest panels, both done on the theme of *The Sacrifice of Isaac*, arranged

Stone patterns beckon to secrets and wonders.

side by side in the Bargello Museum. My loyalties tend to be for Brunelleschi probably more for emotional reasons than calculated artistic ones. It pleased me, therefore, to find that Kenneth Clark, a noted art historian, had this to say about the two panels, "The Ghiberti relief is dominated by a strong, vital rhythm which forces us to concentrate on the terrible subject (Abraham sacrificing his son Isaac). By comparison, the Brunelleschi lacks a unifying rhythm, in fact the composition is rather awkward. But, when one concentrates on the heads of Abraham and Isaac, one finds something that Ghiberti never quite achieved: an intensity of purpose, a feeling that men's relations with God and with each other is a terrible, and ultimately a tragic responsibility."

Brunelleschi is another one of those troubled geniuses who reaches out to grab my interest and my allegiance. I developed affection for him as I read about his struggles to convince the city fathers that his design for the huge dome of the Duomo was the best one, and for his other architectural struggles throughout the city. Much more about him will follow, but for now I think it is safe to say it was just as well for Brunelleschi that he didn't win the Baptistry door contest, because those massive doors took forty-eight years out of Ghiberti's life.

Once Ghiberti won the contest with an Old Testament subject, he was commissioned to do a set of doors on the north side of the Baptistry which was divided into twenty-eight compartments with scenes from the life of Christ, the Evangelists and other figures. He included a self portrait. It took him from 1403 to 1424 to complete this set. Following that success, he was given a second commission to do the famous east doors which also contain a self portrait. The east doors took him from 1425 to 1452. He had help in the casting and polishing, and was also involved in other commissions during that time, something Brunelleschi, a more single-minded individual probably could not have handled. It's a fascinating story and we all benefit from having both the gorgeous golden doors *and* the monumental architectural achievement of Brunelleschi's dome which dominates not only the little city of Florence but the entire countryside around it.

Toward the back of the Duomo and just across its ring road is the *Museo dell'Opera di Santa Maria del Fiore*, The Duomo

Museum—*opera* means work. The Opera of the Duomo has been responsible for the maintenance of the duomo complex since the fifteenth century. It is my favorite museum in all of Florence. It's often missed by those who are in town only briefly. Here, statues, carved reliefs, busts, plaques and other objects removed from the Duomo, the Baptistery and the Campanile are all preserved for safekeeping. Someone suggested that museums ought to be approached lightly and experienced personally. To me, there are two basic approaches to museums: one, is to carry prepared notes identifying everything, and two, is to go absolutely loose and move as the art pulls me. The Duomo Museum is a manageable museum; I need no detailed plan in hand. I just go.

The first time I visited there, the arrangement was rather lackadaisical. It seemed as if things had been hurriedly carried in and placed wherever a spot could be found. Now, however, it has been beautifully renovated. It even has elevators. Even though it is organized much more fastidiously than before, and maybe a trifle too regimented, it is still my favorite.

Michelangelo's magnificent *Florentine Pietà* broods on the landing of the stairway; as long as it is there, I will always hop off the train passing through Florence to look at it no matter where else I'm headed. The arrangement of this *Pietà* involves four figures: Mary, the grieving Mother who does not hold her dead son across her lap, rather he is supported somewhat by her crouching figure to one side of him, *Maddalena* stands on the other side, but the bulk of the weight of Christ's body seems to be supported from behind by an old man, said to represent Nicodemus. The strong, old man with a hooded cowl forming a soft peak at the top of his head bends over the group supporting the dead Christ with one arm while comforting the Madonna with the other. This figure is said to be a self portrait of the artist at age eighty. What a face! What grief!

This *Pietà* is not made from the white Carrara marble which Michelangelo usually preferred. Instead, the marble is a golden color. The warmth coming from the softer color makes the figures come alive. Once, before the museum was equipped with all kinds of alarms, I walked around the sculpture and briefly touched the back of Nicodemus/Michelangelo. A jolt of energy raced through me. Whatever it was, perhaps my own current of excitement, I trembled, and for that brief moment I was breathing and pulsing with the great artist's energy.

It is said the *Pietà* was meant for Michelangelo's own tomb but in frustration one day he tried to destroy it because "the stone would not obey" him. Luckily, his students stopped him and pieced together the breaks, but Christ's left leg was lost forever. Later in a book published by Phaidon Publishers, Inc., called *Michelangelo*, I found a picture of the original *Pietà* formed in wax and preserved in the Gigli Collection. In the wax model, the left leg of Christ juts out across the crouching figure of his Mother, and the Magdalene figure appears to be more emotionally involved. The jutting left leg gave the overall shape of the group a better proportion. I noticed, however, that the left leg was raised forward on the ball of the foot giving the illusion that its energy was supporting Christ's own body. How interesting. If the stone would have obeyed Michelangelo and he had finished the piece, I just know he would have adjusted that tension in the foot because he was meticulous in dealing with weight in his sculptures. His attention to body balance and where the weight is placed on a figure's foot or leg or hip is why his pieces are indeed masterpieces.

One of the pupils finished the group, evidently Michelangelo had nothing more to do with it. Where the missing leg would have gone, there is drapery roughly filled in, almost as if it were a thick plaster spread on to look like the continuation of the Mother's thigh and gown. The Magdalene figure appears to have been entirely done by a student. The proportion is off. Her body is too small compared to the other figures and both body and face are more like a thirteen-year-old rather than a mature woman. Her body does not appear to be bearing any weight with which to help support the heaviness of the Christ figure. Her head turns away rather than inward as it ought to if she were offering support, or if she felt any grief. Her face is bland; it reveals no emotion at all. The defective sculpture offers a good opportunity to compare the skill and insight of a great artist with that of a journeyman.

The *Pietà* is so moving that I've noticed everyone is pulled toward it if only to stop on a step for a moment to stare. No one passes undisturbed. The outpouring of grief that emanates from this sculpture speaks to anyone who has lost a loved one, or even contemplated such a horror. But, to lose a child must be the most unbearable grief of all. Then, to watch one's child suffer so cruelly and unjustly must be something one could never accept. Yet, whenever I think of this moving work, the grief I recall and feel the most is that of the old man. I can't help but wonder what thoughts Michelangelo carried in his heart as he chiseled this marvelous portrait of his own face intended for his own tomb.

If you were ever wondering where Donatello's ravaged *Maddalena Penitente* is, you will find her in the room at the top of the stairs of the Duomo Museum. Anyone whoever sat in a darkened auditorium looking at slides for Art 101 will remember seeing this powerful sculpture of the *Penitent Magdalene*. He carved her out of poplar and she stands thin and wasted from her thirty years in the desert. Although she is nude, her long hair covers her like a tattered nightgown.

In the 1966 flood, the lower part of the sculpture was covered with water mixed with mud and oil. A coat of brown paint was added in the seventeenth century, and when the statue was cleaned, it was discovered that Donatello had originally painted her skin to suggest a tan from the desert sun and had gilded her hair. Traditionally, Magdalene had long, blond hair and she is usually depicted in paintings with either blond or reddish-blond tresses. It was thrilling to confront this powerful work. Her ravaged, emaciated face with sunken eyes and missing teeth is a far cry from the raving beauty she once was.

In the large upper room, I also found a marble choir carved by Luca della Robbia. The frolicking cherubs and children prance, play pipes and sing in that same wild exuberance that overtakes real children when they get their second wind just before bedtime. You can see their flushed cheeks and wild eyes. Luca carved the choir in marble before he started his lucrative business of painted, glazed terra cottas which are found all over Tuscany. Did he ever regret leaving true sculpture behind?

On the opposite wall another marble choir hangs; this one is by Donatello. His children play and dance to heavenly music as well. It's impossible to choose a favorite between the two, and as long as I can sit on a comfortable bench in the middle of the room gazing from one to the other, it makes no sense to try.

Loitering against the walls like displaced citizens are more carved figures by Donatello and his peers. They had a purpose once when mounted on the outside of the Duomo. There they represented important Biblical figures reminding the faithful of their prophecies and truths. Fortunately, they were rescued from pollution but not before some were severely damaged. They do look pitiful and reminded me once again, that Florence's city fathers have exercised poor judgment for years by allowing motor vehicles into its busy heart. It's madness!

I so love being in Italy. Its lengthening shadow of storied past lays a patina of history, like particles of dust in the aging air upon every relic, upon every ancient monument, as well as on modern activities, giving substance to the old memories and meaning to the new ones. That's why I hate to leave. When I must say goodbye, powerful images such as the *Pietà* or the *Maddalena* tug at me to stay.

On a more practical note, as soon as I walked outside the museum, I realized a pressing urgency to use the W.C. I managed to communicate my need to the guard. He was friendly and forgiving as he released a gadget on the turnstile and pointed the way to the toilet. His kind smile of recognition when I emerged and walked toward the exit started me thinking that perhaps most Florentines didn't fit the disparaging stereotype I had laid on them. The museum guard could have 'forgotten' that I had just exited. I could not forget the time I had stood in a comfortable alcove of a trattoria to use the pay phone rather than face those on the noisy street. My conversation lasted too long, and the workers politely asked me to finish so they could close. Nor could I forget the sweet gentleman from Hotel Concordia who ran after me with the prescription glasses I'd left behind.

Occasionally tired clerks can be rude, and sometimes I long for the American notion that the customer is always right, or for a more practical system uncluttered with bureaucracy in the post office, but the old-world Italy with its warmth and *simpatico* nature of Italians comes forth more often than not. It seems they have an abiding sense of caring about other human beings, not only as potential customers to improve the 'bottom line' on their financial statements, but a genuine desire to take the time for a personal encounter—a desire for one human to meet another human face to face. In short, Italians need to communicate.

Humanism, which rose in fifteenth-century Italy and Florence, is a philosophy that claims that rational human beings can reason together, help each other and live in harmony. I think this philosophy still permeates the psyches of modern Italians. Mary McGrory, a columnist for *The Washington Post,* wrote about the Italians' record during the Holocaust of the Second World War. "Eighty-eight percent of Italy's approximately 50,000 Jews survived. For those who wondered how Italy, *the country of small kindnesses,* could have been part of the Holocaust, the answer is, it wasn't." Several survivors at a conference held in 1993 at the Holocaust Museum remarked that their "Italian saviors didn't preach or beat their breasts. It was somehow taken for granted that they would help an unfortunate fellow member of the human race."

Occasionally, if a person is busy or distracted, his or her first reaction might be brusque, but in a trice, she then sets about to do her best to answer my needs. That brusqueness may just be part of crowded city life. They sometimes wince at my accent or awkward use of their beautiful language, but many take the time to try for a real communication, if only to lock eyes and smile before moving on. Often, they gently correct my usage or pronunciation. When I thank them and suggest that they are my professor or professoressa, more often than not, we both end smiling with a warm handshake.

As I left the museum, my head was bursting with images of the *Pietà,* the *Maddalena,* and the frolicking children in the marble choirs as well as these thoughts of the inherent warmth found in

Italians' breasts. Already I was feeling the nostalgia I would suffer back home, knowing I would long for this place and these people who live vibrantly in the present with daily reminders of their past glories (and follies) all around them. I did not want to leave Florence or any other part of Italy.

༽

CHAPTER NINE

La Mia Casa, a disgrace but what a location.
Santa Maria Novella: green, white and ever serene.
Giorgio's Place. Signor Greyface.
Masaccio, slovenly Tom.
Brunelleschi's Crucifixion *and his Impossible Dome.*

LA MIA CASA WAS A SHABBY HOSTEL, BUT IT HAD A GREAT location because it faced the beautiful Piazza Santa Maria Novella. Although La Mia Casa was within a few blocks of the station, as was my first hotel on noisy Via Nazionale, it lay in a different direction and that made all the difference. As I had been organizing to get off the train two days before, the sign *Firenze S.M.N.* caused me a moment of panic, but a pleasant youngster carrying a cello case strapped on his back assured me it was indeed the main station for Florence. Now it was clear; the station was named for the gorgeous church.

Santa Maria Novella's facade is made of white and dark green (almost black) geometric designs in stone, and lacy patterns and scrolls are carved in graceful proportion to each other. The horizontal stripes of green and white follow along the entire side wall enclosing gardens and an ancient cemetery; the long wall extends toward the station just behind the church. I like to walk beside the striped wall touching the marble like a kid who runs a stick along a picket fence. Tuscany has other exotic, Levantine-striped churches in Siena, Pisa, Lucca, Pistoia, Prato, Arezzo and probably many others, but of those I've seen, Santa Maria Novella is my favorite. Inside, the church is dark and quiet, and there's a friendly touch of identification plaques for the famous paintings. It's almost as if they are admitting that tourists come in for the art. Many churches identify nothing. Signs are there too in several languages reminding guests to be quiet and not stomp about during services along with the usual requests for donations. Who would pay the thousand small fees and donations left discreetly all day long if they didn't have the art? Modern Italians do not appear to support the hundreds of churches in Italy on a regular basis. Thank goodness the Italian state recognizes their value and through its bureaucratic maze does what it can to maintain and restore some of the important ones.

Through the centuries, Florentines have always paid serious attention to the architectural design of their piazzas. This particular one is a beautiful urban place even though some of the buildings along its perimeter seem to have developed without a unified plan. Maybe that's why it appeals to me. Directly in front of the church, a green, grassy space stretches for about one hundred yards with a small obelisk at each end, a pool in the middle and several benches scattered around. People are here in early mornings and late nights.

It's not as bold as the Piazza della Signoria, the city-hall part of town where Michelangelo's *David* stands, nor as balanced as the dignified Piazza Santissima Annunziata where the famous foundling hospital sits designed by Filippo Brunelleschi, but to me the green-and-white facade of Santa Maria Novella and its green space is the prettiest. I never tire looking at it. I'm in good company because Henry James claimed it as his favorite too. The feel here is of an old, comfortable neighborhood. It's a shame that large, bad-smelling city buses make frequent stops beside it, then again, it is one of the nicest places in the world to wait for a bus.

~

If Patricia hadn't already been staying in La Mia Casa, it's doubtful I would have made it past the first few steps. A small brass plaque indicating the name and address was on the wall beside an open stairwell. So far so good. The steps were of a soft, porous stone riddled with large pock marks, and with each step I could feel the depressions made by thousands of feet gone before. Nice. The stairwell was dimly lit, and from the darkest corner near the turning of the steps, the rancid smell of urine rose. Not so nice, but it was raining, and for me, rain is a good omen, so up I went.

At the first floor landing was an attractive mahogany double door with another brass plaque and a bell. Things were looking better. Inside, however, the dark green carpet was littered with lint and dust. The owner, a tall, emaciated man, spoke enough English to indicate he might have a place for me the next day. He seemed preoccupied and hassled and wasn't willing to give me a firm answer as he walked away flicking ashes from his cigarette onto the carpet. Here was an Italian who did not fit the happy-go-lucky stereotype. The assistant manager said she had worked for the Signore twelve years and for his parents before that. She said he could be difficult at times, but that his flare-ups blew over quickly. She spoke less English than he did, but she was a natural communicator. Twelve years seemed a long time to be associated with him. Who knows what story lay behind their relationship? One morning she waved cheerily to me from her own room one level up across the open air courtyard. During my stay, I never did learn how many floors of the building the Casa used, maybe all four upper ones. Except for towers and domes of churches, most buildings in Florence are only five or six floors tall, at the most, preserving its old-world skyline. The rooms were large with high ceilings, the hallways were wide, and the stairway leading to upper rooms might have been rather grand in earlier times, but it had been reworked poorly. This may have been an elegant home at one time. Then again, maybe it never was any better than this.

That evening I finally met with Patricia and joined her and her roommates for dinner. A gorgeous eighteen-year-old from Australia was one of the young women sharing Patricia's room; we thought she was even more beautiful than Elizabeth Taylor had been at that age. Her mother had Spanish ancestors, and Rachel could have been Italian. Her lustrous black hair fell around her shoulders, and like Liz, she had violet eyes. People (usually young men) spoke to her on the street as if she might understand them or at least hoped she would.

We went to a family trattoria called *Da Giorgio*, Giorgio's Place. When we entered with Rachel, all the young men's heads turned to stare. The walls were gray stucco with no decorations anywhere; it was a long, plain room devoted to serving simple fare and lots of it. A two-liter jug of wine along with a liter of mineral water and a basket of earthy, heavy bread were already on each table. After a day with little to eat and miles of walking, we began nibbling the bread immediately, but when the cute waiter, one of Giorgio's sons, announced choices from the first course, we were off to stuffing ourselves. There was no menu and he had to repeat his offerings several times to all of us, but he didn't seem to mind. Years later, I dropped into Giorgio's and recognized the same fellow. He seemed to have lost his energy and bonhomie. Maybe the excitement of waiting on hungry people had worn him down.

Included in the fixed price was a *primo* (pasta or soup), a *secondo* (meat or fish), a *contorno* (salad or vegetables) and, of course, the wine, water and bread.

The young women in our group enjoyed Giorgio's Place because we were the only women there. They went back often. Young working men eat out a lot, but I didn't see any young working women dining without men. Afterwards, someone in our group led us on to Vivoli's, a popular gelateria with the guidebook set. The prices were reasonable; I was too embarrassed to tell anyone how much I'd paid over at Piazza della Signoria. I couldn't eat another bite anyway and had a Hag instead. Caffè Hag is a decaf espresso that comes in individual foil packets; it isn't as good as freshly ground espresso, but a cappuccino made with Hag is not bad.

It was a lovely evening; the rain had stopped and a moon was smiling on Florence. A young American was playing a guitar and singing Bob Dylan songs in the Duomo area. An enterprising fellow, he had set up a portable microphone and sound system; his music drifted gently out over the piazza. Many were out enjoying the evening; for a change, there seemed to be as many Italians as foreigners. After a while, I headed back to my quiet little hotel with plans to move to La Mia Casa the next day.

The landlord of La Mia Casa ran a strange ship; one day a room was promised; the next day, maybe not. No matter what he would eventually decide about me, after a night on Via dell'Amorino, I knew I'd move again. The room had been pleasant enough and the owners were lovely people, but my room looked on a street which I thought would be quiet but turned out to be far noisier than Via Nazionale the night before. At least on Nazionale a constant traffic sound created a steady drone, but on Amorino, people talked beneath my window, then they were quiet, then someone shouted, then they were quiet, then they started cars and roared off, then they set off car alarms, and the final straw was when someone had a joust with garbage cans.

In the morning, I left my bag with the angelic landlady and hurried to the Casa to confirm once and for all whether I had a room or not. When the Signore finally confirmed my space in his establishment, I started back for my belongings. At that moment, the sky opened with a torrential downpour. The doors of Santa Maria Novella were open, and I took the opportunity to make another quick exploration of the vast church. That's when I discovered Domenico Ghirlandaio's lush frescoes covering the entire area behind the high altar. I tried to identify which angel young Michelangelo might have painted when he was apprenticed in Ghirlandaio's workshop.

I heard priests chanting somewhere in a chapel, and I listened to the rain pouring outside. Everything felt right with the world and marvelously mystical.

Never have I changed beds so often in one town, and when I returned to La Mia Casa with my bag, I feared I might be turned away after all. For some reason, Signore was upset with all of us.

He insisted I couldn't be in the room with Patricia even though Anna, one of her roommates, wanted to leave. He wouldn't let Anna go without paying for another day because she had originally indicated a certain length of time. He won the battle, Anna stayed one more night but at what cost in anxiety and stress? It seemed he made it more difficult for himself than necessary. Why couldn't he charge per bed and not worry where the singles slept? It didn't appear that his motive was for money because he had an eager waiting list. It must have been because he'd been doing it that way for thirty years and could not—would not—change.

Signor Greyface, my name for him because his skin had the pallor of a corpse, had a room just off the common room. It seemed to be his office, but he never invited anyone in there to handle paperwork; all business was done at the bar among the cups, espresso machine and bottled water. He slipped into his room, I supposed, to do whatever it took to run a pensione or small hotel. The old word "pensione" is now used loosely. Technically, hotels in Italy are rated by stars and like most on my list, this was a one-star establishment. If they offer at least one meal they can call themselves a pensione; some offer breakfast at exorbitant prices, of which no one partakes, yet that offering permits certain rating privileges. If anyone should request breakfast in such establishments, it is usually brought in from a nearby bar.

Greyface offered a continental breakfast for a reasonable cost, paid for on the spot—he never ran a tab—but his cappuccini were below par and his rolls were stale. To start the day, I preferred to go out for a good cappucino found in almost any neighborhood bar. Sometimes at the end of the day, though, it was nice to plop down for a cup of coffee or hot chocolate and compare notes with whomever happened to be in the coffee room. A pleasant elderly couple was staying in one of the private rooms, and Sarah, was particularly enthusiastic and knowledgeable about Florentine art. Her tips were always welcome.

With unmistakable body language, Greyface made it clear that no one was to enter his room. When he came out, sometimes he didn't quite close the door, and of course I peeked. It was dark and smelled sour and musty. He smoked constantly, no doubt cutting down the blood flow and contributing to his pallor. The office was cluttered with supplies and odd pieces of furniture from who knows how many years (decades? centuries?) of doing business. If he wasn't in sight, we knocked on the door to order coffee or buy a bottle of mineral water. He would heave a long sigh and come out to prepare coffee or chocolate. He eventually smiled and managed a pleasantry or two. In the evenings, he offered free movies in English (old American ones) which many of the youngsters enjoyed. In spite of his grim demeanor, I think he was interested in the youngsters who came through his doors, and he made their stay comfortable providing no one looked into dingy corners.

The women who came to clean wore a profusion of jewelry, lavish makeup and stiletto heels. It was unlikely they did much actual work. We speculated about Signor Greyface and the women, but decided he was too full of smoke, coffee and nerves for any hanky panky.

Water leaked from one of the toilets in the bathroom nearest my room; it was clean water, but I felt nervous about falling on the tile. There were other shower rooms farther down the hallway. En route, I peeked into closets and storerooms. All were incredibly messy and filthy. In a word, La Mia Casa was a sty. He couldn't get away with such sloppiness if he charged more, or if his clientele demanded more. People stayed a short time and were too busy to complain; besides most were incredibly young and probably put up with worse in hostels and campgrounds all over Europe. There seemed to be a tacit agreement among all of us that the price was right, still, we grumbled that he should be reported.

I wished my bed were next to a window looking out onto the lovely piazza. I would have enjoyed looking down on the scene whenever I felt like it—even in the middle of the night—but the young women in beds near the window didn't want to leave the shutters nor the windows open. They said it let in bugs and was too noisy. It was hard to argue with those in control. My corner bed across the room offered some sense of privacy but was stuffy. I had no bedside light so I had to slip into the lounge area where lumpy, overstuffed chairs and reading lamps stood in haphazard disarray, but after a full day of walking the streets of Florence, my bedtime reading lasted but a few minutes anyway.

Before the windows were closed each night, I did lean out and savor the spectacle below. From that perch, I noticed two neatly trimmed walkways cutting an X across the lush grass of the piazza, just one more balanced design to soothe the senses. There's something about these renaissance churches with their precise symmetrical patterns and their colored marbles that speaks of serenity. The church looks Romanesque from the front, but it is Gothic inside. One source calls it a masterpiece of Italian Gothic, and discusses the beauty of the fourteenth-century gothic bell tower. Another, speaks of Leonbattista Alberti's fifteenth-century addition to the front which blended the two styles. Alberti's facade has been labeled Florentine Romanesque and was copied often. No doubt the scholars are correct, but the church reminds me of a beautiful woman flawlessly groomed and sure of herself.

On the left wall inside Santa Maria Novella is one of the most important frescoes of the early Renaissance. In *The Holy Trinity*, Tommaso Guidi, known as Masaccio, showed off his skill with foreshortening and perspective. Although Brunelleschi had taught the young artist his own involved ideas on perspective, Masaccio was an innovator in his own right. The figures in the *Trinity* are arranged in a pyramid. Starting at the bottom are two kneeling figures representing the donors; they are praying to Mary and Saint John standing at the foot of Christ on the cross. Above the Christ is the Father, who stands on platform and seems to hold up the cross. All the figures except the donors are placed within an elaborate architectural space defined by pillars and an arched coffered ceiling. Another arch and its ceiling reaches beyond the first. It looks for all the world as if I could step up into this elaborate chapel and feel the hardness of the walls and the flutes on the pillars. Just as the artist planned it, my eyes were drawn from the small kneeling figures outside the pillars on to a point beyond the Father's head.

Static, symbolic pictures tend to leave me unmoved; in fact, the first time I saw this famous fresco, I came away wondering why it was called *Trinity* having noticed only two of the entities, the Son and the Father. By the time I returned later, I had learned that the third entity, the Holy Spirit, was represented by a white dove. Sure enough, a dove hovers between the heads of the Son and the Father. How foolish I felt when I realized that what I'd thought was some sort of white collar peeking out of God's robes was indeed a dove. Did I need new glasses or was it the dim lighting? Or, maybe I hadn't learned yet to think in religious symbolism.

Tommaso Guidi was only twenty-four when he painted this fresco; he died three years later, yet he is credited with making a huge impact on the course of art. Fillipo Brunelleschi bemoaned his early death at the time. Through the years, many artists studied his works including Michelangelo and Leonardo da Vinci. Da Vinci wrote ponderously, "Tommaso, of Florence, nicknamed Masaccio, showed by his perfect works how those who take for their standard anything but nature—mistress of all masters—weary themselves in vain."

Maso is a nickname for Tommaso, and the ending "accio" is usually considered derogatory; it would be as if you were calling him slovenly Tom. Yet, according to Giorgio Vasari, *the* Renaissance biographer, when people called him Masaccio, it was more of an endearment. Evidently the name did suit him because he was one of those wild-eyed, careless revolutionaries who thought only of his art and nothing of the details of life. Masaccio *was* slovenly about his appearance and seldom collected his debts until he was in dire need, on the other hand, he was known to be friendly and ready to help others. In the 1950s he would have been a romantic beatnik; in the 70s he would have been a talented hippie; in the 90s he would have been an abject failure.

In this one church, one can also find a painted crucifix by Giotto, terra cottas by the Della Robbia family, a bronze crucifix by Giambologna, and a small Botticelli painting of the three magi who resemble three leaders of the Medici family. Would the Renaissance have cradled so many outstanding Florentine artists, I wondered, without the rich, arrogant Medicis to encourage them?

The Strozzi Chapel with its Filippino Lippi frescoes was closed for restoration. Frederick Hartt wrote that Filippino's fresco of *Saint Philip Exorcizing the Demon from the Temple of Mars* is really the painting of a bad smell. Evidently the poisonous odor from the demon is so strong, the king's son falls dead. Several of the people standing nearby are holding their noses. How curious. It is supposed to be one of the strangest paintings of the Florentine Renaissance, and I wanted to see it. This chapel was the fictional meeting place where the young people in Boccaccio's *Decameron* met before making their getaway into the hills to escape the plague. Naturally, when a place is closed for restoration in Florence I am disappointed, but there are more masterpieces in this compact little city than I could see in a lifetime of looking. The problem is solely one of timing.

In Santa Maria Novella there's a small, exquisitely carved wooden crucifix by Brunelleschi of all people. Vasari tells a delightful story saying it is the one made on a dare after Brunelleschi had criticized Donatello's crucifix. Donatello is supposed to have retorted, "Take wood then, and make one yourself!" They were good friends and Donatello probably thought no more of it because, after all, Brunelleschi was only an architect. Several months later, Brunelleschi invited Donatello to eat with him. As they were toward his house, they bought some things in the market which Brunelleschi asked his friend to carry, saying to go on and he'd come in a minute. Donatello went on in the house and immediately saw the crucifix because Brunelleschi had placed it in a dramatic spot with good light. Donatello dropped his hands and out spilled cheese and eggs.

"What have you done? What shall we eat now?" asked Brunelleschi following closely behind to catch Donatello's reaction.

"I, for my part, have had all the dinner I want today," replied Donatello. "You have represented the Christ. Mine is a common man."

There are more tales about renaissance artists by Giorgio Vasari in his books *Lives of the Painters, Sculptors and Architects.* He was a prolific artist himself and a darling of at least two of the Medicis. The more I read Vasari's books about other artists, and about his own accomplishments in painting and architecture, the more impressed I am of his indefatigable energy. Scholars sometimes question his accuracy but he's all we have. As Kenneth Clark says, "He gives us a flavor of what those fabulous people were like and many of his descriptions of art works have been invaluable in identifying those without signatures."

Only an architect! There's another story about how Brunelleschi won the competition to construct the largest dome since the Pantheon in Rome. It was also the highest ever built at that time. It's a good story, but I'll only say that his method (which he wouldn't reveal until he won the commission) was quite simple. Isn't that always the way with genius? A part of the Duomo Museum is set aside to display Brunelleschi's pulleys, ropes and wooden models. It's fascinating to see these ordinary tools that he used in such an ingenious way. His genius is apparent in his other buildings, but for me, it's not the technical ability that attracts, it's the calming influence I feel when I step inside one of his designs.

CHAPTER TEN

Old Sacristy by Brunelleschi.
Professor Hartt's Legacy. Irritating guides.
New Sacristy by Michelangelo.
Santa Croce, a mausoleum for the great.
Michelangelo's tomb, a travesty.

I LIKE TO THINK I WOULD NEVER TAKE THE GRANDEUR OF
Florentine buildings for granted, but one rainy day I entered
the Old Sacristy of San Lorenzo—the Medici's family church—and
it was as if I had never seen harmony and grace before. Brunelleschi
designed this room where the elders of the Medici family are
buried. As I stood in this quiet space, it hit me that I adored this
old guy's ideas. Part of my personal attraction to Brunelleschi was
probably that he had no use for the cold, Gothic churches of northern Europe with their spires that soar to distant heights.
Romanesque arches are more accessible, more for ordinary mor-
tals; they are like rainbows that I might just be able to touch.

According to Frederick Hartt, "Brunelleschi abandoned the
Gothic...as if it had never existed." Hartt was an art historian who
wrote and taught about his passion for Italian Renaissance art for
over fifty years. If I'd only known more about him when I lived in
Charlottesville, Virginia, I thought. If I'd already been to Florence,
or if I had been more knowledgeable back then, I would have
asked Professor Hartt a hundred questions. As it happened, I only
knew of him. He was the eccentric art professor at the University
of Virginia who walked across the campus using a theatrical cane,
wearing a dramatic brown velvet cape with his white hair flowing
over the collar.

Much later I realized Hartt may have needed the "decorative"
cane since he had served in Italy as an Officer of Monuments

in the Fine Arts and Archives Division of the U.S. Army, during World War II. He was a Knight of the Crown of Italy, a Knight Officer of the Order of Merit of the Italian Republic, an honorary citizen of Florence, and a member of the Academy of the Arts of Design in Florence whose charter members included Michelangelo and the Grand Duke Cosimo I de' Medici. What tales he must have told at faculty cocktail parties!

In the Old Sacristy, Brunelleschi's theme was simplicity and light. He held to a two-tone plan: all the flat surfaces were white stucco; the arches, supports and trims were of gray limestone which Florentines call *pietra serena*, serene stone. Pietra serena has a soft, transparent look about it that reflects light the way the opaque surface of a quiet pond does when gray clouds hover above. Various proportions were worked out in the Old Sacristy: 1 to 2, 1 to 3, 2 to 3, and so on. The room was an exact square and variations were used with the windows and arches and columns. The dome had twelve ribs that came together. Symbolism was again at work: three is the number of the Trinity; four is the number of the evangelists; and twelve is the number of the apostles. The sacristy had four sides and on each side there were three arched windows and three medallions. Three times four equals twelve which was the number of ribs in the dome and the number of arched windows and on and on it went.

By holding a detailed pamphlet about the Old Sacristy, I could appreciate the beauty on one level all the while thinking about the design on another. The best part was being able to absorb it at my own pace rather than having to tag behind a guide who would talk too much and not allow enough quiet time. Guides spend too much time emphasizing their own interests and testing new jokes. How would I do it? I would lecture before and after we entered a specific place; while inside, I'd be available to answer whispered questions. I wouldn't stand there droning on boring my own group and disturbing other visitors. Would that method work I wondered? These are the moments that remind me that traveling alone is the most nourishing, and yet, I was looking forward to joining my new acquaintances for wine and pasta later that evening.

A more famous chapel in the San Lorenzo complex is the New Sacristy; it holds two more Medici tombs. These tombs and the entire chapel were designed by Michelangelo. His four famous figures called *Night* and *Day*, and *Dusk* and *Dawn* are here. Most visitors come to the New Sacristy because of Michelangelo and go away without ever seeing Brunelleschi's Old Sacristy. I had been in the New Sacristy a few times, but until I read a small book by Edgar Wind called *Pagan Mysteries in the Renaissance*, I could never keep the names of the four figures sorted out.

The story goes that in 1529, when Michelangelo had temporarily left work on these Medici Tombs, he created a painting of *Leda* for Alfonso d'Este, one of the dukes of Ferrara. When I compared a picture of this painting with the figure *Night,* I could see a strong resemblance as pointed out by Edgar Wind. The poses are, in fact, almost identical. The traditional, classical pose of Leda and the Swan shows Leda lying back with one leg bent at the knee and the swan coming to her between her legs. Here *Night* leans back with her left leg bent at the knee. Her head is bent forward, however, and supported by her right arm which rests on the knee. There is no swan, but there is an owl sitting in the crook of her leg—owls traditionally symbolize night. Both figures by Michelangelo were derived from ancient images of *Leda and the Swan* often found on Roman sarcophagi. According to Wind, Michelangelo had studied ancient Roman works and probably knew that the name Leda was associated with Leto, or Night, the mother of luminary gods. With the Leda image in mind, I can now use *Night* as my guide. From her, I can then identify *Day*, her partner. Across the room are *Dawn* and *Dusk*; and remembering that Dawn or Aurora are feminine names, I can comfortably identify all four figures in this chapel. I feel a bit self-satisfied to have deciphered this small part of the entire complex.

I'm not exactly comfortable, though, with Michelangelo's sculptures of women. His sculptures of the human male are divine; he often expressed his belief that the male nude figure was the highest art form. But, it seems to me that his women figures are hard, muscular men with artificial breasts stuck onto their chests. *Dawn* does have a softer look to her arms, legs, and abdomen; but that may be only because he intended to represent both *Dawn* and *Dusk* as older figures.

Years later as a benefit of attending language school in Florence, I had the chance to accompany an art professor from the University of Florence on a few tours. While in this chapel, he offered Freudian reasons why Michelangelo's *Dawn* and *Night* look more like men than women. His theories were difficult to follow in Italian and seemed contrived. Obviously they weren't entirely convincing because I don't remember the details, but when he discussed Michelangelo's madonnas in relation to Freudian theory, there was a ring of truth. He commented that none of Michelangelo's madonnas engage their child. Most madonna-child figures show the mother gazing at her child either in awe or simple adoration, but Michelangelo's mothers look away. The one here in the New Sacristy, holds her bambino tentatively with one arm while the other is thrust behind her. Maybe she needs that back arm for support, but as the baby turns eagerly to her, her beautiful face turns away from him. The artist's own mother died when he was about six. In Freudian terms, he was abandoned. Certainly, this madonna's body language does hint that she is not there for him.

In Santa Croce, that splendiferous sanctuary of the Franciscan Order, Michelangelo, Machiavelli, Galileo, Ghiberti, Marconi and many others are buried. The Franciscan Order is one that ostensibly embraces poverty and asceticism. Some of Giotto's works are here as well as in the bedazzling double church in Assisi built to honor the humble Saint Francis. So much for asceticism, yet how nice it is for art lovers that Francis' ideas were mostly ignored. After all these years, maybe the gentle saint would forgive and enjoy along with us. But, poor Michelangelo, how distressed he would be to walk into his own parish church and see the ludicrous tomb designed in his honor.

Vasari meant well in designing this tomb. He had the greatest respect for Michelangelo. They were acquaintances, possibly friends, if one can take Vasari at his word. In his book about artists, Vasari paid great homage to Michelangelo with a lengthy introduction saying Michelangelo was the answer to the "Divine Ruler of Heaven's" prayers for a creature on earth to have an "universal ability in every art and every profession..." His homage in marble, however, is another thing.

Sitting on the ledge that supports Michelangelo's sarcophagus are three marble figures, one seems to be weeping, the other two in artificial poses. It's true that Michelangelo developed grandiose ideas himself, but the gold-fringed, red canopy draped over the white marble monument is garish. Two adult angels languish against a medallion on the top of the marble while various putti play under the folds of the red canopy. A painting is framed by the upper part of the marble shrine which may be a pietà of some sort. There is a nice marble bust of Michelangelo, probably taken from the bronze bust by Daniele da Volterra found in Casa Buonarroti, but all in all, the tribute is ornate, undignified and silly.

It was a different story when Vasari was given the task of remodeling *Gli Uffizi*, the State Offices for the Medicis. Those same offices became one of the most famous art museums in the world. Giorgio Vasari would never have been remembered for his paintings or sculptures, but for his architecture and his books, he will always be respected. His writing style is as tedious and as dull as his art, nevertheless the gossipy stories about some of the most famous artists of all time make for fascinating reading.

On one of the side walls in Santa Croce is a sculpture of *The Annunciation* by Donatello It's more of a bas relief than sculpture, and the tabernacle holding it looks for all the world like a porch of a classical Greek temple. Made from a soft, gray-green limestone and terra cotta edged in soft gold, it is simple and perfect. Donatello's virgin bends courteously toward the kneeling angel; instead of looking shocked, she seems to accept the strange business with style and grace. A Florentine family commissioned the work and in an unusual gesture, they did not insist themselves into the scene.

Outside and to the side of the church, Brunelleschi's famous Pazzi Chapel stands alone. It was closed. Another time, I sighed.

Santa Croce is like a mausoleum with somber memorials and burial stones, but outside, the piazza in front of the church is a bright open space. It must be as big as a football field and designed for life. There are benches all around the periphery on which to sit and admire the surroundings. A huge statue of Dante stands in front of the church to the left. Inside, of course, is his empty tomb. All during the time he was in Ravenna writing his famous *The Divine Comedy*, he longed to return to his beloved Florence, but he had been banished on pain of death. Now, they claim him, but the Florentines will never get his bones back!

Santa Croce glowered unfinished over the piazza for five hundred years; the present-colored facade wasn't added until 1863. The marbles are similar to the Duomo's in red, green and white geometrics, but since it is smaller, it seems more of a piece than that of the gigantic Duomo. It is a neighborly space with buildings on the two long sides of the rectangle. They are full of apartments overlooking the piazza. Frescoes are still visible across the upper section of one immense building extending along the south side. The sepia designs look so pretty on the beige-colored stucco. Some say these frescoes were done by twelve painters working overtime to complete the facade within thirteen days; others say twenty-one days, but whatever the number of days, Signor Antella, the owner, was in a big hurry for some long ago reason.

Other buildings framing the piazza are of a soft gold-colored stucco with dark green shutters, colors so typical of Florentine buildings. Along with the golds and greens, Brunelleschi's grays and whites are also popular color combinations found repeated throughout the city. At the far end of the piazza, opposite the church, a small decorative fountain plays beside a busy street called Via Verdi. The streets running parallel to Verdi leading off from the side of the piazza and church grow quieter—not necessarily less busy—but mostly filled with cyclists and walkers.

A mammoth corner building on the piazza, closest to the church, is of a much brighter gold color with big, loud green shutters. It appeared to house numerous students who lounged night and day on the wide window sills of eight-foot-high windows. Each time I passed by, I wanted to shout, "Be careful! You'll fall to your death!" Naturally, I didn't and naturally they would ignore me anyway.

The ground-floor shop of this gaudy, gold building sells gold jewelry, but most of the rest of the area's shops deal with leather. Tourists are led here in droves. Inside the cloister of the church, a leather school has gorgeous, buttery-soft items for sale, not necessarily cheaper than shops outside, but all beautifully made. A wee apartment overlooking this piazza would not be hard to take, I thought, not hard at all.

As I mused about this friendly space, a soccer ball smacked me in the middle of the back and took my breath away. A couple of boys laughed and then half-apologized. No doubt in my surprise, I must have looked funny to them. Were they embarrassed or did they rather enjoy the "accident"? After the first moment of shock, I waved to them remembering the antics of my own three boys. In moments like this, I am reminded of why I love the place so much. Florence and all of Italy offer me the storied beauty from the past along with the smashing energy of the present.

⌒

CHAPTER ELEVEN

San Miniato. Piazzale Michelangelo, the best view in town.
Santo Spirito, Brunelleschi again.
Brancacci Chapel, Masaccio's influence. Rachel's big upset.

I WAS THRILLED TO BE IN THE CITY WHERE THE ITALIAN
Renaissance flowered, but finding a place to use the toilet was a
constant problem. I needed to do as Italians do. They walk in to a
coffee shop, find the toilet and make no apology for not buying
something. It's unnerving in small bars where I cannot pass by
unnoticed; to save face, I usually buy something before leaving. If
the large department stores are open, they offer relief without
embarrassment. In the outer foyer of the Palazzo Pitti Museum,
restrooms are labeled W.C. Sometimes other places will have a sign
toletta or *gabinetto*, old-fashioned names for toilet, but usually it is
W.C., an obeisance to the intrepid and demanding British travelers through the centuries. This time at the Pitti, there was no stern
woman to take my money or parcel out a meager amount of toilet
paper. I learned early on to carry toilet tissue in a plastic sandwich
wrap and was in the habit of replenishing my stash before setting
out each morning. With toilet paper and a map, I am invincible.

The Palazzo Pitti lies a few blocks straight ahead after crossing the Ponte Vecchio. It is a huge museum which sprawls forever
and offers enough art for months of wandering. Organization is
best for an immense place like the Pitti or the Uffizi, otherwise I
wander from room to room and my mind dulls before I reach the
best works—best to me anyway. With a cheat sheet, I can skip
entire rooms and aim for a chosen few. That day, however, was a
day to walk outside; the sun was bright and the crisp autumn air
energized me. On the hill behind the palace many people were
already there picking their way among the elaborate shrubberies

and statues of the Boboli Gardens, so I aimed for Forte Belvedere, a former Medici fortress. In spite of Medici patronage through much of his life, Michelangelo was a lover of the Republic at heart, and one time, he joined the republican forces in direct opposition to the Medici. He not only helped fortify this very area against military forces led by the Medici Pope, Clement VII, but he was put in charge of the city's defense. In the long run, the Republicans lost and members of Clement's family were brought in to rule Florence again. Evidently the pope had made a self-serving deal with the French in order to regain control of Florence, but that deal probably saved the city from devastating damage.

When his side lost, Michelangelo ran for his life. Rumor has it that he hid in the cellar beneath the same chapel of San Lorenzo he'd been working in for the Medici family. Later, he was pardoned by the ever practical Clement who simply wanted him to finish working on his family chapel. Michelangelo did the work and then left for Rome, never to return to Florence.

As I walked up the hill, I smelled wood smoke from little houses hidden behind trees, but the road on which I walked had no shelter and the sun was burning. I longed for a sun hat. My nose would be red and splotchy for sure, but I plodded on expecting to reach the famous overlook called Piazzale Michelangelo. It was considered the best view of the city. Maybe I'd find a cold drink there. I'd taken a wrong turn, however, and overshot my destination to arrive at Piazzale Galileo instead which overlooked the Boboli Gardens and Palazzo Pitti. Fortunately, I saw a road on the other side that led toward the overlook. The road down was shaded by trees, and I sighed with relief as a delightful breeze dried the sweat from my face.

In no time at all I reached San Miniato, a true romanesque gem. From the outside, the church looks like a miniature Santa Maria Novella all covered with dark green and white marble; or should I say Santa Maria Novella looks like an enlarged San Miniato? After all Miniato has been there since 1013, possibly before. The crypt is different from most, it's not below ground level, rather the choir is raised above it. The pavement in front of the altar all the way to the entrance has exquisite marble intarsia panels with signs of the zodiac and animal motifs. Classical and pagan symbols are interwoven throughout this Christian building.

They say that most of the interior is in its original state. The ceiling, the carvings and the altar are all small and all beautiful. Under Michelangelo's guidance, the Republicans wrapped this church with mattresses and wool to protect it from the pope's cannons.

It was cool and dark inside and paradisiacal to be there listening to someone playing the organ. I wondered why no one else was there. Outside a young monk stood facing the city; he was serenity itself clothed in a dazzling white robe and brown leather sandals. Many young Italian men are beautiful with their smooth, olive skin and large, liquidy eyes, and this monk in white knew just how gorgeous he was.

The famous overlook was a short walk down from the church, and that's where the crowds were. I sometimes pooh-pooh trite, popular spots where tourists gather, but in the end, there is usually a good reason for their popularity. Standing at Piazzale Michelangelo, I couldn't miss the massive dome of the Duomo, and it was easy to identify San Lorenzo's smaller dome nearby and the lopsided tower of Palazzo Vecchio. From this spot across the river, Arnolfo di Cambio's massive tower looks perfectly in proportion to its surroundings, but when I stand down in its piazza looking up, it appears heavy and forbidding. The asymmetry of Arnolfo's building is a nice touch amidst the balanced proportions found in most of the other buildings; could it be the architect planned it that way to keep the civic center off balance and ever agitated?

Certainly that space saw turbulence and violence in its day. Girolamo Savonarola, the fanatical priest, convinced citizens to toss their rich, ornate possessions into a huge fire down there in the belief that austerity was the only way to be Christian. His fervor for simplicity was really aimed at the hierarchy of the church, and eventually he angered the Borgia Pope, Alexander VI, who excommunicated Savonarola. Not long after that, the fickle

114

citizens of Florence turned against Savonarola, and he was burned at the stake in the same place where his "Bonfire of the Vanities" had taken place. Now, there are rumors that the church is considering him for sainthood.

From the overlook, the Synagogue appeared to be one of the largest buildings, yet down in the city, sitting as it does off to the side, it's not so noticeable and keeps an unobtrusive low profile in Florentine life.

In the center of this Piazzale Michelangelo is yet another copy of *David* looking back at his city. He does have the best view in town. Lodged in my memory, though, was an even more spectacular place overlooking Rome. Would I ever find it again or had it been a dream?

While still across the Arno, I visited Santo Spirito built from a design by Brunelleschi. It is plain stucco on the outside except for its comfortable shape—a later modification of Santa Maria Novella's design. And, like a noble dowager who decides there's no need for outward adornment, the pale cream-colored church surveys her park-like piazza. Her neighbors and sometimes a few tourists come to sit around a simple fountain or gather for a chat on benches under the trees. Morning markets spread along the far end, and one Sunday a month a flea market spreads over the entire piazza in good weather and bad.

Inside, is an anonymous wooden crucifix from the 1300s brought from an earlier church, and also a painting of the *Madonna and Child* by Filippino Lippi. Although he does paint beautiful angel faces, Lippi is not one of my favorite painters. His paintings seem too pretty and too busy. An elaborate *baldachino,* a permanent, ornamental canopy, stands over the altar, and, as usual with these ugly monstrosities, it hides whatever beauty might be behind it. The art work in most other areas of the church did not speak to me; I had really come to experience the overall proportions anyway.

Santo Spirito hadn't been built exactly according to Brunelleschi's wishes. The spatial integrity in relation to its outside placement had been spoiled. In spite of the gracious park in the front of the church, it was crammed into its allotted space toward the rear. Brunelleschi had the bad habit of planning to be around during construction and didn't commit enough details to paper. Sometimes while he was away in Rome, for example, his subordinates made mistakes which sent him into fits of anger on his return.

In the case of Santo Spirito, however, it was more devastating because he died before its construction. He had wanted the church to face the Arno and sit back far enough from the river to allow a graceful approach. It would have enhanced the skyline looking across from Florence proper. As often happens with urban development, certain influential men who owned property along the riverfront managed to alter the plans. Now, it faces in the exact opposite direction. What might have been a pleasant vista beside the river is an ugly jumble of buildings all crowded behind the church at the water's edge.

Inside, though, it retains Brunelleschi's renaissance touch. It is all gray and white with arches, arches, arches and rows upon rows of soothing columns crowned with Corinthian capitals. The plan is a Latin cross—short arms and a long nave—with a dome over the crossing. I counted thirty-five columns which trace the entire shape of the Latin cross creating an unbroken arcade. Thirty-eight chapels formed within semicircular niches are all around the perimeter. It is quietly amazing.

~~~

After walking up and down the hills under a burning sun and over to Santo Spirito and back across the river, I could barely drag one foot after another up La Mia Casa's worn old stairs to collapse with a cappuccino. I sat in a heap dreaming of a sleek leather purse I'd seen in a shop on the Ponte Vecchio when Sarah bounced in all enthused about Masaccio's frescoes.

"They've been newly restored. They're over at Santa Maria del Carmine."

Oh no, I thought. Not only was my flesh weak, but my spirit was withering from art overload.

"The frescoes absolutely sparkled," she said. "You must go. It's a chance to compare his work with his partner, Masolino."

Patricia appeared just then and caught the excitement. Of course, we went back across the river. The hour was late, and we hurried. It was the first time I felt irritated with her. She was cross and expected me to know the exact location of the church. Maybe I had shared—bragged about?—my knowledge of all things Italian once too often. We were both tired and probably should have postponed the venture. When we found the Church of Santa Maria del Carmine, we had to wait in line to buy tickets for the Brancacci Chapel.

Patricia was testy, I was exhausted, and the guide was cranky, but the frescoes were worth it. Sarah was right, the colors and emotion of the figures painted by this young genius were amazing. I felt revitalized and was pleased to see how excited Patricia was too.

In one corner of the chapel, Masolino's *Temptation* shows Adam and Eve in a serene, static pose with a friendly serpent hovering above her head. Adam looks off in one direction, and Eve dreamily gazes in another draping her arm casually around the same tree on which the serpent curls herself and beckons. Oddly enough, the serpent has the head of a benign woman! Like a punch in the stomach, on the opposite wall, Masaccio's Adam and Eve crouch away in anguish. An angel, in a fiery red robe with red wings, hovers over them. Red wings! In *The Expulsion from Paradise*, the angel wields a wicked sword as if to prod them out of the garden. I could almost hear a menacing rush of wind from those wings. Adam forgets his nakedness and covers his face in shame instead. Eve has a haunted look on her face. Her eyes are drawn into a searing frown and her mouth is open as if she's howling into an emptiness. Her howl reminds me of the anguished face in Edvard Munch's *The Scream* done centuries later. Had Munch seen this fresco?

The idea of someone like Masaccio, who died at age twenty-seven yet had powerfully influenced art with his *Trinity*, in Santa Maria Novella and *The Expulsion* and *The Tribute Money*, both located here, reinforces the notion that geniuses do spring full blown at birth. Most artists work and struggle to accomplish in a long lifetime what a chosen few achieve in short bursts.

Some art speaks instantly while other art speaks after repeated study. Both voices are authentic and pleasurable, but the one that captures me instantly turns that encounter into a personal connection. Masaccio's *Expulsion* was like that; the sight of their devastating pain and remorse grabbed at me immediately. After such a personal encounter, I bristle when someone criticizes "my" artist and take offense when an expert pronounces even the slightest censure.

More relaxed with each other and glad we had pushed ourselves to see the chapel after all, Patricia and I sauntered back chuckling about how often Italians use the all-purpose word, *allora*, meaning "well now" or "so then" or "in that case" or "my, my." From that evening on it became our pet word. Patricia tried on a pair of funky shoes that looked like boots but not quite. They were just becoming fashionable in Italy; like many Italian fashions, they caught on back home a year or so later.

"Allora," by the time we reached Ponte Vecchio, I'd made the decision to buy that elegant purse with its soft, buttery texture. We went to our separate rooms to rest before dinner, and my sagging cot in the corner felt like a queen's divan.

When I went in to gather everyone for dinner, Rachel was going through everything she owned, pulling out drawers, cupboards, and crawling under beds. She was in a frenzy. She couldn't find the turquoise belt she'd bought in Mexico; she adored that belt, but then she adored all her purchases. Finally, she was forced to admit that someone in the Casa had stolen it. She was crushed, not only to lose it but to think it had been someone among us. She had started her trip around the world with $6000 saved from her "nanny" money and was adorning herself with purchases from everywhere. No doubt someone was either jealous of her things or of her beauty. Rachel's trip was about shopping. Silently, I clucked my tongue. Then I reflected that a young woman of fifteenth century Florence might have been just as upset over a lost belt.

A subdued Rachel planned to leave soon for Rome; Patricia considered going with her but dithered. She even considered skipping the Eternal City and going directly to Paris. Either way was fine with me. Patricia was a good egg, but by then, solo travel looked better and better to me. The stories about vagrants and gypsies hanging about Rome's train station had upset her. Evidently, gypsies would swarm around a tourist; their children would distract a person by holding out pieces of cardboard at waist level with something written on them. During the confusion with the cardboard as a cover, they would be into and out of one's pockets in a flash. If we kept our money under our clothes, surely the little rascals couldn't get at it, I kept telling her. In spite of myself, I began to take on her anxiety. No matter what happened, though, I was determined to see Rome again, and like Scarlett, I decided to leave that worry for another day.

CHAPTER TWELVE

La Mia Casa gone! Noisy streets.
Casa Buonarroti: Michelangelo's investment.
Andrea Castagno's Last Supper.
Bargello's masterpieces.
Brunelleschi looks up at his stupendous Dome.

ALTHOUGH I NEVER STAYED AT LA MIA CASA AGAIN, ON each return to Florence, I looked for the plaque and wondered how things were going up there with Signor Greyface. Each time, I put off going up that dark, odorous staircase to find out. It had to happen, of course, and the last time I checked, the little brass marker was gone. Major reconstruction was in progress. What had happened to him? Had he smoked himself to death? Had the pen-sione police put him out of business? I regretted not having stopped by just once. He wouldn't have remembered me, but because the strange, hollow man was always in my mind when I was in the area, I felt a personal loss.

Through the years, the thrill of seeing Florence's architecture and art treasures has never diminished, but the noise bouncing off the stone buildings into the narrow streets, and the crushing traffic make me crazy. Those who live in the city lament that it used to be a nicer place to live when they were young. Laura, my landlady of an apartment I rented two years in a row said,

"When Gabriele and I moved here thirty years ago, it was a lovely place. We could stroll through the streets without worrying about the crowds and noise."

She and Gabriele have no intention of leaving their beloved Florence, of course. And, travel books from the eighteenth, nine-teenth and early twentieth centuries invariably report the city's inhabitants were saying the same thing then. Aside from the unpleasantness of having to dodge vespas and autos or having to shout to a companion to be heard over the street noise, what real-ly upsets me is my selfish fear that this perfect urban place is being ruined. Naturally I want it to stay the same. I want to go home and know that the skyline will remain just as I left it, that the colors won't change, the paintings and sculptures will be safe and the outdoor markets will still be there waiting for me. The gorgeous countryside of Tuscany is seductive and has been a favorite haunt of expatriates for years, but my heart lies in urban centers.

Ambling along, it struck me again that this is where the Renaissance happened. And, what a happening! It was a special time in history. Were the artists of that time more gifted than any other time or did the gifted ones emerge because the climate was right for them? It was the fashion for powerful, moneyed mer-chants to encourage the arts. The church with its vast resources was in on the act too. Most buildings in Florence are either beau-tiful or interesting or both; to me the city itself is a work of art.

It is also a confusing maze. The Duomo is huge and I always expect to be able to see it for orientation, but the streets are narrow and the buildings are so close together they often hide the massive dome from view. After beginning and ending in exactly the same place twice, I finally found Casa Buonarroti on Via Ghibellina. While living in Rome, Michelangelo Buonarroti bought this house as a family investment, he never lived in it himself, but his nephew did, and it stayed in his family after his death. There, in a room alone at the top of the stairs, hangs an exquisite, diminutive, wooden crucifix. The figure of this Christ is delicate and youthful. The body appears to be that of a teenager, not a mature person of thirty-three years. In the next room is a dynamic marble bas relief with straining figures. Both these pieces were done before Michelangelo was twenty!

In 2000, this crucifix was moved to Santo Spirito across the Arno. Evidently, it had been originally created for that church, and after all this time, they asked for it back. First it was restored and then placed in the sacristy as its centerpiece. If the church wanted it, it seems to me it should have the honored place at the main altar, but, of course, typical traveler that I am, I want it back at the top of the stairs in Michelangelo's house where I first saw it.

A polished wooden model made for the facade of San Lorenzo is in the house too. To his great disappointment, it was never used. In the Medici part of Florence, the massive church still sits with its uneven brickwork waiting for the facade he envisioned in marble. Naturally, Michelangelo would conceive the facade in marble. From the looks of the model, it would indeed have been beautiful with classic lines balanced by his own renaissance shapes for windows and cornices. I've seen several rough, unfinished facades here and there in Italy, and to me, the uneven patterns of the bricks are beautiful just as they are. When the sun hits them at the right angle to create shadows from the protruding bricks, those old "unfinished" fronts speak of untold hours of labor done by common workers participating in their own glorification to their God and to their city.

The guard at Michelangelo's house that day was a cold bitch. All she wanted in the whole world was to sit hunkered over a corner radiator and read her book. I managed to interrupt her four times. It wasn't done with that in mind, but she epitomized the old adage, 'You get what you resist.' If she'd been willing to offer full information in the first place, I wouldn't have bothered her with just one more question.

Back on the streets, I found myself tracing and retracing my steps in a quest to find Palazzo Davanzati. Davanzati had been an affluent merchant in the fifteenth century and his home on Via Porta Rossa 13 is now a museum supposedly showing furniture and household goods from those fascinating days. A bored young man standing in a doorway smoking a cigarette explained there are two sets of numbers, red ones and black ones: red indicate commercial addresses; black indicate residential. He sent me on my way again. I was eager to hurry away from his smoke, but my body was crying for respite. I almost dreaded finding the palazzo. When a sign in front had the words *Chiuso per restauro*, Closed for restoration, I was relieved.

On Via dei Neri is a small *salumeria*, a delicatessen. The name Via dei Neri might go back to the time when the political party of Guelphs had split into blacks and whites, the blacks being responsible for Dante's exile. The plural for the word black is *neri*. It could also be named for one of the patron saints of Florence, but according to R.W.B. Lewis in his book *The City of Florence*, the street name is a change in spelling of the name Nori, a family who lived on this street at one time and who was devoted to the Medicis. At the *salumeria*, I bought part of a roasted chicken, a ball of cooked spinach and fresh bread. The chicken, roasted with herbs, was deliciously salty and greasy. On the way home, it started to rain. Italians are funny about rain; they worry so about getting a slight chill. Up go the collars and umbrellas for the slightest mist, not enough for Oregonians to remove their sunglasses. It was a warm, gentle rain but it ended their evening passeggiata immediately. In other ways, the Italians are hardy, tough people, especially these Tuscans. Maybe it's merely the vanity of city dwellers.

In an unfamiliar part of the city, I finally located *Il Cenacolo*, by Andrea del Castagno. This *Last Supper* is in a former Benedictine monastery called Santa Apollonia on the corner of Via Santa Reparata and Via XXVII Aprile. Formerly called Via Santa Apollonia, the street was renamed in the nineteenth century. The twenty-seventh of April commemorates the day in 1799 when French troops were turned back from Tuscany. In most cities, some Italian streets are named for certain dates, usually political events. An important one named Via XX Settembre commemorates the day Garibaldi and his troops conquered Rome. That was the day in 1870 that brought all of Italy into one united kingdom. Such an ancient land, yet United Italy is almost one hundred years younger than United States.

Castagno's painting was so beautifully preserved that I assumed it had been recently restored. Right away, I made plans to return with my camera because there were no cards or posters for sale, and the bored custodian was vague about where they might be purchased. It isn't as famous as Leonardo's *Last Supper*, but I was thinking maybe it should be. It is high on the wall of the former refectory, a normal position for these paintings, and yes, it was the original paint applied in 1445 according to a faded placard placed halfway across the room. Evidently the Benedictine Order's rigorous rules had kept it hidden from the outside public until the Kingdom of Italy expropriated the monasteries. Authorities had taken the trouble recently to install an apparatus to measure the temperature and humidity of the room in order to preserve the work, but the outside door stood wide open.

The student cafeteria of the University of Florence occupied the rest of the building which was faded and deteriorated. But, inside the museum, the colors were brilliant. The individual faces around the table are craggy and superb. The famous group is seated within a simple architectural treatment that mimics the refectory with its two windows at the right of their long table. The frescoed room depicting *The Last Supper* appears to stand alone within a separate structure with a Tuscan-tiled roof. It's as if a wall has been removed for us to view the scene.

I had to move forward as close as possible to determine whether the background wall behind Christ and his disciples was made of genuine marble slabs or not. The most flamboyant "slab" imitates swirling streaks of reds, blacks and splashy whites often found in actual marble and happens to be placed immediately above Christ's *and* Judas' head. The brilliance of the background is distracting yet it draws the eye immediately to Judas and then to Christ. It's a disturbing trick.

This presentation of the famous scene was unique to me. It tells the story almost in a caricature of itself. Everything is over-dramatized. Eleven disciples sit artificially posed on a decorated bench behind the rigid table. They all face us. The twelfth, Judas, sits in profile on a three-legged stool on our side of the table.

Not one utensil is in sight and only a few hunks of bread lie on the plain table supported by plain columns all covered by a plain white cloth. The stark-white cloth hangs so straight from the edge of the table that it looks more like a board than a cloth except for an ever so slight bit of a fold at each corner. Underneath the cloth, the men's long robes and feet show. Each disciple's name is written near their feet, but without the printed names, it would be obvious that the one who holds his chin in one hand gazing to the heavens with a questioning frown on his face is Doubting Thomas. Every other disciple is probably revealing something unique to his own legend as well. John, the youngest, sits to Jesus's left fast asleep with his head lying on his hands. Jesus looks down at him with a smile that seems both patronizing and, well, a bit disgusted.

Judas' feet do not touch the floor; he sits stiffly on his high stool as if concentrating on keeping his balance. His hair is jet black, he has a sharply-pointed black beard, his nose has a pronounced hook and his ears have grown into a sinister shape; in short, his characterization is overdrawn and on the verge of being ludicrous. The work seemed to me a bit off, even comical.

Later I discovered that this isolation of Judas was a device used by medieval painters, long before renaissance painters tried their hand at the traditional scene, but for me, in that first look at Castagno's version, it was new and powerful. When I found *The Last Supper* by Domenico Ghirlandaio in the monastery of the church of *Ognissanti*, All Saints, I realized that Castagno's arrangement was indeed the more accepted scheme rather than a revolutionary one. Judas also sits on our side of the table, and the disciples strike almost the same poses as in Castagno's painting. In Ghirlandaio's fresco, no one can miss the isolation of Judas because all the figures wear a halo except him.

There's a bit more activity in Andrea del Sarto's rendition which resides in the refectory of San Salvi, a long bus ride to the eastern part of Florence. One evening I sat in front of Del Sarto's *Cenacolo*, Last Supper, listening to baroque music. Most all attendees were Italians. The music was superb, but my vagrant mind began to muse about Italians and their coats. Surely, they must be trained from birth never to sit on them. I never see Italians drape coats over the back of their chair. They either fold their coats and place them on their laps or lift them out of the way before settling down. The woman in front of me wore a fine, warm, tweed coat, but as she sat down she lifted it a bit to the side. She sat through the concert on the cold, hard, plastic chair. As she leaned back, the coat was crushed—but never sat upon!

After comparing these three famous Last Suppers in Florence to Da Vinci's in Milan, I began to understand why Leonardo's is the unique interpretation after all—and the most moving. The figures in Da Vinci's painting are caught up in the very moment of being told about the betrayal. Their agitation is almost palpable as it is juxtaposed to the calm resignation of the Christ figure.

For almost thirty minutes I had the room to myself then a small German tour group came in. They listened quietly to their guide but seemed more interested in grabbing every available seat. Poor tourists, she had probably gotten them out at the crack of dawn and now it was approaching lunchtime. I waited them out and soon the small museum was mine again.

On my way out, I noticed an oil painting of a madonna and child in the vestibule. It too sparkled; the colors were brilliant and

jewel-like. When I looked closer I surprised myself with a loud guf-
faw. The guard poked his head around the corner, but as soon as
he satisfied himself that I hadn't slashed the work, he turned back
to his sports newspaper—I could tell he was reading sports
because it was printed on pink paper. "Crazy tourists," he probably said to himself.

Neri di Bicci's Madonna sits on a throne with saints surrounding her. Nothing humorous about that. Her scarlet gown is gor-
geously draped and a blue mantle edged in sparkling gold match-
es her halo and her babe's. She has one of those palest of pale
faces, powdery white, the kind seen in holy paintings suggesting
purity. She balances her babe as he wobbles up to a standing position on her lap and reaches down the front of her gown to play
with her breasts. She smiles benignly at his antics. Babies sometimes do this even when they are not hungry and mothers sometimes allow it. The funny part is that the babe has an ugly, old
man's face.

The ancient *Badia*, Abbey, is only a fifteen-minute walk from the
museum. The Badia has a famous fresco series by an unknown
artist called the Master of the Cloister of the Oranges. The orange
trees are gone, but supposedly some frescoes remain. The
Benedictine Badia is one of the oldest structures in Florence; parts
of it go back to the tenth century. The idea of the Badia fascinated me, but it seemed that every time I stopped by, it was closed.
Opening times listed on a side door were limited to a couple of
hours on *some* afternoons and Sunday morning services.

In Florence, there's always another attraction, and just across
the street from the Badia is the Bargello Museum housing match-
less sculptures by Michelangelo, Donatello, Giambologna and
Ammanati. In fact, Donatello has a room almost all his own
upstairs; it is sometimes off limits. Through a tall window on the
street level, I could see an immense sculpture by Giambologna. It's
doubtful that he ever did anything on a human scale. Probably his
most famous marble sculpture is the *Rape of a Sabine Woman*
standing in the loggia at Piazza della Signoria. It is a three-figured

theatrical piece that holds everyone enthralled as they walk around and marvel at how those three beautiful bodies—woman, defender, and conqueror—are interwoven into a single carved group. But, my favorite Giambologna is *Nettuno*, Neptune, the centerpiece of a fountain in the main piazza in Bologna. Now, there's a heroic figure. Copies of *Neptune* are in Florentine art galleries in an elegant shopping area near the Arno, and I've often wondered how he would look in my back yard!

In the Bargello, his *Florence Conquers Pisa* is movingly beautiful, and I wondered whether Giambologna might have been a feminist at heart because Florence, the conqueror, is a woman subduing Pisa, a man. She is powerful but retains a feminine grace that Michelangelo's women never achieve, yet, I never weary of spending time alone with Michelangelo. His *Bacchus,* for example, is both enchanting and disturbing. The off-balance stance of young Bacchus as he holds up the cup of wine is subtly sinister to me. His soft belly protrudes suggesting dissipation, but it is his eyes which bother me most. They look sorrowful and evil at the same time. The little satyr with cloven hooves and goat-like legs gobbling grapes behind Bacchus' leg is charming too in a perverted way. As usual, with Michelangelo, there's much to contemplate here.

Bartolommeo Ammanati's work is also in the Bargello; he tried ever so hard to emulate old Michele. His *Leda with the Swan*, a sculpture done from a design by Michelangelo reminds me of Michelangelo's figure of *Night* in the New Sacristy of San Lorenzo. There was a time when Michelangelo had mentored Ammanati and felt that "he worked with faith and with love," but after he saw Ammanati's awkward, *Neptune Fountain* that sits in the Piazza della Signoria, Michelangelo said he had brought forth "something naked, provocative and lecherous." I've walked around that fountain at the corner of the Palazzo Vecchio several times, and although it is impressive from a distance, Michelangelo was right, there is no motivation for the figures, and they do seem pornographic and naked for the sake of being naked.

Upstairs in the Bargello, Donatello's room was open, and a group of Germans was clustered around his *David*. This sculpture

has a certain fascination. Here is a vision of David entirely opposite from Michelangelo's heroic concept of the young man caught
in a thoughtful moment before his conquest and different from
Bernini's fierce idea of the hero caught at the exact moment of
throwing the fatal rock. Donatello's bronze *David* stands with his
foot already on Goliath's severed head, yet the pose is anything but
heroic or fierce. David wears a silly hat with the laurel leaves of a
hero festooned on it, and except for knee-high boots, he is nude.
The stance is curved and almost off balance. He looks effeminate
as he holds a small rock in his hand perkily placed on his tilted hip
and a big sword in his right.

It was impossible to get close enough to see the figure well. I
stepped back hoping for a better view, but the group formed such
a tight clutch that it was still impossible to see it from across the
room. After a solid fifteen minutes, I asked a guide to request them
to move. They loosened their knot slightly, but never appreciated
the idea that others had the same right to access as they. They were
sketching and listening intently to their leader and exuded a strong
sense of entitlement. Yes, that fit, I thought, they were "the entitled
ones." Most groups traveling together tend to forget the world
outside their chummy unit. Certainly large groups of Japanese
marching through Florence's narrow streets two by two seem
oblivious of the world outside their coterie, but because they
spend lots of money, shopkeepers welcome them with open arms
and fixed smiles. And, they *are* quiet compared to groups of
Germans or Americans.

As I approached the Trinity Bridge designed by Ammanati, I tried
to understand why architects consider it special. The arches are
flat and the immense wedge-shaped pylons make it almost too, too
solid. Maybe from a distance it looked graceful. Frederick Hartt
wrote that the tension and power of the flattened arches probably
came from Michelangelo's help and Ammanati may have softened
the details. The local art professor suggested that the odd flattened
arches could be traced directly to those used on Michelangelo's
tombs in the New Sacristy. The bridge had stood from 1566 until

the retreating Nazis blew it up in 1944. As in Verona, rescuers salvaged pieces from the river to rebuild it according to the original plan. These were fascinating bits of information to have in my head while walking across the Arno.

Later, when I re-crossed the Trinity Bridge, I saw a banner stretched across the gigantic Strozzi Palace straight ahead. It lured me into an exhibit called *Engineers of the Renaissance*. Every school child knows about Da Vinci, not only for his Mona Lisa but for his drawings of a man with attached wings trying to fly and for his peculiar habit of writing backwards so that his notes had to be read through a mirror, but Brunelleschi was the reason I went in. His dome is considered one of the greatest construction achievements of all time; surely it is Florence's most outstanding architectural prize because it is, to this day, the largest vaulted structure built of bricks in the world. Brunelleschi's vulnerable personality—his fierce pride, his quick temper and tendency toward paranoia—makes him real to me and may have had something to do with my succumbing to the technical exhibit. It was certainly not the pulleys, wooden screws, drills, grapnels, pumps, gears, ratchet wheels and wondrous representations of cross-sections, elevations, graphs, charts, and measurements.

His tricky method of winning the commission for the dome after having lost to Ghiberti for the baptistery doors is intriguing. He *knew* he had the answer for constructing such an immense dome but didn't dare reveal it because once he did, the committee would think it too simple. They would have said anyone could have thought of that. How clever he was to understand human nature and make it work for him.

Later he had to trick the committee into dumping Ghiberti from a joint architectural commission on the dome. Brunelleschi played sick until it was clear Ghiberti couldn't proceed without him. Ghiberti told the story differently in his boastful autobiography, but no matter how talented Ghiberti was with brass work, he was not an architect. Brunelleschi had given up his own goldsmithing and sculpturing to specialize in architecture, and in doing so he was bound and determined to raise the dome free of

Brunelleschi, gazing at his dome in Florence.

supervision. Once he finally had the sole authority, he then supervised all aspects of the project, a system rather unheard of in those days. A lumpy statue of him is on the sidewalk to one side of the Duomo. There he sits solidly with his feet flat on the pavement holding his measuring tool in his lap gazing up at his glorious dome. I like to give his knee a loving pat whenever I'm in Florence.

～

CHAPTER THIRTEEN

The best little bar in town.
First foundling home: babies on a Lazy Susan.
Santissimma Annunziata. Famous asparagus.
A 120-year-old restaurant in a church.
Pazzi Chapel, Brunelleschi's masterpiece. A bizarre Emerald City.

SURE ENOUGH THE BAR, RECOMMENDED BY THREE JOVIAL Aussies I met in a trattoria, makes the smoothest cappuccino ever. Some days the *Bar L'Innocenti*, Bar of the Innocents, has fresh *bombole*. A *bombola* is something like a doughnut stuffed with creamy custard, but unlike greasy, heavy doughnuts, *bombole* are as light as sugary bubbles. When a bar or pastry shop has a sign in their window saying *Bombole Qui*, Bombolas Here, it means they have 'just that moment' made them fresh. It's worth it to stop in your tracks and get one or three.

In *Bar L'Innocenti*, the coffee and pastries are fresh, and the ambience is simple, clean and cheery with no blaring music. Not one table is in sight. This is a no-nonsense-stand-eat-drink-and-run bar. In the mornings, it's always crowded and spotlessly clean. With so much sugar spilled on the counter tops in these bars, it's amazing that I never see ants. Here, as in most nice bars, polished brass containers sit on the counter with two wells of sugar. Long-handled brass spoons arch from the mounds of white crystals. I don't use sugar, but I love those shiny gold containers with their sparkling white crystals of sugar; they are the first thing I look for when I enter an unfamiliar bar. People crowd around to get their coffees and reach across each other's shoulders to spoon sugar, lots of it, into their tiny cups of espresso or cappuccini.

This bar would be my breakfast bar from now on. The handsome, white-haired owner picks up the cup from the barista, turns to me in one graceful motion and sprinkles chocolate on its top. *Oh no! No cioccolata!* I blurt. I hate chocolate sprinkles on cappuccino, but he is so handsome I say okay, *Va bene*. His pure white hair complements his ice-blue eyes. How could I be upset with him? Next time, however, he remembers, and ever after, teases with, "*Cioccolata?*" as he hands me the un-sprinkled cappuccino.

It was time to investigate another of Brunelleschi's handiworks at the Piazza Santissima Annunziata. The church called *Santissima Annunziata*, roughly translated as the Holiest Annunciated One, contains enough art for a semester's study, but the true centerpiece of the whole piazza is Brunelleschi's *L'Ospedale degli Innocenti*, The Hospital of the Innocents. I located the place on the porch where the abandoned babes used to be placed on a kind of lazy susan, *La Ruota*, which spun the children into the hospital/orphanage. I shivered at the thought of having to put my child on that turntable never to see it again.

These foundlings were cared for, educated, and given vocational training through age eighteen at the expense of the city fathers. In the 1400s it was one of the first such institutions in Europe; it seems that Florence had a lot of firsts involving humanitarian efforts. Their charitable institution called *Misericordia*, which gives help to those in need and operates an ambulance service today, was founded in 1244. Their office is across from the Duomo and volunteers still make the organization work for the community.

Some historians suggest that the city fathers contributed to the orphanage out of guilt for having sired some of the "innocenti." Many orphans were children of slaves—often from Slavic lands—who were kept as servants in wealthy homes throughout the city. These children were all christened and given the surname of Innocenti or Innocenzi. From then on their pedigree was clearly known and duly noted by society, but over time, the name lost its stigma. I counted 691 Innocenti listed in the current telephone book.

It's possible to visit the inside of the institution by buying a ticket to their small picture gallery. Among their collection is a glowing painting by Ghirlandaio showing the Magi visiting the Madonna. Ghirlandaio could certainly paint real faces and a real infant, with a genuine baby face. After the gallery, I peeked into many classrooms. Though empty, they appeared to be currently in use. Is this still a foundling institution, I wondered? Silly me, I should have asked, but I didn't want to admit I'd been snooping.

The church of the Santissima Annunziata is venerable and goes back to the 1200s when it stood in the fields outside a second ring of ancient walls. A religious brotherhood called the Servitors of Mary established an oratory here. An oratory can be a place for prayer, and it can be a society for secular priests who do not take vows. The Servitors of Florence are a home-grown religious order. The short, straight street leading from the Duomo to this church is named Via Servi. It all started out modestly but the cult of the virgin was rife throughout Tuscany, and when a fresco performed miracles here, pilgrims came by the thousands with votive offerings and candles. The church was enlarged several times to accommodate the crowds and more monastery buildings were added as well. Miracles were big business.

After a couple hundred years, a large church complex had developed, some of it under architects Michelozzo Michelozzi and Leon Batista Alberti; later Filippo Brunelleschi was brought in. He designed the foundling hospital which forms one entire side of the large piazza; other buildings were added later following his plans—somewhat. As usual, if the designer wasn't around, changes were made, even so, the square became one of the most pleasing of all renaissance spaces. Some admirers claim the hospital was the first true renaissance structure. When I perch myself on the steps of the building across from it, no matter how agitated I might have

felt when I plopped down, a sense of calm soon smooths my ruf-
fled feathers. It's the spaciousness, the order, the graceful arches,
the blue Della Robbia medallions placed between the arches, the
two small fountains, even the equestrian statue of an arrogant
Medici that all work together to evoke a psychic comfort something like the perfect final chord at the end of a piece of music.

A church service was already in progress when I arrived at the
church, so I waited in the atrium to look at frescoes. What a huge
vestibule. It needed to be large to accommodate crowds of pilgrims. Formerly open to the elements, the roof now has a frosted
glass covering, but the frescoes showed signs of damage too extensive to be cured even by the most modern restoration techniques.
On the walls were full-scale works by such early sixteenth century
painters as Andrea del Sarto, Jacopo Pontormo, and Rosso
Fiorentino, the red-haired Florentine. The names were certainly
familiar, and after seeing their work first hand, I was inspired to
delve into further study of these less famous artists. If one stays
long enough, Florence has a way of nudging one up another level;
not only is the city a work of art, it is an art course as well.

In one of the chapels in the old church, were two frescoes by
my new friend, Castagno. Call it coincidence or synchronicity, but
it seemed as if I were seeing his work more and more. "Chance
favors the prepared mind," is a favorite saying of a dear friend; certainly I felt favored in The Church of the Santissima Annunziata.
On one side of the chapel's altar is a fragment of Castagno's fresco of Saint Julian. According to legend, he is deep into self guilt
for having murdered his own parents in a darkened bedroom
thinking it was his wife and lover. That is a weighty sack of guilt.
Unbeknownst to Julian, Christ hovers just above his head. One
need not know the story or understand any Christian symbolism
to be stirred by the powerful communication between them. On
the other side was Saint Jerome, but he is hardly recognizable.
Usually Jerome wears a voluminous scarlet robe with matching
broad-brimmed hat. Typically, he sits in a contemplative mode happily translating the scriptures. Here, Castagno strips him of his red
robe—his red hat does lie at his feet—and places him barefoot in a

stark desert. He has just finished flagellating himself and holds a fragment of the bloody rock used to beat his chest. Two somber followers, fully clothed, are beside him; his trusty lion stands close by.

Above Jerome, also dripping blood from his wounded side, is Christ, with his arms outstretched on the cross; God farther above, in a flowing red robe, extends his arms out to the ends of the wooden plank and looks grief stricken at what's happened to his creation. The Holy Spirit, a white dove with wings also outstretched, hovers in the space between God and Son. This Trinity is scrunched up to the very top of the scene, and part of God's head is hidden by the arch. Two strange putti had been added later, and their red paint is smudgy and peeling. Although their purpose is puzzling, it doesn't change the disturbing effects of Jerome's vision nor the anguished look in God's eyes.

The miraculous picture of the Annunciation, the original reason for enlargement of the church, has an elaborate shrine built around it. It sits in the far back corner of the church on the left as one enters. The building is deceptively immense. About half of the seats in the church are arranged to face the shrine and the other half face in the opposite direction toward the main altar which looks miles away. An abundance of aisle space is all about, not to mention numerous chapels around the entire perimeter as well as within the ambulatory encircling the large altar.

Four Corinthian columns frame the sumptuous entablature arranged around the miraculous shrine; lacy, grillwork supports an ornate railing which holds countless shiny gold and brass candle holders. All are lit. It is a startling sight. When I first entered the dim church and saw all those flickering candles, my wayward mind remembered the lights of Las Vegas as they appeared to me out of a dark desert. Somewhere behind this dazzling display was the famous fresco, but too many people were milling about to see it. Another time, I sighed, another time.

Across the river, Ringo's had been recommended by the Australians for having super hamburgers and other delights. Not a hamburger lover, I decided to investigate anyway because their recommendation on the coffee bar had been so good. Evidently, Ringo's was the first cafè to offer American-style hamburgers in Florence, at least twenty years ago. The bistro was all in stainless steel and glass, the prices were high and the music was loud. Down that same street was another place more appealing called Mamma Gina and the house red was excellent. What I thought would be a small *bruschetta* turned out to be two full slices of stout bread toasted on a grill, decorated with chopped tomatoes and spices and a sprinkling of luscious green olive oil. Heaven. I do eat meat occasionally, but I told the waiter I was "*una vegetariana*" and asked his advice. He suggested the special asparagus from Piavè. "*È famoso*," he said. Famous indeed, those five spears cost 18,000 lire (about $12), but they were elegant and delicious.

Back into the center of old Florence, I discovered Natalino's. In autumn, Natalino's served a homemade gnocchi made of pumpkin drenched with delicious green olive oil and seasoned with leaves of sage. After frequenting Natalino a few times, the owner took good care of me. I've never found a restaurant in Italy that serves wine by the glass, but they do offer one-fourth of a liter—about one and one-half small glasses— served in a small pitcher. Instead of my usual quarter liter of the house wine, he sometimes offered a better wine already opened— at no charge. It's the Italian way to recognize a client for being faithful. Ristorante Natalino has been there for 120 years and is situated in a former church called *Santo Piero Maggiore*, Saint Peter Major. Ancient capitals are still on some pillars inside the main dining room. On the back wall, a homegrown fresco depicts a long table where the original owners sit with their backs to the diners looking out on a painted view of their Florentine countryside. Like most Florentines, they probably talked a lot about loving to be in the country, but in reality they were urbanites through and through.

Nearby on the corner of Via Verdi was a large branch post office. A bunch of government workers were standing around chatting with each other. No, I take it back, there was one energetic woman willing to help me. According to a sign in the lobby, stamps were sold at windows numbered 21, 22, and 23, but there were no such numbers. Strange. When I asked, someone pointed farther into an area that looked like an "employees only" section, perhaps a sorting room. That's when the woman came out to ask what I wanted. She said that I should go to window number 15. I told her the sign indicated other numbers and besides window 15 was closed. She was good enough to walk back into the main lobby with me and agreed about the sign and that window 15 was indeed closed. She found someone to serve me. What a strange system. I wondered who put the original sign there. I knew I would never know nor would anyone else.

Following Via Verdi towards the river, I soon came to Santa Croce again and this time Brunelleschi's famous Pazzi Chapel was open. I thought I had understood purity and balance when I looked into his Old Sacristy of San Lorenzo, but it was nothing compared to the restraint in the Pazzi Chapel. Evidently Brunelleschi and Donatello had fallen out over work done in the Old Sacristy because while Brunelleschi was visiting Rome, Donatello had added heavy decorations to "his" two simple doorways there. Brunelleschi was furious but it was too late. After all, Cosimo de' Medici, who doted on Donatello, had commissioned the work. Once again Brunelleschi had lost control.

In the Pazzi Chapel, however, it was clear that Brunelleschi was in complete control. All was quiet, simple and elegantly geometric. Only the blue and white of Luca Della Robbia's medallions and a few other touches of color in a small frieze broke the calmness of his gray-and-white space. Best of all, I had at least ten full minutes alone before a scattering of tourists arrived. This can only happen in late autumn.

Once again at the San Lorenzo complex, I wondered how I had ever missed a third Medici Chapel? On previous visits, I must have walked blindly past its entrance into the New Sacristy containing Michelangelo's *Dawn, Dusk, Night* and *Day*. Or, maybe I missed it when I went into the Church of San Lorenzo proper and entered Brunelleschi's Old Sacristy. No matter, I was therre now and the *Chapel of the Princes* was absolutely astonishing.

I felt as if I'd entered the Emerald City. It is a huge cavern of a room. The floors, the walls, the ceiling are entirely covered with glowing marble; the predominant color is a rich greenish blue not quite aqua, not quite teal, and enhanced with touches of gold. What a tour de force created by Florentine craftsmen. It is said that their expertise in the use of marble, mother of pearl, and precious-stone inlays is now a lost art. One needs to stand in the middle of this space for at least five minutes just to gasp, and then another twenty minutes to walk around inspecting the exquisite designs. There's no need to understand how the work in *pietra dura*, hard stone, was done or what all the symbols mean, or even who did it, it's enough that it is there.

How crass and worldly I felt later to barter for a leather belt in the market just outside San Lorenzo. But no, not really, because that has always been the flavor of Florence, art and commerce side by side. Inside the Duomo, is this same juxtaposition: a serene Saint Mary sits high in the rose window, and down on the wall of the Duomo, side by side, two mercenaries sit astride their horses. One fresco was done by Paolo Uccello and one by Andrea del Castagno. Both were commissioned by the city fathers to commemorate two captains who fought to preserve Florence's commercial livelihood. The Florentines were religious, political and mercenary, but not necessarily in that order.

⌒

CHAPTER FOURTEEN

Etruscans all around: The Chimera.
Signor Obeso and Gold.
Etruscan art and Cellini.
Inside Palazzo Vecchio: town meetings for five hundred years.
Lardo, pure fat at its best.

THE ARCHEOLOGICAL MUSEUM IN FLORENCE HAS ONE OF the finest Etruscan collections in Italy, and I spent hours admiring objects I'd only read about before. The Etruscan wing had been ignored for almost thirty years because everyone paid attention to the ravages of the 1966 flood which struck more harshly elsewhere in the city.

The François Vase has a room all its own with excellent lighting. In 1844, an archaeologist named Allessandro François found it shattered in an Etruscan tomb. I have tremendous respect for those who spend their lives reassembling precious, ancient finds. It must be like working a giant jigsaw puzzle except there is no picture on the box to prop up before them as a guide. They must call on their own creativity to achieve their results. This exceptionally large vase—more than two feet tall—was found in the Chiusi area, another Etruscan city about one hundred miles south of Florence. It was probably used to mix water and wine for large banquets. It may be the most famous Attic black-figure piece found in Etruria. Six bands go around the vase with over two hundred figures from Greek mythology. According to an information sheet provided for each room of the museum, the inscriptions on the vase identify all two hundred figures as well as the potter, Ergotimos, and the painter, Kleitias.

Hundreds of objects in the Florence museum were found in Chiusi, and I wondered what could be left in Chiusi. Later, I found more than enough were still in Chiusi's own museum. Signed and dated 570 B.C., this crater is just one example of the many ceramics coming from Athens at the time when Athens was trying to take the Etruscan market away from Corinth.

Antiquity began weaving its spell for me again. The Etruscans were fascinated with Greek artifacts and collected them with a passion. It's been said that more ancient Greek vases were found in Etruscan tombs than are preserved in Greece itself. Etruscan artists began to make exquisite copies and also developed their own styles. Only the experts can tell the difference between the Greek vases and the Etruscan copies. When it comes to the sculptures, especially the little bronze votive offerings called *bronzetti*, it's easier to distinguish between Etruscan and Greek because of the Etruscans' wild abandon with proportion and their tendency to resist "classic" perfection. Even though Etruscan artists had always adored anything Greek, when the classical art of Athens arrived, it left them cold. It was too balanced, too regular, too tame. It took the rest of the Mediterranean art world by storm, and still does. Who hasn't felt quiet awe while walking through the Greek section of a museum? But, the Etruscans were temperamentally different from the classical, moderate Greeks. They delighted in the grisly, the eerie, and in gaiety. Moderation did not appeal to them. They would have preferred Picasso to Raphael.

Their love of life comes through; Greek sculptures are beautiful, but they are cold and almost too perfect. Etruscan ones pulsate with energy and exaggeration. Unlike the Greeks who often defied their gods, the Etruscans felt that they were under the thumb of their gods, that their lives were preordained. Their motto may have been *Carpe Diem*, "Seize the Day," "Go for the Gusto," or however they would have said it in their elusive language.

Some figures were carved from a stone called *pietra fetida* which means bad-smelling rock. A sulphurous odor is released when it's cut or wet. Sometimes, just being close to them is enough to smell the sulpher because even a little dampness affects the stone. Some of the urns are hollowed out and some are equipped with a removable head in order to put in the deceased's ashes or small grave gifts. Most Etruscan funerary objects are of terra cotta, but some beauties are made from alabaster which still show traces of the original colors painted on them after all those years.

Signor Obeso, Mr. Fatso, is a favorite of mine. He lies stretched out in a confident, leisurely manner thoroughly pleased with himself and his belly. He was made around 200 B.C. during a time when they were carving actual likenesses of the deceased rather than symbolic figures. Etruscans thought fleshiness signified well being, but to the Romans and Greeks this was just one more proof of their degeneracy and lack of control. Of course, the Romans held this view before they themselves became decadent and let their empire slip through their own fat, greasy fingers. The most lovable thing about Etruscan art is its honesty. Signor Obeso is a good example. He certainly didn't have the ideal figure of a Greek god, and he didn't try to hide that fact when he hired his sculptor.

As soon as *L'Arringatore*, The Orator, a full-sized bronze figure, was found near Perugia in 1566, he was spirited across the border of Umbria into Tuscany and sold to Cosimo I de'Medici, who kept him in his private room in Palazzo Pitti. Later, *The Orator* moved to the Uffizi Galleries and then to the national museum. If it weren't for the Etruscan inscription on the cloak, he might be mistaken for a Roman figure because the clothing and stance are more like noble Roman statuary than Etruscan. To me, he doesn't have the old flare and verve from earlier Etruscan times; he was created around 80 B.C. when the Romanization of the Etruscan nation was well under way. In a sense, *The Orator* is a sad symbol of the beginning of the end for the Etruscan way of life.

The *Chimera* was just back from restoration and in glorious form. According to Vasari, this fourth-century B.C. bronze masterpiece was found in 1554 when fortifications were being built in Arezzo, Vasari's hometown. Right out of the ground in one piece came this four-foot-long, mythical creature with the lithe body and head of a lion. A goat's head springs from his back and a snake's head is on the end of the lion's tail. The snaky tail arches over the body as it reaches for one of the horns of the goat. What a weird, absolutely beautiful beast he is.

From the inscription on his right foreleg, the *Chimera* was recognized as Etruscan and whisked away to Cosimo, the Grand Duke of Tuscany, whose Florentine palace was in the very heart of the region which took its name from the ancient Etruscans. There was a renaissance mania for the past, and artifacts from Etruscan tombs inspired pride in their local ancestors. Benvenuto Cellini, a brilliant metalsmith of the Renaissance, spent many hours working in the Grand Duke's chambers restoring his Etruscan objects. One of the Etruscan statuettes he worked on could have inspired Cellini to create his own ten-foot-tall bronze *Perseus and Medusa*. Experts enjoy comparing its similarities to a small bronze Perseus made by an anonymous Etruscan artist in 350 B.C. They point out the same stance, the nudity, the winged-shape cap and the sickle-shaped sword. Cellini, the ultimate egotist, whose autobiography leaves no doubt about his self-worship, made sure his work wasn't anonymous. He put his signature on a strap across the chest of his Perseus much as young Michelangelo had done to his *Pietà* in Rome when he slipped into Saint Peter's one night to carve his name across the virgin's chest fearing his work might not be recognized. After that one time, however, Michelangelo never bothered with signatures again.

Cosimo's fascination with antiquity probably helped further the drive for rediscovery, but it was a family trait of the Medicis to collect all kinds of art objects including delicate, ornamental filigree, ceramics, jewels, glass, and works of gold and silver. Florence can thank the last of the Medicis, Anna Maria Lodovica, for keeping their vast collection together. After her death in 1737, it was discovered that she had donated the entire collection to the city with the proviso that no part of it leave Florence. This marvelous collection displayed in both the Uffizi and the Pitti Galleries is there because of her wisdom. I was surprised to see a horrid statue of her stuck in an out-of-the-way spot behind the church of San Lorenzo with not one word about her magnificent contribution.

In the archeological museum, I walked and looked, looked and walked, and felt inspired just being near these ancient Etruscan things. Then came the gold. Thin, thin gold so delicately worked.

Tiny gold granules decorated many of the pieces. Many have said the pieces were overdecorated, but Etruscans were bold wearers of bold jewelry. The granulation process was probably first learned from immigrant artisans from Greece or Phoenicia; it seems to have originated in Mesopotamia three thousand years ago. The Etruscans mastered it and surpassed their teachers. It's a tedious process of meticulous melding of infinitely small spheres of gold onto other gold objects. A magnifying glass is needed to see all their intricacies. I used my reading glasses, and by leaning close to the cases I could identify most of the tiny bits of gold on the jewelry.

The Etruscans loved jewelry, lots of it, and wore oversized earrings, large necklaces and elaborate decorative pieces across their chests, one more reason for the Romans to cluck their tongues. For a moment I thought I was alone in that part of the gallery, but as I went up the steps to see more gold, I smelled garlic. A guard was opening his lunch pack; suddenly I was starved.

A cute corner bar stood near the museum and I ducked in for a bite—a mistake. Every noisy car and bus in Florence screeched past that corner. To make things worse, raucous music blared into the tiny space over which patrons had to shout their order to the proprietor who had to shout back. Insanity. Another rule for traveling popped into my head: stand inside a bar or restaurant and take a sounding before committing oneself. Vivoli's gelato shop was nearby and it seemed appropriate, even Etruscan like, to indulge in a bit of decadence. Chocolate gelato with a raspberry scoop on top was my combination that day, but I'd probably go back to my favorite of chocolate with zingy lemon.

Back to the heart of the city, I entered Palazzo Vecchio. An awards ceremony was in progress in the grand hall called the *Sala dei Cinquecento*, the Hall of the Five Hundred. Following a suggestion from the fanatic monk, Girolamo Savonarola, a new legislative body of the Republic had been formed in 1495 to meet in this hall. Later in 1540, when the Republic had degenerated back to an oligarchy with the Medici family in firm control, Cosimo I moved his family into the palace. People called the building *Palazzo Ducale*, The Duke's Palace. When he bought the Palazzo Pitti from the bankrupt Pitti family and moved his family across the river, the Duke's Palace became known as The Old Palace and it's been called Palazzo Vecchio ever since.

Above the Hall, most paintings and architectural treatments in the Medici's private quarters were either created or at least designed by Vasari. He was the darling of both Cosimo I and later of Francesco, his son. Vasari's art is overblown and boring, but his books are another story. Although he knew only a few of the hundred and fifty or so artists he wrote about, he is considered our first art critic. Without his books, art historians would be bereft of most of their knowledge of Italian renaissance artists. His stories are gossipy and exaggerated and some have been proven inaccurate, nevertheless, experts consider his information invaluable especially his descriptions and dating of lost works. He must have been an affable fellow to be privy to so much information, but then having a duke or two, a cardinal or two and a pope as patrons probably didn't hurt.

Around the perimeter of the Hall of the Five Hundred were various sculptures, one of which was *The Victory* by Michelangelo. It is yet another version of David in an interesting pose. In Florence at that time, David represented defiance against powerful outside forces of invading emperors or popes. Here, his upper torso is twisted into a profile showing bulging biceps as he holds his sling across his back and looks over his shoulder. The face is serene without emotion. The head seemed too small, and I asked myself if this were really by Michelangelo. The lower half of his nude body is in a frontal stance with one knee leaning on the crouching, subdued figure of Goliath. It did not move me.

The ceremony was winding down, and the five young courtiers dressed in red-and-white leggings and fancy jerkins came to life. They'd been standing in a stupor behind the dignitaries the entire time yawning and teetering from boredom. Finally, two of them got to raise their flags, while the other three blew their horns.

There was a fanfare of sorts; their intonation wasn't keen, but they were pretty. As the crowd of city dwellers rose to leave, the courtiers marched off rather higgledy piggledy. My sentimental bones were tickled pink to see community ceremonies in this magnificent room where other events like this have been happening for over five hundred years.

Lardo, now there's a name to conjure by. It was a new taste and totally different from chocolate or lemon gelato.

"Please Signore, what is *lardo?*"

"Signora, it is the white part of bacon," he says. His smile reveals even, white teeth and he never believes for a minute that I will order it.

Soon the young waiter returns, and there, perfectly aligned on a dark blue ceramic plate, are five thin strips of the whitest bacon fat imaginable. Surrounding the glistening strips are leaves of dark, green arugula, a small mound of lightly-seasoned, chopped red tomatoes and three small pieces of crusty, grilled bread. Is that it? Am I paying 12,500 lire for five strips of fat?

It is delectable and I gobble up every tasty morsel. The bacon, or rather the fat, shows but a few signs of finely crushed pepper, so the real flavor must be achieved through a special curing process. The simple spaghetti which follows is fine, the dry red wine is fine, the mixture of bitter salad greens is fine, and I am one fine satisfied customer.

The only problem will be to find the restaurant again. Once is probably enough for lardo, but the trattoria itself is worth another visit. As with many hole-in-the-wall places, it is dusky and dark inside. Customers and waiters must weave in and around each other because the kitchen door opens behind the small reception pulpit standing immediately at the front door where people come in, mill around, let their eyes adjust to the gloom, hang their coats on pegs, all while waiters are bustling out with steaming plates of zuppa, pasta or lardo.

Along the street side of the dining area, tall windows, nine or ten feet high, reach down to table height. It had begun to rain, but they were left open. The large overhanging cornice of the ancient building protected both diners and passers by. How could one not drop in?

ᔦ

CHAPTER FIFTEEN

Standa, a no-service supermarket.
Learning with students from around the world.
A trip through the Vasari Corridor.

SEVERAL YEARS AFTER BEING IN FLORENCE WITH PATRICIA, I attended a language school for foreigners. With the school's help, I found an apartment in the Santa Croce area. What a quiet place it happened to be. My area was at the back of a renovated old convent building with thick walls. An elevator had been installed for the owners who lived on the third floor; they gave me a key to use the elevator, but I was only up one flight and it was easier to walk up. People who lived below had a garden over which I could look, and a tree was loaded with ripening *cachi*. I should have cultivated a friendship with that family, maybe they would have shared with me, but I preferred to keep a low profile because every now and then I could hear unhappy sounds of screaming and yelling coming from below. For the most part, however, it was a quiet haven to come into from the noisy streets of Florence. It was a treat to play house Italian style for two months, and a relief from the confines of hotel rooms and restaurant meals. But, on October 31st, the night before the Day of the Dead, *I Morti*, I made the mistake of going shopping at *Standa Supermercato*.

I Morti is a huge event in Italy, and Standa was packed with shoppers. People travel across Italy to join family members in honoring their dead with flowers and wreaths at the cemeteries. Possibly even more important to celebrants is the consuming of a huge meal at the house.

Standa is a chain of stores something like K-Mart or Walmart; some are supermarkets exclusively, some department stores, and some a combination of both. They are ubiquitous throughout Italy. I've shopped in Standas in several cities and small towns, and have yet to find one I like. This one was handy to my apartment; without a car to reach the suburbs, I was willing to put up with its minor inconveniences. Friends with cars told me that other supermarkets have express lines and are more service-oriented, but not Standa. "Service" is not a word they speak there.

That evening no shopping carts were available. When I walked in, two people were already waiting to grab an empty cart. I, too, held a five-hundred-lire piece ready to hand to someone in exchange for their cart as they left the store. Normally, the carts were chained together with a gadget attached to each so that one could slide a coin in a slot to release it. When finished, the coin is retrieved by snapping the gadget back in its slot. It might help keep theft of carts down, but it's a nuisance when one doesn't have a five-hundred piece in hand. The first time I tried the system, a friendly checker made change for me; another time, however, a tired employee snapped at me and pointed to a change machine on the wall which I hadn't noticed before. It's hard to be green, but after the first embarrassment, how quickly we switch to a certain smugness in knowing the ropes. Luckily, on the eve of *I Morti*, I knew how to weigh and price vegetables before bringing them to the checkout; there are no scales at checkout. I'd been through that routine of being sent back to lay my apples or zucchini on a scale, push the proper button, wait for a sticky label printed with the price, and then go to the end of the checkout line again.

Since the layout of the store did not provide separate space for the checkout lines, the food aisles were crammed with shoppers trying to fill their baskets while others stood with full carts waiting to check out. Someone pushed through, caught the corner of my basket and jammed it into my stomach. The person wasn't aware until I involuntarily said, "Oof." Then he looked back, he didn't apologize but made a face shrugging with a fatalism that said, 'what can you expect?'

~

Mingling with the young in language classes, some of whom are my eldest grandchild's age, felt strange, even daunting. They came from Japan, Germany, England, Australia, Romania, Sweden, Denmark, Greece, Turkey, Gambia, Columbia, Israel, Palestine, Argentina, and the United States. It was obvious that many were sent by their parents rather than having chosen to study Italian themselves. They skipped classes or arrived bleary-eyed from their late nights. Others wanted to be there, and some needed to learn the language in order to enter Italian universities—a desirable opportunity for many. Whatever their reason for being there, all seemed to have a great time and adapted quickly—that was the daunting part for me.

Many of the girls advertised their budding bodies and seemed foolish in their efforts to be noticed. Boys and girls alike were young and beautiful to my eyes, but they didn't realize it. Instead they carried around heavy loads of insecurities. Most were quick witted, and their mental agility could be intimidating. I had to remind myself that Grandmas could learn too. Although I was motivated, learning about art was much easier than learning a new language, yet the school was stimulating and provided an instant community and a sense of purpose.

In my limited experience of other language schools in Italy, the one in Florence pleased me the most. After the standard grammar and conversation classes held in the mornings, the optional lectures and art tours offered in the afternoons are more extensive in Centro Linguistico Italiano: Dante Alighieri than elsewhere.

One of the teachers, Marisa, who was a native of the city, discussed the illustrious Medici family in after-class lectures. She loved her subject, in fact, she seemed to worship anything connected with the Medicis. Like a mother hen, she took a few favorites under her wing to make sure they fared well far from home. Fiona and Amanda, both from England, were obviously a couple of her chicks that term.

Fiona was a willowy, pale, blond English lass who already spoke two or three other languages. She was intelligent as well as sweet; she literally exuded goodness. Amanda was a well-made young woman with lustrous, dark skin and abundant black tresses streaked with gold which she wore dramatically upswept except for a few strands slipping down in attractive wisps. Along with her wit, she was full of life, exuberant, a bit raucous and utterly charming. They met in Florence and became instant buddies. What a beautiful pair they made striding across the bridge *Ponte alle Grazie* each morning on the way to school.

Another lecturer, Massimo Borelli, an art professor from the University of Florence, came in the late afternoons to talk about art, politics or Italian culture. He usually dressed casually in ordinary jeans and sweaters but wore exquisite leather moccasins on his feet. His sweaters looked as if they had been balled up and stuffed into a corner of a drawer. He was short, compact and bounced into class exactly fifteen minutes late and dived right into his subject matter. He threw American idioms into his lecture— current ones—and was proud of his extensive knowledge of American mores and politics. He rocked up and down on his toes in a sort of dance as he lectured. When finished, he gathered his things and waltzed out. If someone did ask him a question, he was gracious, but we had the idea that it was best not to interrupt his "show." And, it was truly a grand show.

Fiona said, "I feel sorry for his wife, how could anyone live with such control and arrogance?"

I told her that when she was absent, he mentioned something about living alone. We agreed that must surely be the case. As usual, it was fun to speculate about others' lives.

～

At the beginning of the term, one of the opportunities listed on the school's bulletin board was a visit to the Vasari Corridor, which runs all the way across the Arno on top of the shops built on the Ponte Vecchio. Oh, how lucky I was to be in this school program, I thought. Silly me, I politely waited for the sign-up sheet to appear at the front desk; by the time I asked about it, I was told it was already full. Let that be a lesson. Next time something like that was posted, I would march up to the office counter and find out right away. I was so disappointed, but the more I thought about it the more I was determined to go. Marisa was leading the group, and someone might not show up on the appointed morning, so I cut my grammar class to find out. Having explained to Marisa what I was doing, I waited in the back of the group until all the names had been called. Sure enough, a few people were missing, and those of us on standby were allowed to go. Our total number seemed to exceed the requisite twenty-four, but Marisa managed to convince the official guide at the Uffizi, and she accepted all of us. What luck!

It was thrilling to go directly from inside the Uffizi Galleria on the north side of the Arno over to the Palazzo Pitti on the south side all above "the hoi polloi." Feeling privileged and special, we looked down on those unsuspecting folks who were merely buying gold and diamonds in the shops of Ponte Vecchio. The walls of the corridor were crowded with self portraits by famous painters from all over Europe. It was a sight. The collection began with Vasari's own self portrait and was arranged chronologically from the sixteenth century on. At first, they were mostly Italian self portraits, but gradually painters from all over Europe wanted to be hung in the Vasari Corridor. Some of them were Rubens, Rembrandt, Van Dyck, Velasquez, Hogarth, and also some nineteenth century self portraits by David, Delacroix, Corot, Ingres and others I didn't recognize. In the last section, a group of seventeenth and eighteenth century portraits of royalty filled the walls. Historical but boring.

This corridor served as a way for the Medici family to avoid hostile crowds. Originally, it was created to allow the Duke to go from his office at his new home in the Pitti to his office in the Palazzo Vecchio without having to mingle with the town people. During these years, Vasari was something of an in-house artist/architect for the Medici family. He designed the corridor and supervised its construction all within a five-month period. The rush was because of a grand wedding festival for the Duke's son,

Francesco, and Joanna of Austria. The construction speed was incredible then, but today, the planning permits alone would take that long. The corridor has windows which offer excellent views up and down the river, and Marisa reported that since it was the only bridge left undestroyed by the Germans during World War II, some Florentines used it as an escape route during the final days of the Nazi regime.

Just before the corridor came to an end, she told us to look through a window into the church of Santa Felicita. We could see directly into the private chapel used by the Medici family. If the family had been worshipping that day, we would have seen the back of their heads as they sat hidden from the view of common worshippers on the floor below. We arrived in the "backyard" of the Palazzo Pitti near a grotto designed for the Medicis by Vasari and built by Bartolommeo Ammanati and Bernardo Buontalenti. Abandoned now, it was the epitome of artificiality. Even in its best of days, it must have been pretentious.

Marisa glanced at her watch and decided we had time for one more treat. Her small feet and slim legs led us back across the Arno to a tiny chapel called San Martino. There Domenico Ghirlandaio had painted the life of Saint Martin, known mostly for his efforts to help the sick, especially victims of the plague. The chapel had already closed for siesta, but she rapped on a window and spoke to the keeper who happened to be there. He peeked out and graciously allowed us in for a quick look. It was a small space, confining for the five of us left from the original group, but we were proud to see one more Florentine treasure off the usual path. The one who enjoyed herself the most was dear Marisa.

That day was a jackpot day for me. After a quick bowl of soup in a cafè near the school, I joined another tour through the San Frediano Quarter with Cecilia, the school's energetic office manager. She was not a native of Florence but obviously loved her adopted city and claimed that the "real" natives lived in San Frediano in Oltrarno, across the river. She pointed out places where the local people worked; especially interesting were the woodworkers who sawed and planed in the streets in front of their tiny shops. *Casalinga* means housewife, and Cecilia showed us where the wives of that quarter went for their household items. They were drab little stores called *casalinghe*. But, while in one of them, I was able to replace a crucial part for my coffee pot that I had accidently thrown away.

Tourists do go across the Arno to see Masaccio's paintings in the Carmine and occasionally visit Brunelleschi's San Spirito, but for the most part the Oltrarno is left to itself. Historically the region was the poorest section of town. They say before the last war the police hesitated to brave it alone. The neighborhood was closely knit and people tended to look after each other. Vasco Pratolini dramatized this phenomenon in his novella, *Le ragazze di Sanfrediano,* The Girls of Sanfrediano. It is a surprising story of life in the years right after the second world war when a group of young women turned on one of the womanizers of their neighborhood.

"Roberto"—not his real name—was a handsome fellow who resembled the Hollywood star of the forties, Robert Young. All the young folks in Sanfrediano nicknamed him Roberto, and it went to his head. He slicked back his hair and strutted about breaking one teenager's heart after another with no thought for her feelings or reputation. Finally, a couple of the more sophisticated girls incited the others to set a trap. They lured Roberto to a secluded place in the large park across the river called *Le Cascine.* They managed to tie him to a tree. They tormented him with words and whips. Just when their unleashed fury was becoming dangerous, one of the girl's defused the situation and released him. Soon afterwards, Roberto went back to calling himself by his real name, Alberto, and settled into a less glamorous life.

The weather was crisp, the air was clean, and when we finished our tour, some of us joined Cecilia for a few minutes to sit on the parapet of Ponte alle Grazie to soak up the view. Alle Grazie was the bridge Fiona, Amanda and I crossed every day to school. We sat facing eastward with Ponte Vecchio just behind us; it was a photographer's dream. We could see Piazzale Michelangelo up the southern slope and above that San Miniato. At night, the church was lighted and became a true romanesque jewel overlooking all of Florence.

That autumn, I had the time of my life with excursions and lectures on art, history, politics, and opera all in Italian. I had the chance to read—with the patient help of a professor—parts of *The Name of the Rose* by Umberto Eco and even a smidgeon of Dante's *Inferno* both in their original language. It was heady stuff to learn first hand of things I'd been passionate about for such a long time.

It doesn't get any better than this, I thought.

~

CHAPTER SIXTEEN

The Uffizi—from offices to art.
Are Titian's women goddesses or seductresses?
The angry Arno threatens. The Ancient Badia. Dante's House.

ON WEEKEND MORNINGS, THE STREETS OF FLORENCE ARE blessedly quiet; no vespas, no cars and few buses. For a few delicious moments, the city was mine. The redolence of an Italian city—a blended fragrance of fresh-roasted coffee and hot sweet chocolate—was in the air like a heady perfume. I set off for my favorite bar. Later, while lazing my way across Piazza della Signoria, I noticed the line outside the Uffizi Gallery was short so I seized the opportunity to go in.

Originally designed by Vasari for the state offices, *uffizi* means offices, this museum is not the usual blocky pile of stone. With a narrow alley between the museum and Palazzo Vecchio, the gallery extends all the way to the river coming back to form a grand U. At the river end, the upper gallery goes above the street across a Palladian-style arch through which the Arno can be seen. The symmetrical wings of the long U create a funnel effect. With Palazzo Vecchio at my back, I saw the green hills across the river through the stone arch. Nice. Sometimes I like to stop for a moment to stand and look, but then arches anywhere are pleasing shapes. I remembered how delighted I was to find a perfect archway leading from our dining room into the living room of the house we inherited when my father-in-law died. He had fastened a wooden beam across the arch and covered it with heavy drapes, but a little bit of Italy had crept into that 1940s Oregon house.

Begun by Vasari in 1560, the Uffizi is mainly a picture gallery, with but a few rooms for sculpture. As in all huge museums, one needs to conserve physical and mental energy. Naturally, the best plan is to organize for a leisurely visit to a few rooms at a time and return often. Knowing all that, I usually try to cram too much into one visit. There are rooms after rooms including a thirteenth century room, a Giotto room, a fourteenth century Sienese room, and a fourteenth century Florentine room. There are separate rooms for Botticelli, Bellini and Giorgione, Rubens, Corregio, Caravaggio and Rembrandt, Raphael and Michelangelo, Andrea del Sarto, Pontormo, Titian and many more. Since I hadn't expected to go, I didn't have my list, and I didn't want to follow the program offered at the entrance, so I tried a new approach. Taking a few deep breaths to relax my mind as much as possible, I moved through the rooms almost in a dream-like state stopping only when something reached out to me with an irresistible force.

One such painting was Masaccio and Masolino's *Madonna and Child with Saint Anne*. The step, the throne, the Madonna and Child and one or two angels holding the curtain behind the group were done by Masaccio; Saint Anne, sitting just behind the Madonna and child. and the other angels were done by Masolino. Frankly, I could not have told it was done by two different painters. I might have ventured a guess that Masaccio had his hand in it because, as in his *Trinity* in the church of Santa Maria Novella, there's a strong pyramidal force. There was something, too, about the Madonna's bulging eyes that reminded me of other paintings by Masaccio, but here, Masolino's Saint Anne, Mary's mother, is the hovering, dominant presence. It is a static painting, yet for some reason it drew me in. For me it was the faces. Each figure looks in a different direction; the grandmother, Anne, with her head completely draped in white wimple and rose robe, looks down toward the baby's head over which her hand seems to be in the act of blessing him. The mother, Mary, with her golden hair showing from under a light blue mantle, stares outward, but not at us. Both faces foreshadow grief. The pudgy, blond-haired baby, faces a different direction from either his mother or grandmother. He almost looks at us and raises his hand in a beckoning motion.

Fra Filippo Lippi's Madonnas are exquisite and he usually allows at least one character in his paintings to look directly into our eyes, generally a mischievous angel. The portraits of the Duke and Duchess of Urbino, painted by Piero della Francesco in 1465, are in stark profile. The Duke has perhaps the most famous broken nose in all of art history. Any veteran of Art 101 will recall the Duke Federico di Montefeltro with his cylindrical red hat and kinky black hair curling out from the edges. Also in profile is his Duchess Battista Forza with her artificially high forehead (the style among noble women was to remove hair to create those odd high foreheads). She wears a stiff collar of pearls and jewels. As a student, I was told to take note of the harsh, clear light which leads the eye to the effects of perspective and shows the two nobles' domain in the background. But, my wayward eye comes right back to their fascinating faces. The two paintings were mounted in the middle of the room. What had not been explained in my Art 101, was the scene on the reverse side of each portrait which is even more formalized and mythologized. Each noble rides on a triumphal cart accompanied by allegorical figures there to emphasize their humanistic philosophy. My granddaughter, Sara, would be delighted that the Duchess' cart is drawn by a pair of unicorns.

Sandro Botticelli's *La Primavera*, The Spring, and *Birth of Venus*, are always big draws with their mythological figures, their flowing, frothy veils and heads of reddish-golden hair a mile long, but to me, if you've seen one Botticelli, you've seen them all. His *Annunciation*, although pretty, seems ludicrous. The virgin sways gracefully away from yet leans toward the angel kneeling before her. Both her hands and his are delicate and dainty and poised in ballet-like positions. Both are swathed in voluminous, billowing

155

robes, and while her long strawberry-blond hair is contained in a graceful ropey scarf, the angel's rusty-blond hair is left to fall in curls around his shoulders.

Although Pietro Vanucci—known as Perugino because he was from Perugia—was Raphael's master at one time, I tend to pass by Perugino's works. They seem insipid. Perugino devised the turning or dipping of a figure's head to suggest motion or thought. Fine, but soon every figure in all his paintings have their heads held in such a way. Some of Raphael's early figures also use what I call the "Perugino dip."

One of Perugino's paintings, however, is effective as well as puzzling. It's in the church Saint Mary Magdalene of the Pazzi. It is a three-part fresco of the crucifixion well preserved on a wall beneath the street. Of the five figures standing or kneeling below the Christ figure, only a lovely Mary, mother of Christ, stands with the traditional dip, but it is only an imperceptible turn of her head. Two other figures are looking up at Christ, and to be fair, they do not have that coy bob to their heads either. As I stood there deciphering the painting for myself, I realized that only one figure had a golden halo, the female to the left of the cross dressed in rather drab colors. All the other figures, including the female figure directly beneath the cross which must be Magdalene, had transparent halos. The drab woman with the golden halo would surely be the Virgin mother, yet how strange that the woman kneeling beneath the cross wears a blue gown and crimson cloak, traditional colors for the Virgin Mary, yet she does not have a golden halo. Could it be that Perugino was telling us there had been a closer connection between Christ and Mary Magdalene than the scriptures indicate? Some recent authors have even suggested that perhaps Jesus was married to Magdalene. Interesting.

Back in the Uffizi, *The Annunciation* by Leonardo da Vinci was interesting in a different way. For a long time it was thought to be by Domenico Ghirlandaio, then some said maybe by Ridolfo Ghirlandaio or even Andrea Verocchio. The experts discuss endlessly the background and perspective. I only know that Leonardo used spirals and coils in many of his paintings; his workbooks are full of them. Certainly the young Virgin's hair in this annunciation fits that criterion. Also, her heavy eyelids and puffy underlids seem much the same as his other women, including *Mona Lisa.*

One of the few paintings done by Michelangelo is here, *The Holy Family,* usually called *The Doni Tondo* because it is painted and framed in a circle and was done for the Doni family. Except for the babe, the family is fully clothed in beautiful draperies which, of course being Michelangelo, manage to reveal the solidity of real bodies beneath. It seems it was impossible for Michelangelo to paint or sculpt anything which didn't include athletic, young, nude males somewhere. In the *Doni Tondo,* they are lounging and chatting on a balustrade behind the holy family. Some critics suggest that they represent the profane or pagan which somehow blend in with the idea of the sacred family. Maybe. We'll never know. Michelangelo didn't like to talk or write much about why he chose to do what he did.

A charming painting by Raphael called *Madonna of the Goldfinch,* is in a soft, pastoral setting. The Madonna holds her child who reaches for the little bird held by his cousin John the Baptist. And, a powerful portrait of *Pope Leo X with Two Cardinals* shows Raphael's artistry in portraiture. Supposedly, this picture was done almost entirely by Raphael himself as opposed to so many of his other works. By the time he got to Rome, Raphael was almost an industry. He was a busy fellow and laughingly took on more than any one person could ever achieve alone.

Evidently he was a likeable person who could move in all circles with ease. He never seemed stressed by the problems of his art as Michelangelo was known to have been. One shouldn't have to anguish and suffer for art, I suppose, but I have to admit my bias for giving short shrift to Raphael. My criticism is not rational; he was extremely talented. Yet ever since I made a connection with Michelangelo, I haven't liked that young man. I've even grown jealous of him for Michelangelo's sake. Raphael was able to work fast, he was willing to ingratiate himself and pay court to officials, cardinals and popes and didn't mind letting lesser artists in his retinue do most of his work.

Ah, Titian. His *Portrait of a Knight of Malta* is one of those paintings that interrupted my dreamy stroll. After much discussion, this painting has been finally attributed to Titian. It's interesting that many artists had not signed their work; was it lack of confidence? No, I think it was just the opposite; they expected their work to be unique and recognizable—certainly Michelangelo seems to have felt that way. The face of this knight is poetic and magnificent. The background is dark, almost solid black, and the man's face is framed by his own dark, long hair and full, dark beard. He wears a black, velvet coat, and there is just enough of a triangle of white, lacy shirt exposed to throw a spotlight on his pensive face. Truly a magical face.

Also in the Uffizi are other provocative portraits by Titian, one is the gorgeous *Flora* with her off-the-shoulder filmy, white gown. She has Titian's favorite reddish-gold ringlets of hair flowing across her plump bare shoulder. She is a show stopper; no one passes her without halting to stare. Two of Titian's Venuses are here as well: *Venus and Cupid* and *Venus of Urbino*. Of these two, my favorite is *Venus of Urbino*.

There she is lounging on her bed in all her soft nudity looking most frankly into our eyes. She is a living renaissance beauty, not a copy of a classical piece of marble or an idealized mythological goddess. Naming these paintings for goddesses was done long after Titian's time. Letters found between Titian and his patrons indicate they were painted to be seductive and intended for private bedrooms. This *Venus of Urbino* is fully human. She has stretched out after a nap or maybe a leisurely bath. Her long golden hair falls across one shoulder in rippling waves of light with a section that has been braided into a crown across her head. She wears pearl drop earrings—at least one is visible as she turns her head to gaze into our eyes. Her lips are rosy; they match the color of the dainty flowers she holds beside her breast. The only other articles she wears is a small ring on her little finger and a delicate jeweled bracelet—possibly made of fragile Venetian glass. Although created for the Duke of Urbino, who lived on a hilltop away from the glassblowers by the sea, Titian was very much a Venetian.

Quiet Return to Trastevere.

A field of sunflowers.

KATHY JOHNSON

Above: Delicate carving on Orvieto church.
Left: Colorful facade of Orvieto church.
Below: Twisted columns on Orvieto church.

KATHY JOHNSON

KATHY JOHNSON

Left: Palazzo Vecchio—the tower.
Below: Uffizi—exterior.

Piazza Navona in Rome.

Posto Magico, Villi Pamphili in Rome.

View from Gianicolo Hill.

One of Rome's elegant buildings.

Country path in autumn near Rome.

Roman aqueduct.

FRANK AMATO

DEANNA HUNT

San Domenico in Arezzo, home of Giorgio Vasari.

FRANK AMATO

Moses—*Golden glow of interior of church.*

View of Florence from Piazzale Michelangelo.

St. Peter's dome rising above the Vatican garden.

St. Peter's, a few columns.

St. Peter's, the embracing colonnade by Bernini.

From a garden on Aventino Hill in Rome.

A view of Arezzo not far from Florence.

Cypress trees in countryside of Tuscany.

Glorious, golden Piazza Santa Maria in Trastevere.

Miles of marble hallways in the Vatican Museum of Rome.

The Roman forum.

Right: Ammanati's
Neptune Fountain
in Florence.

Below: A wet
pigeon dries out on
one of Neptune's
cohorts in
Piazza Navona
in the heart of
old Rome.

Right: Marlene in
an Etruscan tomb
in Orvieto.
Below: Views of
6th Century B.C.
Etruscan tombs
beneath the walls
of Orvieto.

MARLENE HILL

MARLENE HILL

One of many Medici Villas.

Sarcophagus of the Married Couple. Etruscan, terra cotta
from 6th Century B.C. now in Villa Giulia, Rome.

Scenes of the Palio in Siena.

With her maids searching for a gown and other finery in a chest at the rear of the room, her nudity seems more voluptuous than if she were presented naked on the grass as other goddesses were. Her little pet dog snoozes on the linens at her feet assuming his honored place with her. The color of her skin is amazing—a tour de force of technique I'm sure.

The strange *Youthful Bacchus* by Michelangelo Merisi, known to us as Caravaggio, is placed in a dramatic position at the end of a corridor. Caravaggio used himself as a model in many paintings and this one is no exception. His hooded eyes look at us, but I'm not quite sure if they actually see clearly. He holds a large goblet of dark wine most delicately. I can't help but think of some genteel person holding a fine china cup of English tea instead of a goblet of lusty red wine. His thumb and first two fingers grasp the stem and his two other fingers, especially the little one, crook outward effeminately. One muscular shoulder and arm are bare while the other shoulder and arm are draped with a soft, gray fabric. A crown of green, yellow, and deep russet autumn grape leaves rests atop his head of thick, black curls. Along with the other oddities here, he holds in his hand a black velvet bow. Enchanting and bizarre.

This is definitely a strange and arresting painting by an equally strange young man. I suspect he wanted to create a scandal with his paintings. Certainly, some of his religious paintings were brutal visions of Biblical incidents. Caravaggio was known for his swift mood changes, for his wild behavior and for brawling and fighting in the streets. Often held in jail, it is thought that his early death came about because of infections from an escape involving knife wounds. Nevertheless, his forty or so surviving works have been studied, respected and copied by artists through the years.

Exhausted and satiated with the incredible riches of the gallery, I left and moved past the stone figures of famous renaissance persons who stand along the porches of one side of the Uffizi's lengthy U. They are like stone portraits and it was interesting to look at how they may have appeared in real life as I read their names carved on each pedestal. When I reached the Arno, it was yellow and swollen from the rains and seemed angry about something. It is said that the water reached as high as fourteen feet in these streets during the flood of November 1966. As far away as the Piazza del Duomo which is on ground up an incline from the river, there's a plaque indicating how high the water had come. With an arm extended above my five by five inches, my fingers barely touched that mark.

In my favorite novel about Florence called *The Sixteen Pleasures,* Robert Hellenga tells the story of a young American restoration expert who finds a rare, bawdy book from the 1300s while helping in the massive cleanup after that flood. *La Badia* plays a big role in the background of the novel because the heroine's mother had taken her there as a child to see its famous frescoes.

On one of the few days when the Badia's doors were open, I entered to look for those frescoes. It was late afternoon and dark and eerie inside. No one was around. The switches on both sides of the inner door didn't work. Just enough light came through a window high above to see *The Vision of St. Bernard* by Filippino Lippi. Considered to be one of the famous paintings of the fifteenth century, it was pretty as all Lippi's paintings are, but I wanted to know where the famous orange-tree frescoes were. Here I go chasing fictional images—a habit of mine when traveling. It's as if it had been my own mother who brought me here as a child.

Workmen were tearing up an inner courtyard just outside the doors to the sanctuary. Was that the famous orange-tree cloister? In despair I realized it was too late in the day to see anything. A Sunday morning visit was in order.

The next Sunday I arrive in time for the service. When the priest has droned his last words in a gravelly, bored voice, he disappears and a choir which had stood behind him moves forward. They regroup for a mini-concert directed by a slender Japanese woman from her seat at a portable, electronic piano. During the concert, I lay my plans.

It is a good performance and as usual, the congregation shows its appreciation by clapping and calling out "Bravi!". After being exposed to the Calvinistic notion that enjoyment is not an accepted form of worship, I'm always amazed and delighted at such exuberance. I love that Italians do not lock their passions outside the church door.

As soon as the music finishes and people rise to leave, I slip up the steps that lead to the main altar, and follow the directions given in the novel. Through a nondescript door on the right, I cross a small sacristy where choir members are changing. Through the next door on the right, I go up the dark stairs. There it is. At last I've found the upper portico of the cloister where the master's frescoes show the miracles in San Benedetto's life, but there are no orange trees below and the silence is heavy.

The thick walls muffle all sounds coming from the people below—have they left already? Will I be locked in? After all my bravado I feel nervous. The idea of being locked in the cold church for twenty-four hours (or more) is frightening and I rush around the inner balcony like a mad woman. Where is the crow who knocked a poisoned loaf of bread out of the saint's hand just as he was about to take a bite? Where is the goblet that broke in his hand just before he was about to sip the poisoned potion? I see them in a blur and rush back down stairs.

As it happens there is plenty of time because many remain below gathering children and coats and scarves. Next time would be a cinch.

In the hallway just beyond the main church door, lay-people are handing out bread to some poor parishioners. They appear to be those pasty rolls and twists that never taste good to me, but every bite helps if you are hungry. A lump forms in my throat to see the bread being passed from hand to hand. Hands touching hands. These are church people practicing what they preach and not some anonymous organization supplying bread in plastic wraps.

The church door opens onto Via Dante, and a few steps away is Dante's house, or what could have been his house. It is a tall, narrow building. Documents are framed and mounted in several rooms on three different floors. Some are translated and explain various transactions and events that had happened either to Dante or to others of his time. Drawings and etchings of old Florence with excellent explanations and maps are attractively arranged. It is intriguing but freezing cold in "his" house.

I hurry back to my own warm place where I pull out a bottle of Brunello di Montalcino I've been saving for a special occasion. The hearty red wine is a perfect accompaniment to a bowl of homemade bean soup patched together from the remains of a roast chicken, a can of seasoned white Tuscan beans and cubes of leftover Tuscan bread. As I indulge myself with the wine and hot soup, I re-read portions about the Badia in my well-worn copy of Hellenga's novel.

⌇

CHAPTER SEVENTEEN

La Certosa, a calm retreat. The city's lessons.
Fiesole, the first Florence.
Ghirlandaio's Fifteenth Century Snapshots.
Tomorrow and tomorrow.

LUCIA, A FRIEND FROM SCHOOL, TOOK ME TO SEE *La Certosa*, one of her favorite places. The Charterhouse was a Carthusian monastery located in the outskirts of Florence. She

La Certosa, a quiet refuge for monks and all passersby.

explained that the Carthusians are a monastic order founded by Saint Bruno of France in 1086. They live as hermits within a community and do nothing that puts them in competition with others.

"Their work is prayer," she said.

A city bus dropped us off outside the lower gates, and we walked up a gravel road to the huge complex. We were met by an elderly monk who led us and a group of architectural students up a long flight of steps. We reached a great hallway where lush frescoes by Jacopo Pontormo filled the huge walls. Here he had indulged in those brilliant oranges and greens that seem to be his trademark. The gigantic figures moved as if in another realm of color, but unfortunately, we had to move along with the group much too soon.

The old fellow was a kindly soul but had no concept of how to project his voice amidst a large group. The students' teacher was intent on making her own importance known by asking quiet "private" questions to which the elderly monk replied quietly. As a result, I got little out of his discussion and began to feel anxious and frustrated. The calmness of the place must have worked on me because gradually I let it all go and enjoyed what I could. No matter where one stands at *La Certosa*, at any window or any balcony or any stairway, one can look out on soft hills and ravines tinged with varying shades of gray and green punctuated by tall, dark cypress trees.

An exquisite lavabo *carved from* pietra serena
stands in the cloister of La. Certosa.

There are eighteen apartments, too spacious to call them cells, and every one of them has a choice view. My first reaction to the arrangement was, all this for eighteen monks? Lucia gently suggested another way to look at it. She felt that the purpose was never meant for just a few; it was there as a spiritual and physical refuge for any traveler who passed by. And, it provided steady work for the local people.

Then she whispered almost to herself,

"I think these walls are consecrated by thousands of prayers."

After climbing down from my pragmatic, high horse, I began to sense a certain holiness within the *Certosa's* walls; even the vistas seen through the arched windows of the silent refuge seemed holy.

After having been annoyed with Florence, I was falling head over heels for her and began to notice some lessons she'd been offering all along. One lesson was to accept my clumsiness with the language. I hadn't started studying Italian until I was fifty-nine, but as long as the schools would admit me I'd keep on. My role model was an elderly Englishman who began his efforts at seventy-nine in order to speak with his Italian-speaking grandchildren. As I stood in an archway of the cloister and gazed across the soft fields, I sensed a heavy load slip from my shoulders. In that moment, my efforts to learn the language changed from being a struggle to a joyous adventure, a lifetime journey.

Another lesson showed me how closely Italian Renaissance Art could be linked to my beloved Etruscans. Every now and again, I saw their same quirky approach in modern Tuscan art as well. The less famous artists of the Renaissance were also emerging as a lesson. My assignment for the coming year was to go home and take a look at those extraordinary "lesser" artists. Those who had always been there in the background of the Florentine tapestry but who were eclipsed by the giants Giotto, Donatello, Ghiberti, Brunelleschi, Leonardo and, of course, Michelangelo.

Yes, Lucia was right, The Certosa was indeed intended for more than just eighteen monks. Even thousands of miles away, if I close my eyes and whisper, "*La Certosa*," my neck and shoulder muscles let go and for that moment all my receptors are quiet. It had been her personal refuge, and it was there for me too.

Back in Florence in 1990, Patricia and I said goodby to Rachel at the train station. Patricia didn't go with her after all because Rachel was going directly to the airport for home, and Patricia felt nervous about staying in Rome alone. Then too, I suspect she was intrigued with the idea of exploring the Etruscan tombs in Orvieto with me on my way to Rome. What had happened to my resolve to go to Rome alone? Obviously, I was too weak to do anything about it. Instead, I vaguely hoped it would "all work out."

Since the city bus terminal is located at the train station, I decided to catch bus number seven up to Fiesole, the village overlooking Florence. Patricia went elsewhere for the day. The Etruscans had settled high on the hilltop as was their custom and had been there since the fifth century B.C. Only after the Romans conquered and destroyed most of the Etruscan town did Florence come into being. In 59 B.C., Julius Caesar is credited with founding the colony beside the Arno; he named it Florentia.

When the bus reached Fiesole, I crossed the street toward the left which started me off in the wrong direction from the famous view that everyone had talked about. The first sight I came upon looked in the opposite direction from Florence and was a fine vista of rolling hills. A breeze rippled through the upper branches of deciduous trees and tall, dark cypress trees inserted themselves among the bronze leaves like staunch sentinels monitoring unruly cadets. Best of all, it was blessedly quiet. The bustle of Florence was exciting, if only someone would turn down the volume. The noise of the compact streets was stressful. There on the back side of Fiesole, the stones and pillars from a Roman theater were inviting. I could have bought a ticket to walk into the grassy area and wander among the ruins, but I left that for another time. Instead, I continued on the main road which I hoped would lead all the way around the hilltop.

A pleasant surprise appeared beside the road—the remains of an isolated, nondescript Etruscan tomb. While I was crawling around and peeking inside, an elderly woman spoke to me. When I told her how beautiful Fiesole was, her face beamed with pride. She had been born there and had lived no where else. How had she spent her long life, I wondered, in such an isolated place? What had it been like up there during the Nazi occupation?

I thought back to the village in Nebraska where I grew up and knew I could never have stayed until my eighties. But, there was an enormous difference between the two villages. Hers was full of revered ancient monuments with exquisite vistas in every direction. Mine was a dusty little farm town surrounded by a few wheat fields fading off into the barren Sand Hills.

The road did not completely encircle the hill after all, but she took obvious pleasure in leading me across a playground where children ran up to her, some of whom could have been her great-grandchildren. Then she guided me through an old iron gate and pointed toward a gravelly road to town assuring me it would lead to the bus stop. We waved goodby. Soon the quiet was again intense. In no time at all, I came alongside a small curved wall, and when I looked down, Florence was spread out below. Even from so far away Brunelleschi's dome still looked too big—gross, but beautiful.

Patricia was off with another friend, and I would leave early the next morning for a day in Siena. Traveling freestyle was agreeing with me, and I wondered again why I made a date to meet her back at La Mia Casa before going on to Orvieto. Was it my ego? Was I flattered that she wanted me to reveal what I knew about the Etruscans? With only a few hours left in Florence, and with that old worry that I might never be able to return, I struggled with choices. In the end, I entered Santa Maria Novella one more time. A men's choir was rehearsing, and didn't they sound glorious? Their music created the perfect atmosphere for looking at the glowing faces painted by Domenico Ghirlandaio. Both Bernard Berenson and John Ruskin had given him short shrift because his scenes were too pretty and because he didn't meet their requirements for greatness. That may be, but those faces, figures, colorful clothes and heavy draperies tell vivid stories of real people walking across the Biblical stage to play their roles. Much like pictures in a photo album, they show the Florentines of his day as they really were.

Not many people were behind the main altar that rainy afternoon, but enough of us to keep the light meters fed. In last moments like these, I always try too hard to embed the beauty I see, yet in the end, it's only the "memories" of beauty that are embedded. On a later visit to Florence, the area behind the altar was off limits. What a fortuitous choice I'd made after all.

The postcards for sale in the sacristy couldn't begin to capture the essence of the originals, but I bought some anyway. The bored young clerk mumbled that the cloister was not open, "*Domani*," he said, "*Domani*." Once again I'd missed seeing Paulo Uccello's fading frescoes. But, there would be other tomorrows for Uccello. There would be other tomorrows for Donatello's sculptures in the Bargello, for the strange frescoes in *La Badia*, for climbing up inside of Brunelleschi's magnificent dome and for Michelangelo's *Pietà* at the top of the stairs.

PART III:
Siena's Horse Race and Orvieto's Tombs

CHAPTER EIGHTEEN

Siena's Duomo, like the Arabian Nights.
Insipid Sculptures by Michelangelo.
Siena's Palio, the only show in town.
The Police Chief's private tour.

AS MY BUS FROM FLORENCE TO SIENA WOUND
through the lush hills of Tuscany, I settled in for an hour of pleasant reminiscing. Dark cypresses and umbrella pines slipped by my window, and it took no effort at all to slip back six years to 1984. I'd gone alone to Siena—if going on an organized tour could be called alone. Still, after waiting for over twenty years, it was a start. At least I had traveled solo for ten days in Rome after the two-week expedition with the Earthwatch group.

In a small pensione outside of Siena, eighteen middle-class Americans sweated together digging in and around the cistern of a monastery. We were searching for connections to a chain of Saint Augustine hermitages founded in the eleventh and twelfth centuries. After completing our early morning chores, we washed off the cistern's red dust and caught a bus into the lovely, brown-brick city spread over several hills. Nelda, my favorite colleague in the group, often went with me to poke into shops along the narrow walking streets of the city center.

During the two weeks spent on the dig, we had time to visit the National Art Gallery, where Siena's golden madonnas including some by Duccio and Simone Martini are preserved. But, the unfinished Duomo of Siena was the most appealing of all. With its exotic black and white marble horizontal stripes, it was reminiscent of Middle Eastern architecture. The tall bell tower had horizontal stripes on all four narrow spires as well as their pyramidal caps.

Siena and Florence competed and fought each other for centuries. When not actually fighting with swords, they held ongoing jousts of church building. The bubonic plague struck Siena particularly hard in the middle of the fourteenth century, and soon after, its financial fortunes collapsed. Grandiose plans to remake their Duomo into the biggest in the world came to a screeching halt, but a huge arch and part of a striped wall, still stands in unfinished splendor.

It's hard to imagine how they could have improved on their magnificent church already there. An unusual feature of the Sienese duomo complex is that instead of erecting a separate building for their baptistery—the norm for most cathedral ensembles of the time—they built theirs under the apse of the Duomo. It served as part of the church's support on the edge of the hill where it was situated. Many visitors miss the Baptistery altogether, and we found it almost by accident. Bronze panels done by Ghiberti and Donatello on the baptismal font were worth finding. Ghiberti's *Baptism of Christ* is just next to Donatello's *Herod's Feast*, and it was interesting to see how different their works are. Ghiberti's is beautifully made, but Donatello's scene emphasizes perspective, the new hallmark of the Renaissance. Except for these two Florentines' input, most of the Sienese artists saw perspective as a plaything. Their viewpoint may have been influenced by patrons who continued to ask for pointed arches and golden backgrounds.

One exception was the Sienese sculptor Jacopo della Quercia whose figures in the *Fonte Gaia*, Gay Fountain, at Piazza del Campo show his awareness of the renaissance movement in Florence. They twist and turn within their niches and their draperies lap over the edges, an innovative approach to sculpture and bas relief. Some of della Quercia's panels are in the baptistery as well.

Upstairs in the cathedral, Nelda and I encountered stripes and stripes and more stripes of black and white marble giving it a sumptuous, eastern look. The two rows of striped pillars which advance down the center of the church are not individual, fat pillars; instead, they are made of smaller columns clustered together and each column in the cluster is striped separately. My eyes were dazzled trying to absorb the lavish use of stripes on columns, arches and the decorated walls supported by the banded posts.

Intricate carvings are overhead. On both sides of the center aisle, we looked up to see one hundred seventy-two heads representing all the popes from the beginning of the papacy to when the church was constructed in the thirteenth century. These are individual faces—not stylized, and they protruded from the frieze to stare down on all below. They were freakish.

That's not all; the floor is laid with stone mosaics in brilliant geometric designs giving it the appearance of being scattered with Persian carpets from the Near East. Five sculptures by Michelangelo are mounted in the elaborate Piccolomini Altar: Saint Frances, Saint Peter, Gregory the Great, Pope Pius I, and Saint Paul. Usually my emotions respond immediately to Michelangelo's works, but I was surprised to feel nothing from these. Even more surprising is that they were carved during the same years he made his *David*, world-famous for its intense drama. These five figures wear cumbersome drapery and stand in stylized poses; obviously, he hadn't been given free rein with this commission. Saint Paul was the most interesting of the five probably because his nose and frown lines reminded me of *David*.

In spite of all the sumptuousness and elegance, to me, the most fascinating part of the Duomo is its inlaid marble pictures on the floor. Evidently they had been made by anonymous artisans over a two-hundred year period and were absolutely exquisite. These pictorial reliefs of Biblical scenes and historical legends put me in mind of fine appliquè needlework except all were in polished black and white stone. Fortunately, most of the reliefs were protected by markers to keep people from treading on them. We felt we had stepped into the Arabian Nights.

The Siena expedition was cleverly planned to coincide with *Palio*, the bareback horse race which is devilishly dangerous. Etruscan

Parading in velvet before the big race.

terra-cotta panels have been found in the area showing scenes of horse races with jockeys riding bareback. Certainly, the ancient hills of Siena were once inhabited by Etruscans. The race takes place in the sloping, shell-shaped Piazza del Campo, Siena's heart and soul. The beautiful herringbone brickwork on the floor of the Campo is divided into nine pie-shaped slices (representing the city's medieval government of nine). They aren't equal slices; I walked across all of them once when the Campo was almost empty and discovered that in each of those sections, the color of the brown bricks appears to be slightly different. The pattern is so perfectly done that when I sat on the balustrade surrounding della Quercia's fountain placed at the highest part of the shell, the brick sections looked raised in places and uneven. I would swear that I'd have to step up and over certain rows of bricks. Yet, they are all smooth and level.

For the race, the perimeter of the brick pavement was strewn with sand and straw, but even so, those curves are perilous because

Parade participants before the race.

buildings stand close to the "track" all the way around. They tie mattresses against the sharper corners, but inevitably riders are seriously injured and often horses too.

Each year during Palio, rumors abound of the drugging of horses, bribery of riders, and of vast sums of money won and lost. Most important, however, is the pride and honor of each of the seventeen *contrade*, divisions, of the city. That pride has been riding bareback each July 2 and August 16 since 1238.

Palio! What an event. Banners waving everywhere, horses being blessed *inside* the churches, people wearing scarves representing their contrada around their neck, around their waist, across their shoulder, or through their belt. I wear the one representing *Nicchio Contrada* for no other reason than it has brilliant blues and a pretty symbol of a large sea shell.

*Hearts stop as pounding hooves roar around the
Campo at Palio in Siena.*

This is an event which involves the Sienese all throughout the
year. There are meetings held and strategies are forged in each of
the separate parts of the city. The loyalties are fierce and they carry
over to families; they've been known to arrange it so that babies
are born in the "right" contrada. In the past, a marriage between
two people from different contradas was considered an "inter-
marriage" and carried the same taboos and hardships as marriages
between different religions and different races often do.

During the week before the contest—especially the evening
before—tables are set up in the various districts for pre-race drinking and dining. No doubt the winning contrada has a royal celebration all night long after the race; chances are the losing ones
hold wakes all night long. Soon after the final Palio in August,
committees are formed for the next year.

In the days just before the race, banner throwers march
through the streets dressed in costumes depicting their division's
colors. On the morning of the race, each contrada holds a ceremony at their parish church. Some of us from the expedition hear
about this and go to one of the churches to watch them lead their
horse inside to be blessed. No one seems to think this is a bit odd,
least of all the priest. Immediately prior to the race, a grand parade

*Riders hang on for dear life as they round the
treacherous curve in Siena's Palio.*

marches around the Campo with all seventeen contradas even
though only ten get to ride in any one race. The selection process
is of Byzantine complexity and judiciously controlled. More than
one book has been published about the regulations.

Men in armor and colorful velvet costumes guard The Palio
which is a painting of the Madonna on a pale cloth. A new design
is created for every race. The cloth flutters on its tall frame and
wobbles on its mounting fastened to the bed of an ancient wood-
en cart pulled by four tremendous white oxen. The oxen lead the
parade. There is not a cloud in the sky and the sun is burning
everyone—in fact it is relentless, but I would never consider leaving. My heart begins to pound in anticipation, and I feel so lucky
to be here, in this Campo, at this very moment.

From my place in the middle of a surging crowd, it is difficult
to see all that is going on. If they didn't use a small cannon, I
wouldn't know for sure just when the race actually begins because
of the complex system followed for lining up the horses at the
starting point—it's all in a book called *La Terra in Piazza*, by Alan
Dundes and Alessandro Falassi. I begin to envy those more

fortunate than I who stand in windows, on balconies of the buildings and on rooftops overlooking the Campo. They are privileged either by owning the apartment, knowing someone who owns the apartment or having paid a hefty price ahead of time for a good spot. The balconies have colorful banners draped over them. I see people standing with wine glasses in their hands. What a festival.

When the race begins I cheer as furiously for my choice as the Sienese do for theirs, but, there is a big difference in all this frenzy. When it is over, I don't burst into tears as the other losers do.

Birds fly up when the cannon goes off, drums roll, church bells ring, brilliant colors sparkle in the bright air, it's Palio!

Friends and I from the dig always found our way back to the pensione, but none of us really made the streets of Siena "ours." The Police Chief of Siena owned them, however, and since he was friends with the manager of our small hotel, he stopped by often for a coffee or drink. He always spoke courteously to any of us who happened to be in the bar after dinner. One evening he invited me to join him and another couple from our group, whom he already knew, for a tour in his official vehicle. I was thrilled to be included. He was our personal guide as he walked us through the Campo and all around the Duomo in the moonlight ending in his rather palatial apartment on one of the hills overlooking the city.

That was a heady evening. Peter and Doris were fluent in Italian. I knew only a few phrases from a pocket phrase book, but with a few nouns and infinitives, lots of smiles and gestures, I imagined I was communicating with the handsome Police Chief of Siena. When he brought us back to our hotel, I was glad I had memorized, "*Grazie tante per questa bella serata*," Thanks so much for a pleasant evening.

Few trains go to Siena and buses aren't particularly frequent which helps keep the little city's isolated charm intact. It might be nice to return and take a class there, I thought, but I knew I'd not be satisfied to be away from the urban delights of a larger city. Now that I was learning to travel on my own, the memory of those two weeks showed me what a protective bubble of make believe we had been in. It had been wonderful, but it was a narrow, hedonistic experience completely insulated from the frustrating logistics of transportation, lodging and meals. Traveling solo is harder but much more satisfying.

It was pleasant to be back for a day, and I wandered about leisurely refreshing my memories. Before leaving for Florence and then to Orvieto, I sat in the Campo with a coffee and wrote Nelda a note reminding her of our good times together years ago.

~

CHAPTER NINETEEN

Dreamy Orvieto floats above the plains.
The Etruscan League of Twelve convened here.
Orvieto Classico, white ambrosia.
A cathedral made for astonishment.
Luca Signorelli's macabre frescoes.

THE HILLTOP CITY OF ORVIETO WAS MAGICAL AS I KNEW IT would be. In 1990, when Patricia and I arrived, we crossed the street from the train station below the little city and entered the funicular which lifted us from the valley floor to lofty Orvieto. Another dream of mine was about to unfold. Orvieto rides one thousand feet high on a magnificent outcropping of tufa left from a prehistoric volcano. Soon we would see Etruscan tombs from the sixth century B.C., and medieval streets and the famous church that took seven hundred years to complete. As the gondola swung out over the valley, we watched our little train roar off toward Rome. If you were to sit on the left side of the train heading north from Rome, you would see Orvieto floating up there on its unique pedestal. How could you not stop for a few hours, a day, or the rest of your life?

For most people, it takes a few days of vacation time to relax and let go of life's cares; in Orvieto, it takes minutes. Winding through the medieval streets or walking among the Etruscan tombs, opens my spirit to other realms. Ever since that first time in Orvieto, no matter where my plans take me, I always take a side trip to this magical spot to let my soul catch up to my body.

Once we began talking about traveling together, it was hard for me to say no to Patricia. The inner struggle was obviously one of my own making, and I needed to be more clear with others and myself about what I wanted. Much of the time, she was a bright, cheery companion, and usually I enjoyed our evening meals together, but there were times when she was out of sorts for no reason that I could figure. Since we were now together, however, I reasoned it might be fun to share with her some things I'd learned about the Etruscans.

Orvieto was a sixth-century B.C. stronghold belonging to the powerful Etruscans; they had taken it over from the Umbrians there before them. Both peoples were probably attracted to this site for its defensive advantage. Because of the nature of tufa and its water supply, this particular settlement has been inhabited for at least three thousand years, probably longer. Two Etruscan women could have stood right where we stood looking out over the wall to the rich lands below. The volcanic soil in the fields all around is probably why Orvieto's white wine is respected everywhere.

The Romans took Orvieto from the Etruscans around 200 B.C. and assimilated it into their growing empire. From the Middle Ages and into the sixteenth century, Orvieto was sometimes a retreat for popes on the outs with other powers in Rome. While here, Etruscans built strong walls and dug deep wells using the natural caves in the tufa for storing their famous wines. While here, popes built beautiful palaces, dug more wells and used the same caves for storing their own wine collections. Orvieto manages to retain its wonderland atmosphere because its height and ancient walls tend to keep it separated from twenty-first century Italy. People can take the bus or drive the narrow road that winds up to the open staging area, and the funicular is also available, but because of its relative inaccessibility, its small, brooding streets have remained barely wide enough for the ubiquitous Fiat.

⌒

We stepped from the gondola and walked up a gradual incline to Piazza del Duomo. I pulled my cart and Patricia wore all her belongings in a backpack weighing heavily on her slim hips. She'd been having back trouble and had pulled her mattress onto the floor each night at La Mia Casa. She was a passionate runner but it seemed to me her mania for running was why her legs, back and hips ached much of the time. Although she was only thirty-nine, she seemed set in her ways. For a change I kept my thoughts to myself and reflected on just why we all get "fixed" in our ways.

⌒

As we turned the corner onto the Piazza del Duomo, prickly electrical charges danced down my arms and I had to give them a quick rub as if I were trembling with cold. This is truly a cathedral made for astonishment. If my grandsons were here they'd say, "Grandma, it's awesome!" This shrine is so fancifully radiant, however, it inspires lightheartedness instead. Another reason for the town's fairy-tale look is the abundance of honey-colored palaces built by the rich to get away from it all. Many of these palaces are now hotels and museums. The reigning beauty, though, is the Duomo. Its facade reminds me of a stone castle in the sky with shades of blue, pink and gold mosaics and all glittering. Up close, the marble sculpturing tells Biblical stories—some whimsical, some gruesome—a few steps back and the marble tracery becomes lace. Facing west, the front sparkles in the afternoons, and people gather to be amazed again and again.

Everything on the outside looks majestically gothic. Like the Duomo in Siena, it has horizontal black and white marble stripes running all along the sides of the building. Inside is a different story. The church is romanesque with the flat ceiling of a basilica with more black and white stripes. The stripes dominate as one walks toward the altar; all the inside walls, all the immense pillars, and all the arches proceed up to the altar with their wide black and white horizontal stripes of stone. After the radiant facade outside, it always seems dark and brooding inside until one comes to the chapel filled with Luca Signorelli's brilliant frescoes. But, when we reached the chapel gate that first time, nothing could be seen of Luca's work except a colorful poster tacked in front of shrouded scaffolding. Restoration again. Like Michelangelo, Signorelli was fascinated by the nude body especially when in motion, and here the action looked exciting, at least it seemed so from the poster.

Over the next several years, I made five more trips to Orvieto, but the frescoes stayed under wraps until 1997. The restorers had aimed for the seven-hundred-year celebration in 1990, but after having missed that deadline, evidently they lost their sense of urgency. But, who would want such delicate restoration work rushed? When it was complete, the chapel opened for a few hours each morning and a few in the afternoon and tickets were needed to enter. The first year it was finally open, I bought two.

The end of the world is here in all its delicious, gory detail. First, on the large wall to the left of the entrance is an unusual scene depicting an innocent-looking anti-Christ standing on a pedestal speaking to people crowded around. A demon, whose horns emerge from the sides of his head, is whispering to the anti-Christ figure—obviously suggesting evil ideas. Sources claim that the woman taking money from a wealthy man is a portrait of Luca's mistress; others claim that famous characters are repre-sented in the crowd including Columbus, Boccaccio, Petrarch and Dante. Naturally I wanted time to identify each one.

It is a busy scene as are the other scenes in the chapel, incred-ibly busy. I was glad I had two tickets because there was too much to absorb in one session. But, I couldn't miss the two figures at the far left standing there in stark black robes. One is a self portrait and the other is a portrait of Fra Angelico. The two painters stand solemnly surveying the scene, perhaps critiquing their work. Their portraits are a form of signature painted by Luca when he com-pleted the work. Fra Angelico had started the fresco cycle. When he died, Bernardino Pintoricchio from Perugia was given the job, but for some reason that didn't work out so they hired Signorelli.

How lucky for everyone because Luca created a thrilling piece; Pintoricchio's would have been soft, lovely and boring.

Many scenes show macabre skeletons becoming flesh right before the eyes. Some of Signorelli's nude figures climb out of holes in the ground to become redeemed, others drop from "fallen" angels' clutches or ride on their backs. I couldn't miss their anatomical perfection. They say Michelangelo didn't miss it either and that he drew inspiration from Signorelli for his *The Last Judgment* in the Sistine Chapel, completed in 1541. Possibly. Surely Michelangelo had been inspired already by classical models he'd seen while growing up in the Medici household and later in Rome. Creative spirits absorb ideas from everywhere. When they come forth later, who can say where they came from?

In 1499, Luca was hired for one hundred eighty ducats to finish the part that Angelico hadn't finished. Contract details show that he was then hired to complete another part, and after that was approved, hired again for another section. A later record shows ninety ducats more and again another ninety-three ducats until finally he was given the commission to paint the entire chapel for a total of five hundred seventy five ducats. The Works Committee supplied the gold, the blue, the plaster and some other items; Luca paid for all other colors—gold and blue were the most expensive. Also, a dwelling with two beds was provided along with two measures of corn (wheat) a month, and eighteen hundred liters of wine a year. That's almost five liters a day, who drank all that wine I wondered?

The ducat of Venice and the florin of Florence were standard coins; both were used interchangeably throughout Europe for several centuries. It's almost impossible to determine accurately what a ducat or florin would be worth now. Both weighed 3.5 grams of gold and might be worth at least $26 in current American dollars, but in a world where barter was commonly used, a ducat bought much more than it would in our time. For example, the cost of living for an average person toward the end of the fourteenth century was about twenty ducats per year. It would seem that Signorelli was adequately paid; ironically, the restorers of his work probably received much more.

Walking out of the cathedral and into the streets, one forgets mundane things as ducats, florins, dollars and now 'euros' because Orvieto, like Camelot, is a place that inspires ideals and dreams. In addition to Orvieto's historical fascinations are her paths, tombs, caves and cisterns all recalling the mysteries of the Etruscans.

For years, scholars have wrangled over whether Orvieto had been the site of the vanquished *Volsinii*, the most powerful and influential Etruscan city of the fifth and fourth centuries B.C. The latest report concludes that it was indeed Volsinii. Here was held the annual meeting of The League of Twelve and the worship of *Voltumna*, the guardian goddess to whom all the Etruscan city-states paid homage. No doubt, the annual meeting was a time for trade, gossip, athletic games, and games of chance, something modern Italians still consider almost as important as wine and pasta. There must have been good food, pub crawling, whoring and brawling as well—all the usual activities that go with conventions.

All that is known for sure is that the twelve leading cities met somewhere near Orvieto once a year to choose a leader, an honorary post with no real political power. It may have been the only time the famous twelve ever agreed on anything because they were too jealous of each other to work together. One might say that's a familiar trait of modern Italians, politically at least. Their fierce competitiveness was probably a major reason for their final downfall. After destroying Volsinii, the Romans renamed it *Urbs Veteris* meaning old town, and eventually that name became Orvieto.

Much has been written about The League of Twelve. I've noticed that more than twelve towns in this part of Italy hand out brochures claiming connection to The League. Which ones were actually members? I can see now Chamber of Commerce members putting their heads together to find a shred of evidence to prove their community was also one of The Twelve.

~~~

No matter which direction I look over the walls, there are vineyards. Some are owned by large firms, but most are small, family-run farms producing the white wine known worldwide. If their grapes grow in a strictly limited area close to the city, they can label their wine Orvieto Classico. They make reds too, but Orvieto is known for its whites. In this same valley, the Etruscans produced wine. They must have had a good trade going with the Gauls and other Northern Europeans because evidence of wine from this city has been found in Southern France and as far away as Germany. Experts suspect it was much sweeter then because it was made in the natural caves beneath the city where the temperature is perfect for storing wine but too cool for complete fermentation. The advantage of making their wine in that controlled temperature would have been consistency—unusual for their time—and no doubt a good selling point.

~~~

Modern artisans of Orvieto are no slouches; seldom have I seen inferior work on display in Orvieto. Throughout the town, shops display one of the traditional crafts of Orvieto, ceramics. Many of the wares come from the local ceramic co-op. In Italy, cooperatives receive financial help from the state; they offer work to young people who earn while they learn. There are restaurant/hotel co-ops, fishing co-ops, farming co-ops, artistic co-ops, etc. They follow the tradition of the medieval guilds. After they complete a two- or three-year professional course, apprentices work in the cooperative for three more years. In Orvieto, the artisans produce authentic reproductions of traditional etruscan, medieval and renaissance ceramics. Occasionally, I see unorthodox inventions, but the smart artisans tend to produce what the market demands.

Another traditional craft is woodworking. My favorite shop is on Via Albani, a pretty alley with vine-covered arches overhead, where the Michelangeli family's woodworking shop sits. Gualterio Michelangeli's father was a carpenter, his grandfather and great grandfather were too. Gualterio continues to make everything in wood from furniture to all forms of decorative objects, especially wooden animals, huge ones and tiny ones. I might see an owl, a basset hound, a pair of cats, a monkey, a goat or whatever takes the fancy of the artisans currently employed. The clerks are the artisans and know their inventory. Imagination, skill and plain hard work have gone into every object, yet the overriding feeling is light-heartedness, humor and gaiety. Surely the Michelangeli family is directly descended from the Etruscans.

⌐

CHAPTER TWENTY

A screaming landlady. An innocent flirtation.
The little tomb city speaks.
Olive bread, Porcini spread, and House red.
Il Greco the charmer. Hot water at last!

AT THE INFORMATION OFFICE, PATRICIA AND I PICKED UP a map of the little city; it was especially useful because it had hotel and restaurant information on the reverse side. We found a room at Hotel Posta for only 46,000 lire, about $15 each. Not much more than the cost of our rooms at La Mia Casa in Florence, but in comparison, it was a palace. The view didn't compare to Santa Maria Novella, but it did overlook a quiet inner courtyard. Everything was immaculately clean and the beds were comfortable. Patricia continued to drag her mattress onto the floor, and together we lifted it back up on the bed each morning.

We were set, except for our deranged landlady who screamed at everything and seemed perpetually anxious and upset. She screamed when we wanted hot water for showers and she screamed when we asked for blankets in the afternoon. Evidently she didn't want to furnish them until evening. Whatever happened to the notion of siesta? When the lights blew out as I turned on the bedside lamp, she came rushing up to our room. She leaned out

Quiet reigns in ancient Etruscan tombs at Orvieto.

the window and screamed to her son standing at the fuse box in the courtyard. When it was fixed, she screamed at me when it blew as I tried it again. When I screamed back at her in English, she was almost friendly.

With maps in hand, we walked the perimeter of the city hugging the outer wall except for a military area posted with forbidding signs. The views were of idyllic rolling hills, orderly rows of grapevines, and scattered houses framed by artistically planted trees—at least those slender, black cypresses appeared to be purposely placed in dramatic positions.

The map clearly indicated tombs far below but orientation was difficult because it didn't seem to be drawn to scale. We came to the grassy remains of an ancient Etruscan temple and Saint Patrick's Well. Patricia seemed agitated and didn't want to go down the set of double spiraling stairs. Later on, I investigated alone the well designed by the Florentine architect, Antonio Sangallo. It was thought to be the site of an Etruscan well. One set of the broad stairs was for going down, another for going up, the separation had been made for donkeys who were led down to carry water up. Pretty arched windows were cut into the walls all the way down; I could lean over and see the water below or see people climbing up across the way.

185

The perimeter of Orvieto is small and soon we arrived back at the funicular and bus station which sat near a tiny park overlooking the modern part of town below. A spanking clean restroom was in the park. A wizened old gentleman who managed it fell in love with me. From then on each time I stopped by, our friendship or flirtation grew. Whatever the relationship was, it was pleasant and paid off in extra towels and helpful directions.

The guards in the dusty, disorganized Faina Museum opposite the Duomo had told us which bus to take down to the tombs. The bus driver dropped us off at a small sign with the words *Tombe Etrusche*, Etruscan Tombs. Those words on the sign set butterflies going in my stomach. We walked up a grassy lane leading from the road until we saw a shack just around a curve. It must have served as shelter for a guard, but no one was in sight. We signed an outdoor guest book which lay on a simple wooden post; anyone could walk in at any time. The tombs lay directly below and right next to the steep sides of the tufa walls that supported their inhabitants' former city above.

The little gray house-tombs were built of tufa stones cut from their native soil and had the look of a miniature village with clearly-defined streets. Thick, green grass and moss had mounded back over them now that excavators had finished with this part of the necropolis. Family names were carved into their lintels and soft, velvety moss filled in some of the letters. I traced my fingers along the grooves. Some names had faded, but others were carved more deeply by someone's determined hands twenty-six hundred years ago.

My heart took a flip flop. It was as if I'd been there before. All was quiet. We did not speak. No one else was around and we saw no workers about. Each tomb was completely empty. I had to go inside; how to explain such a pull? Patricia strolled on. I sat on one of the stone benches carved into the rock. It might have held a small sarcophagus or an urn holding a loved ones' ashes. All had been stolen long ago or taken to museums. For however long I sat there, it was enough time to "see" a somber celebration with smoke and flame—a final ritual of some sort.

Patricia was calmed by the tombs too and didn't seem in her usual hurry. I found her on another path beside taller tombs. She took an interesting picture of wooden props inserted in modern times to support the roof of one tall tomb. Originally, these Orvietan tombs had no original center posts as some others do elsewhere in Italy. Instead, the ceilings were flat slabs of rock wedged in place against each other forming a modified arch. Those slabs looked heavy yet I had no fear they would crash down; they'd been supporting each other for centuries, but where were the frescoes I'd read about?

It was an easy walk up the hill to the town; it wasn't as far as it had looked on the map. According to our traveling plan, we went our separate ways for the rest of the day. I left Patricia sitting in the sun on the church steps to write postcards and headed straight back to the Faina Museum to ask about the frescoes. They pointed to a large building on the side of the Duomo where I found the unobtrusive entrance to the National Archaeological Museum. The frescoes had been carefully lifted from the tombs below the town and reattached to the museum's simulated tomb walls. The technique needed is delicate because whole slabs of plaster with the paint embedded must be moved. Sure hands and strong egos do that kind of work.

On one hand, I regretted that they'd been taken from their rightful place, but I knew they would have been doomed to disintegration if they hadn't. Here, I could look at the original paintings from the sixth-century B.C. in "tombs" much larger and better lighted than the originals ever were. If only it weren't necessary to have a guide hovering to make sure they aren't touched.

There are banquet scenes with men *and* women dining together and naked serving men bringing them food and wine. The women's skins were pale and the men's a burnished reddish-brown—a common stylistic device also used in Greek art of the same period. Music is playing; people are dancing. One gets the clear idea that Etruscans enjoyed life and planned to continue in the same vein for all eternity.

~

Our first evening in Orvieto, we went to a small cafè that we never saw again, which was just as well. When I ordered a second bowl of the hot veggie soup, the fat little Signora who served us laughed and thought it strange to order two *primi* instead of moving on through the menu toward the *secondo*, the meat course. She tried to argue me out of it. I assured her it was because it was *molto squisita*, absolutely delicious.

She seemed to wear herself out making a separate trip for each item, and her shoes offered no support for her hard-working legs. They were those nothing backless slippers that blue-collar Italian women slap around in every day of their lives. Slap, slap, slap on marble floors everywhere. It's amazing to see them in a country that makes the most comfortably beautiful shoes in the world. Broken veins in older women's legs are a painful reminder of wearing those slippers.

We waited and waited for the bill and finally went to the counter. The in-charge Signora figured our bill by hollering back and forth to her partner across the room. They were jolly women and in fine good humor, but it was the first eating place we'd seen in Italy that was obviously dirty. How would it affect our digestion we wondered? As it happened, our stomachs were fine, but we didn't go back for more.

~

The next day, a white-haired man with an attractive, rugged face stood in front of his trattoria and beckoned us to come in for lunch, but earlier that morning we had bought delectable lunch things at an elegant delicatessen near our hotel. We were intrigued with the charmer. He was small, compact and built like a wrestler. His dark eyes looked almost black under heavy white eyebrows. The lines that curved out from the corners of his eyes and down the sides of his bronze cheeks caught our imagination. Patricia thought his rough-hewn hands and face looked like those of fishermen she'd seen in Greece, and we privately dubbed him Il Greco. We waved saying, "*Torneremo stasera.*" We'll return tonight.

What an enjoyable experience to deal with the two brothers who ran their small, spotless delicatessan. They were patient and obviously took pride in their enticing *salumeria* with its beveled glass door and windows and dark mahogany counters and shelving. Whenever I returned to Orvieto, the same congenial brothers sold the same rich delicacies. We purchased paper thin slices of prosciutto and a small loaf of bread with olives baked right in it. It was the first time I'd eaten olive bread, and I succumbed instantly to the rich taste permeating the loaf. I bought some porcini mushroom spread that cost the earth for a mere spoonful; it was sinfully rich and smooth on the tongue. That was when I understood the true meaning of porcini.

We picnicked on our beds that day. Patricia was cold and tired and refused to try the porcini spread, saying it was too rich. She did try a slice of prosciutto on a bit of olive bread, but then stuck to her dry cereal and fruit. It reminded me of that trip so long ago with my ex-husband who decided to take diet pills while in Italy. I knew she was wise to eat healthfully, but for me, a major part of the trip was to try out different tastes. She may have felt I was inconsiderate to indulge in her presence since she was obviously denying herself. She seemed unconcerned about my gluttony, but from then on, I was more careful about splurging in front of her. It was not a big hardship, merely a reminder that partnerships demand compromise. After lunch, she asked the landlady for hot water for a shower, and there was another scene. We began to wonder if we should find another hotel.

At dinner time, we set out to find the handsome man and his trattoria. His little establishment was on Corso Cavour. Doesn't every Italian town have a street named for Signor Cavour, revered for his part in unifying Italy? The walls of the one-room restaurant were whitewashed, and the sturdy, worn, wooden tables and chairs were almost black with age. The windows were opaque with steam and there were a few colorful travel posters tacked on the walls for decoration, but the warm aroma of garlic and hot, melted cheese was the best invitation to the senses.

My pasta that evening had a smooth, creamy Gorgonzola sauce. It was delicious but maybe a bit too smooth and my stomach reminded me of its richness for an hour or two. Patricia had a Pizza Napolitana, the grandfather of all pizzas they say, since Naples is the birthplace of pizza. It was the simplest of simple concoctions. It had garlic, olive oil, a sprinkling of savory parmigiano cheese and thin slices of anchovy laid on a thin crust baked to a crispy crunch in their wood-fired oven. Our salads were a delicious mix of lettuces and bitter greens. It was a great choice for small cost, and we were in pig heaven.

We took our weary selves back to Hotel Posta where I confirmed with the landlady that I could use my hair dryer the following morning. So far so good, I thought, but when I asked to have hot water at 7:30 in the morning as well, she blew her top and threatened to charge extra. This was outrageous and I indicated my outrage with some Italian words, some English words, some gestures and pantomime hoping to convey to her that other hotels do not charge extra for hot water. I even scared myself. She got the message. She stomped off grumbling over her shoulder, "*Buona notte. E domattina ci sarà acqua calda!*" "Good night, and hot water in the morning!"

In the morning I had plenty of hot water and the dryer worked. Life's little pleasures.

It was time to call Rome for hotel reservations. Given my choice, I'd have waited until I got there, but Patricia had succumbed to the rumors and desperately wanted a secure destination. Face to face with gestures and the friendliness of loquacious Italians, I could usually manage, but I was a total wreck after negotiating through impersonal telephone wires. Aware of my telephone anxiety, she treated me to a cappuccino and a pastry in the prettiest bar in town with its polished woods and beveled mirrors reflecting colorful bottles of liqueurs and brandies.

Then we took ourselves in hand to ask the tourist-office personnel why we had to fight for hot water. Neither of us had ever had this problem in small European hotels before.

"Are we out of line to expect hot water?" I asked.

Immediately, the woman picked up the phone to call Posta.

"No, no, don't tell them we're here," Patricia said.

With the phone already in the crook of her neck, she raised both hands with her palms facing us in what was supposed to be a calming manner and assured us that she would merely ask about their policy. She spoke to Massimo, the son, and we could hear him yelling at her. When she hung up she claimed that all was well, but we fretted on the way back. We slipped up the stairs to our room and found we had hot water in our bedroom basin as well as in the bath down the hall.

One late afternoon, Patricia and I visited an *enotecha*, a wine-tasting bar, and tried Orvieto Classico and Est! Est! Est!, both popular white wines. She preferred the fruitier Est! and I the drier Classico. We came away feeling proud of our new wine expertise, but we headed down Corso Cavour for the rougher house red where our rugged proprietor reigned.

It's lovely the way simple rituals develop between proprietor and clients in friendly atmospheres. Each time we ordered, we would request a half bottle of red, and each time he would bring a full liter encouraging us to drink all we wanted. We'd go through the motions of holding our hand halfway and he'd nod and smile. In the end, he always charged us for half. It was ordinary table wine that had probably been watered down from the huge tuns we'd seen delivered to his back door, but in that cozy trattoria it was an elixir for our souls.

Would he have been insulted if he knew we thought he looked Greek? We guessed that his wife worked in the kitchen and his daughter waited tables—except ours. He was always our waiter, no doubt a tried and true business practice. Once the cook emerged for a chat with some local men sitting near the kitchen; he was a rosy-cheeked, rotund fellow from Naples and certainly knew how to make flaky thin-crust pizza. Il Greco invited us for an early coffee the next morning, but we demurred saying we were off to Chiusi for the day.

"*No problema,*" he insisted, "Why not come in at eight or maybe seven-thirty?"

"*Forse, forse,*" "Perhaps," we said.

⌒

CHAPTER TWENTY-ONE

Bucchero pottery at the Chiusi Museum.
Bold youths.
Alone in a tomb with Gino.
Museum talk.

WE TOOK AN ALTERNATE ROUTE TO THE FUNICULAR TO avoid Il Greco and hoped for good coffee at the train station. Sure enough, when we stepped into the station, the tantalizing perfume of fresh-ground beans promised a great day. Forty minutes later we were in Chiusi. Directions to the archaeological museum were vague but after several questions along the way, we found it at the end of a three-kilometer hike uphill. Naturally it would be at the top because old Chiusi had also been an Etruscan stronghold. Renamed Clusium by the Romans, it was immortalized in Thomas Babington Macauley's poem, *Horatius*. Lars Porsena of Clusium had been held back at a bridge over the Tiber by the Roman hero, Horatius. A century ago, British and Canadian school children were often required to memorize this long poem.

To my delight, the museum was overflowing with vases, canopic jars, urns, and numerous sarcophagi with carved figures reclining on their lids, but there were scarcely any of the little bronze votive figures called *bronzetti*. Some of the lids on the sarcophagi did not always fit and were often out of kilter because the tombs had already been disturbed and robbed long before authorities got to them. They did their best to simulate how they might have been with what objects were left.

After more than 2000 years, traces of color were on some of the artifacts. It was heaven to be there; I could have stayed for hours. From books I'd read, the Chiusi vases were more what I'd expected than those in Florence or Orvieto. Certainly, they were less classical, more playful and more exaggerated than the Greek ones or their Etruscan copies. There were few gold objects. The *bucchero* objects were plain; just plain beautiful. They have so many, would they miss just one?

Bucchero is a special form of terra cotta. In the sixth century B.C., Chiusi was famous for its thick-walled ewers and vases. No one quite knows how they achieved the solid black color; it might have been done by firing the clay at a lower heat than usual. Sometimes the artists polished the bucchero to a high sheen to mimic the look of metal, but most are rather grayish black. Evidently only a few ever emerged from their ovens totally black and beautiful.

There were so many things to dream over that right away I planned to return again. Italy must be drowning in artifacts; the Etruscan relics alone swell the museums. Most objects aren't labeled clearly or at all; they must be short of informed experts and assistants. Part of the reason for poor labeling may be that many of the tombs discovered in the early 1800s were excavated in a haphazard manner. One frustration nagging at me was that both here and in the Orvieto museum, objects were placed in cases by who found them. As a lay person, I didn't care who found them; I wanted to know where they were found, what they were, and when they were originally left there. There may have been a shortage of help to label and sort, but there was no shortage of watchers.

When we first entered, a boorish fellow hung around us trying to ingratiate himself by pointing to some figures and pretending to dance like the figures on the vases. Did he actually think we'd want to dance with him? Then it was clear; he wanted to take us out to the tombs for 25,000 lire (about $17). Later, I spoke with the woman in charge about how one does go to the tombs. She had a couple of other less disreputable-looking fellows, who were "official guides," and they offered their services for 20,000. Clearly, Patricia had quite enough and didn't want to spend more money or time so we passed. It was disappointing, but as we talked with the supervisor, I understood her to say the main tombs were closed for restoration anyway.

It was raining when we returned to Orvieto, and we were chilled through by the time we reached our hotel. Our "gracious" landlady's hot water comforted us before we set out for our last meal at Il Greco's where a group of young military cadets filled the place. In the early evenings they could be seen walking three and four abreast through Orvieto's narrow streets singing loudly to attract attention no doubt and maybe for the joy of it. Their tones resonated nicely from the stone buildings. Their language may have something to do with their voice quality. Italian words end with vowels, and vowels tend to produce head tones so that even untrained voices ring out with rich sounds. None of the citizens seemed to mind; no doubt they benefit financially from these military fledglings.

What a noisy bunch they were, yet harmless. They seemed to get their rebellion and belligerence out of their systems by being loud and boisterous. It was annoying but not frightening, and I sensed no violence roiling beneath the surface. Off duty, these youngsters wore hats, shirts and jackets with English words on them, either U.S. slogans or team names including Lakers or Cowboys, yet they were still very much Italian youths.

I wondered if their musical language might subtly influence a softer group personality. In spite of the Mafia's reputation for violence, it is a gross distortion to dump all Italians into that bag. The truth is I am much safer from violence on Italian streets than on streets in Oregon or most anywhere else in the States. These youths do so enjoy appearing tough, but their method of letting off steam is infinitely preferable to attacking people or trashing property.

If there *are* serious disagreements, it usually involves verbal abuse, threats and name calling. Once, during the evening passeggiata, two fellows grew hot under the collar and were about to explode. Their friends pulled them apart just in time. A few moments later, I saw one telling an older man his side of the story. From his body language, it was clear that his opponent was wrong, wrong, wrong! The man hugged him and whispered something in his ear; the kid smiled and they ended laughing and walked away arm in arm. Touching and hugging among males may also be a softening factor of life even if their testosterone does require all of that strutting and noise.

Little Italian boys get to wear uniforms of one kind or another from early on, much more than little girls. They can look forward to dressing up in all kinds of costumes beginning with altar-boy robes and moving on to various elaborate military or police regalia not to mention the flamboyant medieval outfits worn each year in numerous local festivals. The young military strutters seem silly to me, but the truth is, if a mature man passes by in a well-tailored dark uniform, he takes my breath away.

Other than the young rowdies in the trattoria, there was one quiet couple in a far corner and another table of six mature men—also having a good time albeit somewhat quieter. Il Greco persuaded four youngsters to join their comrades at a long table in order to free a smaller one for us. In Rome we wouldn't be noticed, but here we were a novelty. A couple of the grown men eyed us and one in particular smiled at me from time to time. One's never too old for a bit of attention, is one? It was harmless fun and Patricia enjoyed flirting with the young men. I suspected it gave her pride a boost since things were not going well with a boyfriend back home. Their relationship was dragging on her, and as time went on, her sulkiness dragged on me as well.

Two brash young men came to our table and pulled up chairs for a chat; we suspected they were on a dare from their compatriots. One spoke a bit of English; he played the trumpet and was proud to have been in Chicago once. His goal was to play in a jazz band some day. The other expected to join his father's architectural firm back in Naples. He was the cocksure one, and why not with his tall, dark, good looks and plenty of backing. We speculated that he had never worked a day in his life, would get into a good university, pass his exams and fall into a fabulous career in the family firm.

The occasional eye contact with the older man across the room was flattering, but the young men were absolutely gorgeous and they knew it. We laughed and communicated one way or another. When we left, I shook hands with Il Greco and had good intentions of sending him a postcard from the States, but how could I send him anything? I couldn't read his signature scribbled on the bill.

Within a few minutes after we left the cafè, the man who had smiled at me drove alongside and offered us a ride up the hill. We declined politely, and he went on. He didn't expect us to get in, but 'nothing ventured nothing gained' must surely be an old Italian proverb. No doubt his wife and bambini were snug at home waiting for papa's return. It was two years before I returned to Orvieto. The white-maned, sexy man was gone. So were the perfect pizzas. The cozy trattoria had been refurbished, the prices had gone up and they accepted credit cards. The magic was gone.

It took three years more before I got inside a tomb in Chiusi, and then, it didn't go exactly as planned. A scruffy-looking fellow stood on the steps of the Etruscan museum. He smiled and asked if I'd like to see the tombs. He said it would cost 30,000 lire. While I hesitated wondering how to ask what that amount would include, he lowered his price to 20,000 (about $13 that year).

Gino had greasy gray hair that lapped unevenly over the collar of his blue quilted wind breaker. Many Italians wear those ugly, quilted jackets that are bulky and shapeless—so unlike the usual stylish garb one tends to see. No doubt they were warm and serviceable, but he certainly did not look official. In a country where civil servants wear some sort of uniform or badge of office, it seemed odd that this prestigious national institution had chosen to hire part-timers who looked like day laborers. He wore a blue shirt open at the neck with a frayed collar, his trousers were a dusty black, not necessarily dirty, but the nap was worn so much that they looked gray. His scuffed brown oxfords were a far cry from what natty Italian gentlemen wear in the city.

Before I agreed to anything, he was urging me to go to the tombs prior to visiting the gallery. No doubt he'd lost many a prospect by waiting until they were worn out by the museum. My plan had been to stroll through the rooms first to see my old "friends" lounging on top of their ancient sarcophagi. Then the museum officials would arrange a tour. The first time at Chiusi had been with Patricia, who didn't want to pay the extra money. After all, the Etruscans were not *her* passion. On the second visit, an icy rain had been falling as I emerged from the gallery, but this time I was determined to do it. A familiar voice from the past whispered in my head, "Don't be foolish—a woman alone—better wait for another time." Then I heard my own voice say, "*Va bene, andiamo!*" "Okay, let's go!"

Who knew whether I'd ever get to return? I wasn't getting any younger. Even so, I wondered what I was getting into. When Gino hurried into the museum office to get the tomb keys, through the office window I could see him dealing with the same administrator with whom I had talked before. That was a good sign. In spite of his disheveled appearance, Gino seemed sincere so I trusted my own instincts rather than listen to warnings born of others' fears. The idea of traveling alone to Italy itself was considered dangerous and foolish by the source of those voices—my relations and other nervous nellies.

Gino was a good guide, and really leaned into it. He leaned a bit too close and kept touching my shoulder for emphasis, but he quickly took the hint when I edged away. He was genuinely enthusiastic and took pride in his part of the world. Eager to show his guiding skills, I suppose, he began to extol the landmarks before we ever reached the tomb area. He pointed to Lake Chiusi, the dividing line between Tuscany and Umbria, explaining that the two ancient towers on either side had been built by defenders of those sovereign regions.

He used simple terms and I was able to follow him well enough to know that some of his Etruscan knowledge wasn't entirely accurate, but I wasn't exactly accurate either when he asked the inevitable question, "*Lei è solo?*" "Are you alone?" I fumbled a bit and said my husband wasn't feeling well and had stayed in our hotel in Orvieto. Indeed I'd come over from Orvieto that morning, but as far as I knew, my husband felt just fine back home in Oregon.

At the tombs, we walked across a grassy knoll; he unlocked a black iron gate at the top of steep stone stairs. They led to *The Tomb of the Lions.* The green moss growing on the sides of the walls was soft and velvety. When we reached the bottom of the stairs, there was a massive, wooden door, which had been fitted into the odd-shaped space left by an original stone slab still lying there on its side.

At last, a real buried tomb. I gasped, partly from excitement and partly because I'd been holding my breath all the way down from the gate above. Gino pointed to the lioness, but we could just barely make her out on the upper archway of the room. I was disappointed. The frescoes were faded and flaking because too many like me had tramped through for too many years. But, the banquet scene was visible in vibrant colors of rusty reds, yellows, aquamarines, blacks, browns, and creamy whites.

There they were—my happy Etruscans! Both women and men lounged and dined together, something unheard of by Romans and Greeks. Relaxing in luxury, they were being served and entertained by their slaves. I didn't see a six-stringed lyre that I'd seen in pictures of other frescoes, but some slaves were playing doubleflutes, an instrument that appeared to be two separate tubes attached to one mouthpiece. They held it high with both hands. Fingers of each hand covered various stops to make exuberant music which I strained to hear, and they pranced with their muscular legs lifted high.

Often in profile, the figures at the table seemed noble, but they didn't exhibit the stiffness I usually associate with nobility. Couples were touching one another and some were in affectionate embraces. The Greeks liked to depict young men being affectionate with each other or with courtesans, but never with their wives. The women were draped modestly but wore large earrings, necklaces and rings—more than one finger revealed elaborate rings. The men, both nobles and slaves, appeared to be nude beneath their stoles and short tunics of bright yellow cloth with blue and red borders. The men dancing or performing acrobatic movements had large, well-developed thighs and haunches. I remembered noticing that same body shape in Etruscan sculptures and their little bronzes as well. Definitely not the classic Greek ideal, these bodies were compact and short-waisted with thunder thighs.

Just as in the many pictures I had seen of Etruscan tomb frescoes, the overall impact exuded sexuality, lust, life. In 1932, D. H. Lawrence, author of *Etruscan Places,* drew attention to this ancient civilization when he fell under their spell while touring Italy. From their paintings, it was clear to Lawrence that when an Etruscan man caressed a woman, his caress was beautiful because he *knew* how to touch. Lawrence wrote, "To the Etruscans, everything was alive and it was man's duty to live too. He had to absorb in himself all the life of the world." Certainly, in these older tombs, the idea shines through that theirs was a religion of life. About two hundred years later, when economic downfalls and the military might of the Romans threatened, the art work of the tombs became less positive and more grim.

Lawrence noticed that among Etruscans there seemed to be a poetry of contact between human beings. I think this "poetry of contact" was what I had been noticing among modern Italians, particularly in Tuscany, the land of ancient Etruria. In Lawrence's book, he criticized the ancient Romans and contrasted the Etruscans' art of living with Roman principles. He wrote, "One cannot both dance gaily to the sound of the double flute and conquer the world."

Already seduced by these mysterious people of pre-Roman times, it was electrifying to be there in the tomb with them—at least with their auras. I saw and yet I knew I wasn't "seeing." Oh to be alone with them and tap into the energy I felt might be there for me, but Gino was well into his tour-guide role expounding on the different layers of natural earth; alluvial, creta, tufa, etc. Finally, in the smallest room he was quiet. It was bare of frescoes, but the border of the ceiling was painted a vivid red, still garish with traces of gaudy yellow showing within its frame. Someone had lovingly decorated this little room's ceiling back in the fourth century B.C., 2400 years ago. Maybe for their child.

A tremorous current was building inside me with no place to go; a strange, secret thrill moved under my skin. If only I could turn a cartwheel to release the charge. Instead of a cartwheel, I bounded up the stairs and sucked in a huge breath of Etruscan air while Gino locked the door behind me. Later, I would relive the moment over and over.

~

A man and his small granddaughter were waiting at the gate as we emerged into the brightness of the grassy park. The child asked if we'd seen *la scimmia*, and we laughed saying, "*No, no scimmia oggi.*" "No, no monkey today." Rats! *The Tomb of the Monkey* was what had I wanted too, but Gino insisted it had been closed already for two years because it was too dangerous to go in. Were archaeologists and experts allowed in? No, he said, No one. "*Che peccato.*" What a shame, indeed. Hmm. Sometimes guides say what they think you need to hear. Maybe he had simply forgotten the key to the tomb of the monkey. Maybe another guide had checked that key before us. I would try another time.

We did get to see *The Tomb of the Wanderers.* As we approached, a couple of honeymooners were wandering about outside its gate. Gino chatted enthusiastically with them, but their Italian was too rapid for me to catch it all. He invited them to join us bowing and sweeping his arm toward the tomb as if he were inviting them into his mansion. No money changed hands, he was simply enthralled and wanted to share the adventure.

As we descended another set of steep steps, I now recognized that unique odor wafting out of the door that Gino held for us. It smelled something like the cellar in my grandparents' house, but older. Yes, older, but it was more than musty and damp, in fact, the air was cool and dry. It held an ever so slight hint of sulphur similar to the long molecules of gas emitted from the stone called *fetida* out of which some of the ancient coffins were hewn. Strange to say, it was a smell I would remember fondly.

Once again we were looking at bright red trim around the ceilings. Although faded in the corners, that red paint humbled me. I knew the tomb had been hewn by human hands long ago, and I drew in a breath at the image of someone using such positive brightness for their beloved's resting place.

Three small urns had been placed in the tomb. They were topped with reclining figures in typical Etruscan, self-satisfied poses. They weren't originals but gave the impression of how the tomb might have looked to that lucky person who first discovered it. If I had only followed the lure of the ancient world forty years ago, I thought, I might have been the happy archaeologist to open this tomb.

On the return trip Gino and I talked about our families. When I pulled out a small pocket dictionary and glasses, he pulled his glasses out too. We laughed about the need for spectacles at our ages, he at sixty-one and I at sixty-two. We talked about how young we both looked, and other comforting little lies. Somehow I managed to communicate the advantages of being *una pensionata*, a senior citizen, which earned *some* respect from youngsters and reduced ticket prices. He chuckled. Back at the museum, when I paid him, he gave me a free ticket to enter the museum. He seemed happy with his fee and I knew I'd gotten a bargain.

After roaming through the museum in a state of bliss, I noticed there were no other visitors. It must be closing time, but the curator and his assistant assured me there were still a few minutes left. I dashed back to look at the bucchero pottery one more time. How I longed to touch the smooth surface of one particular black wine pitcher. I wanted to hold it and feel its heft. Some Chiusi bucchero from the sixth century B.C. looks like shiny metal; this one was lovely and uniquely Etruscan.

The curator walked over and began to explain certain objects. It was obvious he loved his museum and seemed delighted to find someone genuinely intrigued. He moved quickly from one glass case to another, pointing out various ewers, pitchers and vases. He spoke no English; we had to rely on my meager Italian.

Did I have any questions? Of course. Where were the bronzetti? Those charming little bronzes which depicted life so energetically and were usually so atypical of their Greek classic models. He shook his own bronzed curls sadly saying that in this area they'd been stolen long before serious excavations had been made, but would I like to see the museum on the lower level? Would I ever! He led me down a flight of steps and unlocked a door to a working area. Both Roman and Etruscan objects from the second century B.C. were lying carefully numbered but not assembled. This was where the real fun lay for the experts.

He seemed eager to talk about the Museum's Etruscan erotic art and used a word over and over which sounded like "shayna." I couldn't grasp his meaning. Later, it came to me, it was simply the word for scene, *scena*. He produced the only two pieces of erotica they had in Chiusi; one was a figure with a huge penis and the other was an erotic "scene" in the bottom of a broken ceramic cup. How did we get on that subject? Maybe he had misunderstood something I'd said. Maybe it was simply a curator's pride in having two rare objects in his museum.

When I asked if he loved his work, his amber eyes shone as he said, "*Si, si, molto, molto.*" The most exciting part of this entire scene was that we had communicated, and I floated out the door.

Timing is all. If Gino hadn't convinced me to visit the tombs first, I'd never have been invited into the off-limits portion of the museum later. By stepping into his battered family car that afternoon, I got to live out another one of my dreams—something that happens more often when going it alone.

~

CHAPTER TWENTY-TWO

Sweet anonymity. An underground tour.
"Prego, prego," but if looks could kill!
An Etruscan bird sings.

ON A SUBSEQUENT VISIT TO ORVIETO, I LAY IN BED ONE morning listening to the absolute silence. How would it be to live here? The day before, I had taken an underground tour which revealed how much like a hunk of Swiss cheese Orvieto's tufa pedestal is with its hundreds of caves beneath the streets. The young woman who led the tour adored her home town and said she had been homesick all the while she was away at University.

Before joining the tour, I had wandered through the oldest medieval section of town where some of the streets were cobbled together at odd angles. Crumbling buildings leaned and support- ed each other so beautifully that tears came to my eyes. Were they tears of some undefined connection or regret that I hadn't been lucky enough to be born here? Would I have stayed? Orvieto is a small, insular town; the permanent population must be parochial in their thinking. The isolation might have felt stifling to me, yet for her it was just right.

~

The Hotel Duomo where I was relaxing that Sunday morning was not as modern nor as spotless as Hotel Posta, but when I learned that the same woman and her son ran the Posta, I opted for some- thing else. My room had a view of the side of the Duomo, which was nice at night when spotlights lit up the building. When the wind howled, the tattered palm tree outside my window made a friendly rustling noise, and it was pleasant to be cozy and alone.

I mused about why anonymity is so comforting. Is it because when I am anonymous, I am not watched? As an only child, I always felt "watched." Mother paid careful attention to all my daily doings: what I wore; what I did in the bathroom; what I ate at the table; what I read, and what I wrote in my diary! Yet with all that watching, my sense was that she knew nothing about me. A hermit I'm not, but anonymity for a month or two is sweet.

About eight, the Duomo bells rang and rang. It was a nice sound and time for coffee. In a comfortable bar, I ordered a flaky pastry and a piping hot cappuccino remembering to ask for it *bollente*, boiling. Some bars let the foamed milk sit cooling to be spooned on top of the espresso for those who prefer a cooler version.

At a nearby table sat a family with a pleasant young man, a charming little girl of about eight and a beautiful but haughty wife. They had spread out over two tables. She got up to order something, and an old man came in. He laid his paper at "her" table and went to the bar to order. When she returned, she sat with her back to the old man. He picked up his paper and moved away obviously sensitive to her behavior. Without thinking, I called to him and said, *"Prego"* gesturing that he should join me. *Prego* is an all-purpose word which can mean "make yourself comfortable," "help yourself," "after you," "excuse me," "you're welcome," or "no problem." He thanked me but drank up and left.

If looks could kill, I would have perished on the spot. Evidently I had insulted her when I was merely being kind to the old man. Did I insult her on purpose? Well, possibly. Maybe I don't like Italian women much. Yet, that's not entirely true. Some are delightful and genuine. Many, however, are so locked in their proprieties that they seem critical of those of us who move outside of their rules. Take fashion, for example, Italian women are elegant to look at, but enslaved by the fashion dictators. It could be my imagination, but it seems they resent independent women travelers. Despite the fact that they hold professional positions and keep their maiden names after marriage, they seem tethered to traditions which allow them few real freedoms. If I ever lived in Italy, it would be a slow process to learn the subtle feminine rules. It might be impossible to make close women friends among natives, especially in small places where newcomers are not exactly welcome.

⁓

Ah, but Orvieto is a jewel mounted delicately on its tall solitaire setting, and whenever I walk among the little tombs below, I have an inexplicable feeling of belonging to this very piece of earth. How does one explain such a feeling? A past life, perhaps, or a longing to be part of something outside of my own ordered one? As I stood in the little dead city and looked straight up at the living one, I noticed some of the crumbling tufa had been propped up with odd-shaped bricks or blocks of stone and huge reinforcing irons. Even those propped-up walls were beautiful to me.

No one was at the tombs that day except a few workers quietly surveying a new area a hundred meters away. When an excavation of a section of tombs is complete, they are turned back to nature again. Gradually thick grass covers their roofs and velvety, lime-green moss gathers in the grooves of old family names. The official name here is *Necropoli Etrusca del Crocifisso del Tufo*. It has an urban plan of straight streets paralleling each other. Of course the Romans took credit for straight streets and city planning, but in reality they learned it all from the Etruscans. Inside the tombs, the ceilings have arched stones. The arches are more like softened triangles formed by layering the slabs of stones at angles similar to tombs found in the ancient Near East. The Romans got their arch ideas from the Etruscans too, but with their brilliant use of concrete and cement they perfected them into stronger, more beautiful "romanesque" arches.

Beside each doorway of the abandoned "houses" a respectful archaeologist had replaced small stone grave markers: a point for the tomb of a man and a globe for a woman. Where the two main streets intersect stands a small obelisk in the shape of a cross. This gives the little city its name, *Etruscan Necropolis of the Tufa Cross*. All the treasures intended for the next world were gone, and all was silent except for an Etruscan bird chirping nearby. It *is* a place to let my soul catch up with my body.

PART IV:
Roma!

CHAPTER TWENTY-THREE

Rome at last. Oh, to be alone again.
The maestro of Piazza Venezia.
Villa Giulia and the Etruscan lovers.
I hear their giggles and laughter.

ROME IS WHERE MY ADRENALINE STARTS PUMPING AS soon as the first blue-and-white sign, **Roma**, appears out the train window. It's where my blood stirs as the train pulls into the station. It's where I feel a surge in my chest, and my breath comes in choppy little gasps. When the brakes squeal to a stop inches in front of the concrete barrier, it's where I whisper to myself, "Roma. I'm home!"

Train stations pulse with romantic rhythms that airports will never have. It's because of the movies of the 40s and 50s when meaningful encounters took place in train stations; dramatic clouds of steam engulfed lovers as dignified conductors called out, "All Abo-a-rd!" Arriving in Rome's station evokes those dreams of adventure I had while sitting in our dusty little movie house in Cedar Rapids, Nebraska.

For most of that first solo trip in 1990, I felt unsure about going it alone. Old psychological baggage came along with me and, at times, held me back. For one thing, my age. Young women one-third as old as I went charging off alone to Europe without a worry, but personally, I knew no women of my age doing it, and Mother and my Aunt never let me forget it. After going in spite of their disapproval, I felt conflicted about teaming up with anyone. It was as if I had let a part of myself down. Nevertheless, there I was stepping down from the train with Patricia in tow.

Anxious people were pushing to get on before we could get off, and a cacophony of hoots from trains, toots from whizzing carts, and squawks from the sound system bombarded our ears. We left the track area moving through turnstiles into a bustling space crammed with souvenir shops and coffee bars. It seemed almost calm. Then we passed into a vast glassed-in expanse with ticket windows, information windows and kiosks. Like a grand foyer, this last area opened into the heart of this restless city.

Maybe those two transitions had been carefully planned as preparation for the powerful juxtaposition of the remains of an ancient Roman wall standing there beside the modern station. Some claim it is part of the wall from the time of Servius Tullius, the sixth king of Rome in the sixth century B.C. The crumbling wall and the modern building never fail to enchant me, and I wanted to shout to the architect, "It works!"

There were no hordes of pickpockets nor gypsies after all; instead, clean-cut, young men and women wearing official tourist badges moved quietly among the arriving travelers. A bright, young woman dressed in a dark blue suit with a crisp white shirt and a badge pinned on her shoulder asked if we had a hotel. She advised against the one we had booked just south of the station. When Patricia pulled out her trusty guide and asked about Albergo Fiorella on Via Babuino near the Spanish Steps, the official nodded her approval. That meant more telephone terrors for me. With a bit of English and a lot of mangled Italian, the landlord and I managed to arrange a double room for 52,000 lire, about $17.50 each. I was amazed at the low price for such a super location near the Spanish Steps. He suggested we take the metro. I wasn't familiar with its stops, but knew my way by walking since it was in the same area I'd stayed years before. He sounded hesitant but agreed to hold the room for one hour.

Patricia hustled, and I could barely keep up. Fear of losing the room spurred her on. When we first met, she had been attracted by my knowledge of Palladio in Vicenza, Etruscan tombs in Orvieto, and familiarity with Rome. Now, it seemed she had begun to notice my feet of clay and had less faith in me. She was almost running. We crossed streets when we shouldn't have, but Romans do that all the time. An impatient driver came through the intersection too close for comfort. His exhaust pipe struck my bag as it trailed behind me causing it to flip over. When he saw I was okay, he cursed and drove on. A small hole was burned in one corner of the bag. I should have waited. It was my fault, but in a childish pique, I wanted to blame Patricia. We arrived frazzled but with time to spare and settled in.

It was a pleasure to show Patricia the *Villa Borghese*, Rome's most famous public park, the Spanish Steps and Trevi Fountain. Trevi is built smack onto the back of a large building and protrudes into a minuscule piazza. My plan was to wind through the little alleyways and suddenly emerge into the small space where this grandiose, rococo fountain dominates everything. The waters would be roaring and the total effect would be amazing. It would be fun to surprise her; she'd never forget Trevi.

As we neared it, she kept dawdling and looking in shop windows bursting with tourist trifles; I grew more and more impatient to present "my" spectacle. Why do I try to force others into my own reality? Finally we came around the corner. And, nothing. No sound, no excitement, no rushing water spraying over horses, demons and nymphs. No one was throwing coins over their shoulder. All we saw was a sign, "*In Restauro.*"

I would show her another spectacle, I thought, and I led her to Via Corso toward Piazza Venezia. There the traffic is like a whirlpool swirling in front of the huge white monument called *Vittoriana,* and dedicated to Vittorio Emanuele II, United Italy's first king. Seven streets converge on this crazy intersection in the heart of Rome, and if we were lucky, we would see a police ballet.

Onto a white podium steps a special maestro wearing a tall white helmet, a wide, white belt with a strap over one shoulder and white gloves with large flared cuffs. With absolute authority, he controls city buses, huge tour buses, autos, small trucks, vans, bicycles, and, of course, the ubiquitous *Vespas* which buzz all over Italy just as their namesakes, the wasps, do.

By design his gestures must be large, forceful and precise, but with lithesome movements he bends and sways gracefully adding

MARLENE HILL

Policeman directing traffic.

his own individual flare to the orthodox choreography. Nothing escapes his notice and those who try to slip by are shamefully chastised in full view of an ever-present audience. We were in luck because the maestro on duty at that moment was skilled in the same bombastic flourishes and nuances employed by all world-class conductors. Surely he could conduct Modeste Moussorgsky's *Pictures at an Exhibition* with ease. He leaned forward gracefully to beckon one congested lane of vehicles, then abruptly stood straight on his toes to arrest the flow of another lane by holding out the flat of his white-gloved palms. Without warning he came down with a furious chop to point a menacing finger at a sleek, silver Maserati trying to slip through unnoticed. Patricia was enchanted.

Our room was on the noisy street side, but on our second night *La Signora* moved us to an inside room overlooking tile roofs and a small, inner courtyard. It's incredible how quiet it can be just across the hall; those thick old walls make all the difference. Breakfast was served by our sweet landlord. His wife had explained the house rules and made decisions regarding who had which room. She seemed in charge, yet he did all the physical work. Was it because she spoke English? We never know about others' arrangements, but that doesn't stop us from speculating. He obviously enjoyed his role of waiter each morning, and every day he came to our table and to ask what we wanted,

"*Caffè or tè? Con limone o con latte?*" Coffee or tea? With lemon or milk?

When I asked for tea with hot milk, it was no problem. Most small hotels tend to use instant coffee so tea is a better morning choice.

As planned, we separated for the day. Pat wanted to run in the gardens of Villa Borghese and shop, and I wanted to dawdle into whatever churches happened in my way. Sometimes the most obscure church had a masterpiece I'd studied long ago. If not, it would have something unique, I was sure, if only a sense of quiet yearning left by thousands of prayers.

One of my goals on that 1990 trip to Rome was to find Villa Giulia. In 1962 I'd never heard of Villa Giulia or Pope Julius III, who had it built, but now I was eager to explore the largest collection of Etruscan relics anywhere. At the bus information booth at *Stazione Termini*, Rome's main train station, I learned that I needed to change buses at Largo Argentina, a lovely little square which protected a sacred area of ancient pillars and foundations from the third century B.C. *Largo* means wide or broad and it's a term sometimes used for city square. Argentina happens to be a busy bus interchange. While waiting for a bus, I can lean over the railings and look down on the ancient past now inhabited by modern Roman cats.

The bus was crowded when it left Termini, and I made the mistake of chatting with a sweet-faced but smelly little man. Foolish me, I blurted out my destination. When the bus pulled in to Largo Argentina, it appeared that he would get off there too. In the crush of exiting, I chose to stay behind because I didn't want to visit Villa Giulia with him tagging along. He looked up from the street with a puzzled look when he saw I had stayed on the bus, I shook my head no; he shrugged and walked away. At the next stop, instead of going back to Argentina for the recommended bus, I walked all the way along Via Flaminia. Flaminia is one of the oldest Roman roads leading north out of the city, but that is its only interesting feature.

At Villa Giulia, a guard followed me through several rooms until he was satisfied I wasn't a vandal. He then lost interest and went back to his post near the front door to follow someone else. In *Views From A Tuscan Vineyard*, Julian More says, "Museums should be approached lightly and discoveries made personally." He is so right, I thought, and I would add they are best approached alone. Except for a casual swish through a museum, it is difficult to share perceptions of art. The intuitive pleasure More speaks of is special and needs privacy.

The *Sarcophagus of the Married Couple* was there in a special setting; in fact, it was the centerpiece of the entire museum. This polished, terra-cotta couple had been my real goal, and if all the rest of the museum had been in wraps, communing with those two would have been enough. They had been found in ancient Caere, now Cerveteri, about thirty miles north of Rome. The two lovebirds are full-sized and recline on their sarcophagus made of red terra cotta burnished to a sheen I never imagined possible with plain old baked clay. It must have been sawn in half and smoothly fitted back together, or more likely, it had been baked that way. They both have pixyish smiles, especially the diminutive wife. They are content with each other. For all the experts' warnings that most Etruscan effigies were stylized, I have to believe the artist molded these two from real life.

In another room, on top of some canopic jars were birdmen and lionmen and wicked little satyrs. A few copies of frescoes from tombs were mounted on easels, sprightly little bronze figures were in glass cases, and a miniature *carrelo* with wheels and axle looked for all the world like a toy cart. There were terra-cotta parts of bodies as well as innards including a heart, uterus, and liver. Perhaps they were left in temples to urge their gods to heal them much as silver ornaments shaped in body parts are left in Roman Catholic and Greek Orthodox churches today. Some figures on the jars were doing strange things. One large, bronze cauldron had little bronze men standing all around the lid; every one had an erect penis. One had none, probably just broken off, but another had a big one pointing straight down. The effect was more amusing than seriously pornographic; most of Etruscan art is lighthearted.

A huge collection of gold jewelry along with glass beads and buttons was in another wing of the villa. The monumental problem of cataloging and labeling artifacts was obvious. Despite looting of tombs through the centuries, there are probably tons of material stored away in dusty vaults and more is being discovered every year.

Etruscan art is unpredictable. Some is superb and some is awkward. Mostly it is exuberant and playful and full of bizarre movement, humor, and pure self indulgence. The work that was strictly theirs (not Greek copies) is at times primitive and simple. Other times it is so distorted that it often looks as modern as a Picasso or—closer to home—as a Modigliani, a Manzù or a Marini. Alberto Giacometti's 1948 rope-thin bronze figure called *Standing Woman* has an uncanny resemblance to a third century B.C. spare bronze of a young boy called *L'Ombre della Sera*, The Evening Shadow. A terra-cotta horse called *Cavaliere* by Marino Marini resembles a horse on a wall painting from the sixth century B.C. in the *Tomb of the Bulls* in Tarquinia. Marini made no bones about where he found his images and once wrote, "I like going to the source of things."

Why do I feel such an affinity toward these particular ancient peoples? They seem more accessible to me than the ancient Egyptians, Chinese or Mayans. The sprightly bronzes, the indulgent reclining figures, the gaudy jewelry, even their cups and bowls touch me. I ache to know them. I know they had the same nasty habits, and the same troubles and sorrows we do, but there's something about their joy of life that rings through. Certainly I admire their hard work of organizing drainage and irrigation systems, their arches, their walls and fine roads, their metal refineries and fantastic goldsmithing, yet what I hear is their giggles and laughter.

By the end of the fourth century B.C., some of the stories on their tomb walls began to change. Pictures of destruction replaced some of the happier scenes. The artifacts were fewer and less expensive; their times were changing. Part of it was a downturn in their commercial climate, but a larger part was because of encroaching enemies. The Gauls were threatening from the North, the Greek sea pirates were hitting both coastlines, and the well-oiled Roman fighting machine was rolling up from the South. Their tomb art became more somber, more grotesque and began to focus on scenes of defeat and dread of death rather than the happy continuation of their good life after death.

Rome's first kings were Etruscans from Tarquinia, and Etruscans' engineering feats were adopted by Romans along with their arches, sewers, roads, city grid systems, and their rules for organizing and founding cities. The man who warned Julius Caesar about leaving his house on the Ides of March was his personal Etruscan Soothsayer. As time went on, however, the Romans denigrated the Etruscans. There were books of both secular and religious rituals including how to lay the foundations of a city, how to make predictions by watching the night skies and flights of birds, or how to divine the future by observing the liver of animals, but they've all been lost. Emperor Claudius, who was married to an Etruscan woman, had researched these books, but his work was lost too in a great fire.

Most Greek and Roman writers gave Etruscans bad press, but they had been their enemies for two hundred years before these authors ever wrote a word. The Greeks particularly disapproved of the extravagant displays in Etruscan temples, but the Greeks disapproved of everything and everyone not Greek. Both the Greeks and Romans wrote that Etruscans were profligate, lazy, and fat, that their clothes were impractical, too elegant, and their hairdos too elaborate. If the truth were known, what really worried them was that the Etruscans had too much fun.

Certainly the stiff-necked, prudish Romans looked down their noses and objected to how the Etruscans dealt with their women.

They actually sat at banquet tables with men and joined in discussions and decisions! The Romans are infamous now for their own extravagances and indulgences, but that all came much later. Early on, they were straight-laced and ordered their society along military lines. Women weren't allowed to drink wine; male relatives, (fathers, brothers, husbands, uncles and even sons) kept tabs on them by kissing them lightly on their lips at every greeting. Etruscan women not only drank wine but danced and enjoyed the whole party scene. The Romans and Greeks assumed they were fallen women; it may have been something like the reactionary Muslim view of modern western women today.

By the second century B.C., their culture had been largely assimilated into Roman life. Before assimilation, the city of Rome had been bilingual, especially when the Tarquins were kings, but when they fell, their language became unpopular and unfashionable. Over time it was completely absorbed into the Roman conglomerate and simply disappeared.

In the middle of the sixteenth century, Julius III built Villa Giulia, and today, it holds the three gold sheets of writing found in 1964 at Pyrgi, the ancient port for Caere. Scholars were excited because they thought they'd found the Rosetta Stone for the Etruscan language, but it was not to be, and the struggle goes on to decipher their language. Their alphabet, derived from ancient Greek, is not the problem. The problem is that not enough different texts have been found for analysis. Out of at least 10,000 inscriptions already studied, most all of them are either lists of kings and conquerors or the same kind of writing we put on tombstones today: names, ages, relationships and gods to whom they prayed. From the gold sheets, however, they did learn that the Etruscan goddess Uni was the same as the Phoenician goddess Astarte and they also deciphered the Etruscan verb meaning "to give."

Oh, to be thirty years younger and take up the search.

⤶

CHAPTER TWENTY-FOUR

No smoking at The Rich Salad.
A taste of Frascati.
Italian churches, an integral part of life.
A contrary door.

MOST EVENINGS, PATRICIA AND I MET AT OUR HOTEL
before going out to eat. She was lying on her bed when I walked
in. Her eyes were red.

"Are you okay?" I asked.

"I'm fine," she lied. "Listen, I think I found a good place to eat
tonight."

L'Insalata Ricca was indeed a cute place. The Rich Salad was a
non-smoking establishment, a rarity in Rome where everyone
smoked all the time everywhere. Located in the Campo dei Fiori
area, Ricca was a long walk from the Spanish Steps, but worth it.
Not only was there no smoking allowed, it was good and cheap. We
returned often.

A typical trattoria, L'Insalata Ricca wasted no space on frivoli-
ties. The walls were whitewashed. A few cheap reproductions of
modern art hung on them offering bright slashes of color. The rest
rooms were down a steep flight of steps into their cellar where
extra jugs of wine, mineral water, and huge cans of tomato sauce
were stored. Energetic waiters dashed down and up frequently for
supplies. Most of the tables were long and narrow reminding me
of a school cafeteria with all the accompanying chatter and scrap-
ing of chairs across marble floors. A few separate tables were
jammed into the far corners of the plain, rectangular room, but
mostly strangers sat elbow to elbow in instant camaraderie. The
kitchen, from which came puffs of steam laden with heavenly
smells of garlic and aromas of grilled meat, was located in the rear.

The hustling waiters were loud and cheerful with both the customers and each other. From time to time, a cook would poke his head out of the kitchen doorway to give the room a once over and welcome someone by name. All in all, it had a lively, friendly atmosphere, but Patricia seemed pre-occupied and impatient with everyone. People kept crowding in, and waiters and customers squeezed between the rows of tables and chairs. Someone bumped Patricia's head by accident and she jerked her chair out of the way with an angry scrape on the floor. The poor waiter apologized profusely but she ignored his placating efforts. Considering the general chaos, I thought the service was quite good. We received our bread and wine right away. It did take a while for our pasta to arrive, but the bread was delicious and I was content to wait. Patricia was not.

"Relax," I said, "we're finally in Rome."

She must have had a bad day because the more I tried to "help," the more she resisted my efforts to neutralize her negative energy. The benefit of a dinner companion was very much in question that night.

Maybe she hadn't had a nap that afternoon. She needed much more sleep than I, but then so do most people I know. I was looking forward to the day when she would leave for Paris. Then, at night, I could stay in my warm bed to read as late as I wanted rather than go shiver in the chilly parlor because she wanted the light off in our room. She "said" it was okay to keep my reading lamp on, but her tossing and sighing until it went off told another story. Still, there were some pleasant times together.

One of our good times was a short trip to Frascati. It was pouring rain on the morning we had planned to see Frascati, but we decided to go anyway. There was no rush, Frascati wasn't far, just ten or fifteen miles away in the Alban Hills. It is one of thirteen little towns called the *Castelli Romani*, Roman Castles. They crown the low volcanic hills clustered around two crater lakes. The rich and famous of Rome have settled there since ancient days. The pope has a summer retreat in one of those villages called Castel Gandolfo.

We went through the rain hugging the buildings with the widest overhangs until we came to the Metro entrance near the Spanish Steps. The rest of the trip to the station was underground and dry. When we got to the train station there were already long lines at the ticket booths. Patricia had to stand in a special line because her train pass required a stamp *each* time she used it. Another boon for the rubber stamp companies, I thought. Mine had needed only the beginning and expiration dates stamped—done once and for all in Milan.

"This ticket is kind of a bother, but less expensive than yours," she said. "*Yes, but...,*" I thought, "*with mine I could hop a train without queuing.*"

When we learned that the track for Frascati's train was in an obscure corner, we raced through the station only to collapse on a bench in a giggling heap as we saw the 11:35 chug away. Then the train jerked to a stop about fifty yards away. We gathered ourselves up thinking we still had a chance, but it slowly sashayed out of sight. At first I felt cross, but realized I was being petty, no harm was done. The energy of the rain pounding on the skylight above us refreshed my spirit, and another train would depart at 1:00 p.m. Now we knew the ropes, so we went for a cappuccino.

It was a quaint little train with about five cars. It wound its way southeastward into gentle hills covered with vineyards. It passed so close to the ruins of a magnificent ancient aqueduct that we could see tufts of grass and fronds of ivy growing in its cracks. Twenty-five minutes later we stepped from the train at Frascati. Just as we turned to look back, the sun came out, and there was Rome spread out below. Her domes were all aglow.

Remembering the sprightly taste of a 1962 jug of Frascati wine, I wanted to try the 1990 version. The barista in a bar on the main piazza had obviously served unprepared tourists before and gladly opened the bottle for us. He also offered plastic cups—for a small additional fee. We walked up to the grounds of a large villa now open to the public. It probably had a story to tell, but that day we ignored all historical facts and relaxed in the country air. Soon we found a trickling fountain near a comfortable bench. Gently I

Marlene holding a bottle of Frascati wine.

placed the opened wine under the fountain wedging it into a handy slot on a slight incline to let the chilly water drip on it. Patricia had brought bread and cheese and we were set. We walked a bit, drank a bit, walked a bit and eventually finished off the crisp, golden wine. Old memories often enhance the truth, but in this case, the new wine seemed better than the one of my memory.

We strolled through the little hill town and found a bar where we used the W.C. and drank an afternoon cappuccino. Patricia was health conscious and seldom indulged in sweets. She had some trouble making her choice, a custardy thing, but making a choice was no problem for me because I had recently discovered candied chestnuts. They were expensive, but when I sank my teeth into the crystallized sugary syrup permeating the entire nut, my urge for sweets, fats and carbohydrates was totally satisfied in one juicy chomp. In a pleasant Frascati glow, we climbed aboard the sleepy train back to Rome.

On the following morning, we woke to a soft Sunday rain falling on the courtyard outside our window. Again, by noon it had stopped completely. We walked along the river where everything was green and clean. Patricia found an earring on the street that she was sure was gold; she was thrilled and planned to take it home to a friend who would melt it down with other gold items she had. She chattered about the design of a new piece of jewelry; I listened dreamily and enjoyed being there beside the river. She seemed relaxed and less impatient than usual. It was good to dawdle beside the river under the plane trees.

As we crossed Ponte Sant'Angelo and neared Saint Peter's, the ambience changed. Crowds filled every approaching street. Finally, standing in the immense piazza, I remembered being there twenty-eight years before, and after the former pope had peeked out at noon to say a few words of blessing, people had shouted, horns honked and everyone moved toward the church as if they were going to a rock concert. Sure enough, the new pope did it too. Standing in the sunshine on the rain-washed stones amidst hundreds of people, I felt embraced and gathered in by those two massive arms of matched columns that reach out from the church. I felt a part of the whole thing being jostled by friendly, joyful people from everywhere.

Attending church is so different in Italy. John Gibbons said it best in his book written in 1932 called *Afoot in Italy*:

"It was not a bit like our own churches at home in England; for instead of a decorous congregation attending at fixed hours, there would be one Mass after another every half-hour or so and a perpetual crowd of people always streaming in and streaming out again. ...And once, I remember, I felt something cold against my hand, and when I glanced down it was a dog's nose; and nobody seemed to think it odd. ...They would come at all hours of the day. The smart young stockbroker's clerk sort of man would drop in almost carelessly for a minute or so, say a prayer, and drop out again... Then, there were the children, and they seemed to use a church as naturally as if it were their own home, the tiny ones playing at the back while their mothers prayed."

I've never felt a cold dog's nose in a sanctuary in Italy, but that relaxed use of church appeals to my idea of spirituality too. It makes it an integral part of life rather than something set aside for best clothes and best behavior.

The current pope spoke much longer than the one had years ago. Then he repeated himself in French. White banners were draped across the entrance to the church with words in French. Patricia surmised the reason for the huge crowd must be canonization ceremonies for a French saint. As we walked up the steps of Saint Peter's, the bells thundered, my stomach shuddered, and for a nanosecond, I thought, "Should I convert?" But, as one of my son's would tease, "Convert from what?"

Inside, we looked at Michelangelo's *Pietà* protected behind a strong glass wall. It no longer stands at the entrance nor is it touchable as it had been in the sixties. The glass barrier diminishes the experience, nevertheless I could stand in front of this masterpiece for an hour. Yes, she does look too young to be his mother, but Michelangelo had his reason. Because she was a virgin, for him, she would always be young. And, she is so serenely beautiful.

We wandered throughout the vastness craning our necks here and there, but except for the sound of its bells and the *Pietà*, there was nothing inside for me. One should visit Saint Peter's, it is too well known to ignore, but its size is overwhelming. I always feel addled because of its many "attractions;" there are more diversions than one would find walking down the midway of a large circus. Not only are there glittering chapels on either side, but the floor is elaborately patterned as well as the ceilings, and the vaults inside the vast dome gleam and glitter and pull the senses up, out, down, forward and back. Saint Peter's is not a calm space. I feel no spiritual harmony there.

~

Back across the river, our favorite delicatessen on Via della Scrofa was closed. Our stomachs had long forgotten our meager breakfast, so we pushed on to our favorite, Ricca, for a lunch of soup, wine and bread. Just as they do in stereotypical movies about Italy, the waiters held fat loaves of coarse bread up to their chest and wielded bread knives almost as big as timber saws. The bread was crusty and looked heavy, but it was light and full of holes—truly Italian soul food. They called it Pugliese after Apulia, the province that forms the heel of Italy's boot. I was a pig and ate four pieces tucking a couple more in my bag for later.

We separated for the rest of the afternoon. Patricia headed for the Borghese Gardens to jog, and I headed toward the confusing streets around the Pantheon. The old, medieval sections of Rome are ever fascinating and usually seduce me to explore on and on, but the wine at lunch had put lead in my legs. My feet grew heavy and thoughts of a nap led me toward home. Soon, I was walking on Via Condotti which leads straight to the foot of the Spanish Steps. Via Condotti, lined with elegant shops, is the Rodeo Drive of Rome but with one difference. On Condotti, the shops are filled with exquisite, expensive things, while on Hollywood's Rodeo, they are merely expensive.

Just for fun, I dropped in to the Hotel Condotti actually located on a side street. Six years before, I had stayed there after the expedition in Siena. It had been a simple place where 25,000 lire had included breakfast on a pleasant terrace overlooking the city. The exchange had been 1650 lire to the dollar making it a marvelous bargain at $15. Now, the exchange was only 1500 lire to the dollar, they had dressed up the lobby, and the room tariff was 220,000 lire ($147). Times had changed. Indeed location is all.

Within a few blocks, I was at our hotel on Via Babuino, and Patricia was already napping when I slipped into our room.

Later that evening at Gran Sasso's, a restaurant near our hotel, the door wouldn't close properly. Each time someone new entered, the door didn't quite catch and chilly, night air swept in. Patricia was cold and finally got up from our table and slammed the door shut in a huff. After we'd eaten and warmed up, her mood lightened. Together we watched the process. Sometimes the proprietor sauntered over to close it. Why didn't he repair the door? We never did find out, but I knew I didn't enjoy having to placate Patricia's petulance once again.

Patricia would talk of moving on to Paris. Then she would stay another day because she too had succumbed to Rome. She would talk of going to visit her mother's friend who lived in Santa Maria, one of the five villages called *Cinque terre* along the Italian Riviera. Then she would stay another day. Even though I longed to be there alone, there was nothing I could do about the situation—that year. But, I was learning. I would never travel with new friends again—probably with no one. In spite of myself, I had let her pouting put a damper on my personal freedom. It was hard to ignore, and I was falling into an old pattern learned from coping with my mother's moods. I kept trying to fix things for her.

At first blush, she had been interested in my plans because I had seemed knowledgeable and because I was heading for Rome. Now that she had seen me make mistakes, lose my calm demeanor, stumble, and probably other annoyances I was unaware of, maybe I had lost her respect. One evening, she announced that she was almost packed and would be leaving the next morning. My stomach took a flip-flop. Did my face show it? I felt guilty for being so relieved because there had been some fine moments together. We talked about her visit to Paris. She could speak French and was eager to get into "her" language. When she left, we hugged, exchanged addresses, and promised to keep in touch. Unlike most travel promises, we actually kept ours.

~

CHAPTER TWENTY-FIVE

My secret courtyard at Galleria Borghese.
Bernini's Saint Theresa in Ecstasy.

HOW LIBERATING TO WALK ALONE KNOWING I HAD A ROOM of my own waiting for me. I walked down Via del Corso noting an old plaque fastened to a wall with the words (gia Umberto I) listed under the name of the current street sign. "Gia" signfied that earlier, the street had been called Umberto I. I've seen similar notices in other cities, and I like to think it was done for sentimental reasons to remind the older generation of the street names of their youth. On a whim, I turned toward the river where I came to one of those hidden spots that offer a gentle surprise to wanderers. Tucked away from the roar of the busy thoroughfare is a group of wooden carts huddled together like a circle of covered wagons. Each day dealers erect their weathered stalls featuring old prints and old books. It was a soggy kind of day, but even when dry, it's a place where tourists are scarce. The display cases have broad wooden awnings that open up and close down efficiently depending on the weather. A person would need to know about antique paper goods because the prices are not cheap.

A block away, a pretty little space called *Largo Fontanella Borghese* opens out, and indeed, a small, graceful fountain burbles there. A stone bench with scattered greenery planted beside it was a welcoming resting place. Through a small opening between buildings, I glimpsed an intriguing courtyard. Could it be a part of the huge Palazzo Borghese said to be still inhabited by remnants of the once powerful family? Before the nineteenth century river embankment project had been completed, the Borghese family would have enjoyed a sloping lawn and an unobstructed view all the way down to the *Tevere*, the Tiber.

Curiosity urged me along the sides of the immense building shaped like a lopsided parallelogram. After moving along three sides of the brick walls enclosing the building—a barrier prevented me from reaching the front of the building—I could not find an opening large enough to look in on that courtyard. In fact, I couldn't even find the original opening where I'd first noticed it. Had I imagined it?

Nearby, a pleasant distraction appeared. Open stalls displayed beautiful fruits and veggies, and a flight of stairs led below the street to a permanent market for meats, cheeses and staples. A huge jar of dry capers in sea salt sat on top of the glass meat case. I hadn't seen dry capers for years and decided to buy some. When I indicated I'd be taking them back to the United States, the proprietor re-wrapped my package more carefully and wished me *"Buon Viaggio."* A man waiting to be served grumbled about the extra time being taken for me. I was amused because usually I was the one ignored and made to wait in other shops.

Streets were tangled and confusing, but in time, I arrived at the riverfront. A small storefront called Galleria Borghese faced the street beside the river called *Lungotevere in Augusta,* so called because the Mausoleum of Augustus is a few hundred yards away. The roads that line the river change their names frequently. Some sections are obviously named for their location: *Lungotevere Castello, Lungotevere Vaticano,* or *Gianicolense.* Others are for people: *Lungotevere Michelangelo, Lungotevere di Cenci,* and old Roman family, and one section named *Lungotevere dei Tebaldi,* was either for the opera singer of the fifties, rival to Maria Callas, or a general from the eighteen hundreds.

This gallery, I thought, just might be attached to the huge Palazzo Borghese that stretched back to the antique market. Entrance was free. I walked in. What a surprise to find not an art gallery, but instead, a carpet salesroom. The vestibule had been set up as a sort of sales area with a large desk on a raised platform to the left; a small wooden balcony was above the entrance behind me. Immediately facing me was a short flight of steps with shabby but once elegant wooden bannisters.

The upper two rooms were long, extending back in the direction of where I thought I'd first seen the courtyard. Surely this was the building I'd been looking for. The floors were covered with lush carpets of all sizes costing *molte, molte lire.* There was a small Persian in a medley of pale greens that might have worked in our bathroom for 2,800,000 lire—only $1,900 or was it $19,000? All those zeros were confusing. Either way, it was too costly for our simple bathroom, but it was fun to consider. There were rugs from China, Persia, Russia, Afghanistan and Turkey hanging on the walls, spread all over the floors and piled on top of each other.

Soon the salesman left me alone. It was pleasant to wander and look at the frescoed ceilings that were peeling and faded. The walls needed attention as well. Gradually, I worked my way around and over piles of carpets to a bank of windows. Through the windows was my secret courtyard, and my imagination took off. Those wealthy Borghesi knew how to live. Graceful statues, shrubs, sweet smelling fruit trees, fountains, mosaic patios, and vines would have all contributed to gracious outdoor living. I could imagine sipping ruby-red wine from a long-stemmed crystal goblet while strolling in the coolness of the walled courtyard before going in to a sumptuous late dinner.

It was sad coming back to reality. At one time, colorful frescoed ceilings had overseen what were probably magnificent marble floors, but now the ceilings showed signs of serious water damage. The floors under the carpets were probably damaged as well. The mosaic pavements out there in the garden were chipped, the statues were broken, the fountains were crumbling and no sparkling water was dripping from them; even the fruit trees looked sodden and ragged.

My own bedraggled look was, no doubt, why the salesman hadn't bothered to pursue me. It was sweet to wander and let my imagination roam, and since the guidebooks hadn't mentioned this place, it was mine. I hugged it to myself.

On Patricia's recommendation, I went looking for Bernini's *Santa Teresa*. I wasn't familiar with this part of town and passed right by her church, *Santa Maria delle Vittoria*, Saint Mary of Victory. It is a small building and it was completely swathed in restoration scaffolding and wraps. Not until Porta Pia loomed in front of me did I realize something was wrong. Porta Pia is a beautiful old gate left from one of the ancient walls surrounding the city. The facade of the gate had been redesigned by Michelangelo; that man was everywhere. Just through the gate, the street abruptly changed into a broad, tree-lined boulevard. It looked inviting. If I ever lived here, this might be a street for me, I thought. I asked an old woman where Santa Teresa was and she pointed behind me. It usually works best to ask old women because they are not in a hurry and are most likely to frequent the churches. As I turned to retrace my steps, I heard screeching brakes, crunching metal and parts rolling in the street. A car must have struck a vespa. The young vespa rider was picking up her crumpled bike. I never did see the car involved. She seemed unhurt, but oh, I felt sorry for her. No doubt there was no bank account set up to pay for such damages. In fact, she probably still owed for the scooter on which she had been hurrying to a low-paying job. And, if she had insurance, she would have to stand long hours in long lines to get it settled. No one stopped to help her, and traffic casually resumed around her. Knowing I could do nothing, I too resumed my search for Teresa.

Santa Maria delle Vittoria is gaudy, a stupendously gaudy church. Not only are marble figures leaning out of balconies built into side chapels, as if in boxes at a theater—certainly Bernini himself had worked as a set designer in theaters—but the use of gold seemed more than excessive. My grandsons would say, "Grandma, it's Baroque to the Max." but then *Saint Theresa in Ecstasy*, was made by Signor Baroque himself, Gianlorenzo Bernini. The overall grandiose look of Rome today is largely due to his skill and tremendous energy.

During the Catholic Restoration period, when the church hierarchy was running scared from the threat of Protestantism, popes hired artists and architects to help make their mode of religion as attractive and glamorous as possible. Bernini was probably the most prolific of all the artists called in. He created churches, chapels, funeral monuments, statues, fountains, and the famous colonnade reaching out from Saint Peter's in that unique embrace which transforms the immense area into a symbolic refuge. For a period of forty years, 1627-1667, three different popes commissioned Bernini to help re-establish a positive, popular image for Catholicism.

There's no doubt he was a master, but for me, his work moves too far beyond the balance of the Renaissance. There is too much flourishing of drapery, both Teresa's drapery and the angel's who stands in golden glory ready to pierce her with his golden arrow. Like the throne at Saint Peter's high altar—also by Bernini—a blinding burst of golden rays electrifies the whole scene.

It is excessive. Yet her figure *is* moving and her drapery *is* marvelously realistic. It's hard to believe she is only cold, hard marble. Her shoulders are arched and her head is thrown back in ecstasy. The most stunning part of all is the look on her face. Surely,

Bernini must have recreated his lover's face at the moment of a magnificent orgasm. The notion that this piece represents piety seems hypocritical. Nevertheless, I can sympathize a bit with artists of that time; most patrons were church leaders and themes were limited to religious subject matters.

～

CHAPTER TWENTY-SIX

Museo Borghese. Lidia's arrival and more compromises.
A theft at the Colosseum.
Fumbling priests in Saint Peter's.
A reluctant courier.

LIDIA, A FRIEND FROM HOME, WAS STAYING IN NAPLES FOR a whole year donating her bookkeeping skills to her Baptist church's missionaries. Italy seemed a strange place for a Christian mission, but I kept my own counsel on that subject. As planned, when I arrived in Rome, we got in touch.

"I thought I'd come stay with you for a few days on my way to Genoa to meet my cousins," she said.

I could feel my face fall. Luckily she couldn't see me through the telephone wires.

"Oh no, I want Rome to myself!" I thought.

Admittedly, we had discussed this idea before we had left the States, but that was before I realized how much I loved being in Rome alone, and I had thought getting in touch would mean a day trip for one or both of us.

"Oh,…well sure. I'll tell my landlady," I said mustering as much enthusiasm as I could.

I had stayed on in the double room shared with Patricia, and I fretted that Patricia's bed would barely cool before Lidia took her place. Friendship requires compromises, I sighed. It's all a matter of timing, and time in Rome had become priceless to me.

~

Before meeting Lidia at the station, I decided to visit the Borghese Museum in the Borghese Gardens. Its graceful umbrella pines and cypress trees were planted to look as though they had always grown there amidst vast expanses of green space. The walkways, fountains and sculptures were near handy benches for admiring the monuments to heroes and philosophers; the area was transformed into a true haven from the noisy city's hum and bustle.

Twenty-eight years earlier, the museum and its formal garden had been a highlight for me, but now it had changed. It had already been under restoration for over ten years with no end in sight. How disheartening to find the once astonishingly intricate garden of years ago lying in complete neglect. A chicken-wire fence surrounded a forlorn plot of stubble and weeds. How could that have happened? Inside, only a fraction of the main floor was open to the public. Some Bernini sculptures were available. His *David*, carved when he was about twenty-five, has Bernini's own face. The figure is vastly different from Michelangelo's *David*, who stands quietly tense before the battle. Bernini's giant slayer is caught in the dynamic moment when he's just about to release the stone from his sling. The dramatic moment of capture in Bernini's *Apollo and Daphne* was striking too. The figures were exquisite. It was becoming clear that Bernini was caught up in drama and dash. I would go back to look again and again because his works *are* marvelous, even if they don't tug at my inner core as Michelangelo's do.

Crowded into one of the makeshift museum rooms, another sculpture that fascinated me was *Pauline Borghese* by Antonio Canova. It is a sculpture of Napoleon's sister, who married Count Borghese. The glow of the marble is incredible. I stood there marveling at how Canova had managed to make the cushions and pillows on which she lies absolutely believable. I wanted to reach out and plump them up a bit. According to John Ruskin, any journeyman sculptor could accomplish such effects. He said that only pure artists create the essence of the subject so that the whole is taken in spiritually and one doesn't stand to gape at such mundane details. Maybe so, but I marveled at the pillows anyway. Carved around 1807, experts consider it one of Canova's finest.

It seemed there was nothing else open to visitors because the building was in terrible disarray. Chalky dust lay everywhere. I was about to leave when I noticed people milling around in a dim, alcove to my right. I stepped in out of curiosity. At first, in the darkness of the room, it was difficult to see a group of paintings leaning casually against the wall almost as an afterthought. It was a cache of six Caravaggio paintings! There was a *David with the head of Goliath* showing a pensive youth holding the gruesome giant's head, truly an anguished self portrait. There were a *Saint Jerome* and *Saint John the Baptist* and a *Madonna of the Palafrenieri*—all impressive but difficult to see crowded together as they were.

The two that captivated me were *Il Bacchino Malato*, The Sick Bacchus, and *Boy with a basket of fruit*. Both were self portraits and fascinating because of the special luminescent skin tones given to the youthful flesh. Even in the dim light, I could see the skin color on Bacchus was tinged with green. His eyes looked incredibly sad or lost or maybe jaundiced. I wanted to stop and penetrate his story. The boy holding the basket of fruit looked pampered, his skin rosy and velvety. In spite of poor lighting, I was excited and looked forward to another day when the museum would finally be finished.

At the station, Lidia was waiting for me. What a lovely woman. She was just so sweet and gentle with her soft gray hair and big brown eyes. She looked like the idea of everyone's mother. During our days in Rome together it was a kick to see her flirt now and then, something I hadn't known about her back home in our Italian class where we'd met.

Lidia's train was early; she said it had left early. A train left early? From Naples? Maybe it was a day late. Only after we were speeding away from the station by Metro did she tell me she hadn't yet arranged her trip to Genoa. I couldn't believe it. We could

have taken care of that moments before. We deposited her stuff in
the room; what a lot for a short trip, I thought, but she wanted to
make a good impression on her cousins whom she had never met.

Then she gave me a fright because she wondered vaguely if
she'd need her passport. Was she joking? The first thing a hotel
manager asks for is one's passport. The Signora of our hotel just
might accept a copy which Lidia "thought" she had with her, but
surely she shouldn't go on to Genoa without it. After more searching in her big suitcase, she found the passport. So this was the way
it was to be, I thought.

"I've been so busy writing letters that I couldn't think about
my travel plans!" she said.

I would learn more about those letters later.

I led Lidia beside the river on Via Ripetta, an old word meaning
"riverside," and passed the ancient Mausoleum of Augustus, a
strange, grassy mound with dark cypress trees encircling it. Once
it had been impressively decorated with marble tombs commem-
orating his extensive family. Now, it's rather inconspicuous, yet an
important site for Romans; he was their first emperor. Augustus
set in motion much of what remains standing from Imperial
Rome.

As long as I couldn't be alone, it seemed a good idea to guide
her on my favorite routes in Rome. As guide and protector, I cau-
tioned her to watch her purse. For example, if someone should
snatch *my* canvas satchel, it would be no loss because it merely
held a cheap camera, a map, spare glasses and, of course, a small
supply of toilet paper. Items of real value, I smugly explained, were
safely around my middle and underneath my clothes. She dutifully kept her purse slung across her chest and covered by her coat.

After a couple of wrong turns in the warren-like maze around
the Pantheon, we came upon that magnificent building. It never
fails to astound me. Inside, we listened to a tape on a machine
which told more facts than a person wants to know. Lidia was fascinated by the crumbling rear of the building which showed clear
evidence of numerous restorations. It was indeed a marvel of

engineering and makes a powerful statement after more than two thousand years.

On the way to Piazza Navona, a sudden squall brought a chill, and we hurried to l'Insalata Ricca for a bowl of hot soup, bread and wine. Lidia kept her purse on her lap as she chatted with a young fellow who sat next to her at our table. I placed my satchel under the chair at my feet. He was putting away steak, spinach, salad and bread at a tremendous speed, but in between mouthfuls seemed happy enough to converse. She asked him where to get an *ombrello economico*, an inexpensive umbrella. His junk business was on a street bordering the Largo Argentina, and he might have one he said as he finished up and left. We found his dusty place where she did buy a big umbrella with a wooden handle for 3,000 lire ($2.00). One could even call it an antique; it was made of heavy canvas, no doubt the best in its time. It was hard to open and would take months to dry, but Lidia was happy with her bargain.

It was pleasant being with someone so agreeable, albeit not so adventurous; Patricia had been adventurous, but often irritable and discontented. Maybe I was the one at fault here. Clearly, I had learned how I wanted to spend my time in Italy, but because I had not said no early on, I too was discontented. In the future, my reply would be, "Sorry, but I always travel alone." Could I manage that next time? Oh yes, I could because being a wimp doesn't make anything right.

⁓

Lidia wanted to go into Gucci's on Via Condotti to look for a purse for her daughter-in-law. The latest style for young women had a gold shoulder chain and cost $850. Of course there were cheaper ones; there was one for a mere $650, another for $450 and a more "practical" price of $290. Lidia would think about it.

⁓

Since the Fountain of Trevi was under wraps, I took her to the Galleria Borghese and told her about the view of the private courtyard from inside the carpet shop. We stepped around the piles of oriental rugs and peeked out the windows onto what was, by now, "my" courtyard. To my delight Lidia caught the excitement. It was raining lightly when we took a bus toward the station, and I noticed the police ballet was in progress as we passed through the congested Piazza Venezia. I pushed the stop bell and we got off to walk back a few yards. This time, the traffic swirl was supervised by the watchful eye of a restrained maestro—a minimalist. He was amazingly fluid in his hand movements. He might have been conducting something by Claude Debussy rather than Moussorgsky.

His podium had been freshly whitewashed and painted with bold black stripes. Rising about two feet above the blacktop, the pedestal was about three feet in diameter at the top curving out to maybe three and one-half feet at the bottom. It looked as though an upside-down mushroom were growing out of the asphalt chaos. Evidently the rush hour was over because promptly at two-thirty, he stepped down and left the traffic to fend for itself.

We caught another bus along Via Nazionale to Piazza Repubblica where the big fountain of nymphs will send water high into the air forever. Some predict that when the fountains stop flowing in Rome, it will be the end of the world. From Repubblica it's but a short walk to the station where we went to make arrangements for her trip to Genoa. Fortunately, the same information clerk who had helped me twice before was available. He must have enjoyed his job. He joked with everyone, spoke passable English, didn't rush, and never, ever made anyone feel stupid. An unusual find among government workers.

At the Colosseum, we leaned against a corner of a locked gate in the outer wall to enjoy the sunshine. It was a nice chance to rest and write some notes. From my satchel, I pulled out a new notebook and tore a page from it for Lidia who wanted to write another letter. Since she had nothing on which to write, I handed her my old notebook already full of comments. Just before we sat down on the steps, I had noticed a buzzer with a brass plate indicating one should ring to contact the office of the on-site archaeologist. We enjoyed the sun and began our writing tasks. A man stepped up beside me and reached up to push the bell over my right shoulder. He seemed to be a tour leader, well dressed, not elegant, but not in tatters either. I didn't turn to look back at him to my right because I "knew" he was pushing the bell. Then he said something to a woman standing to our left. Naturally, we both looked in her direction.

It was another five minutes before I turned to pull out the map and found the satchel gone. It should have been looped over my arm instead of wedged into the corner, but who would have thought someone could lift it from my very side? What a pro he had been! Damn them; they prey on tired tourists. It was little consolation to know how disgusted he would be at his take.

Was I feeling anger or embarrassment? Suddenly, those worthless items took on a great preciousness. I remembered my favorite calculator George had given me; it played *Fur Elise*. Also, I realized my prescription eyeglasses were there along with a small camera, extra pens, etc. The worst loss was the camera; it had an almost finished roll of film of Etruscan places, priceless, but only to me. Fortunately, Lidia held my trip notes safely in her hands.

If only I'd kept my arm through the handles of the bag. If only, if only ... Like a baglady, I rushed around poking through the trash barrels surrounding the Colosseum hoping he would have tossed things away when he realized their worth.

I wanted to leave the area; she agreed. We started toward Saint Peter's, the next site she had hoped to see. I was more upset than I imagined I'd be. It was embarrassing too because I had been the one to preach to Lidia to be careful. She must have gotten weary of hearing me grumble and repeat what I "should" have done, but she kindly said nothing. Along the way a golden-brown, roast chicken was turning slowly on a spit in a cafeteria window. Being robbed must create hunger because I felt starved. The food had a dull, lifeless taste. Doing her best to ease the situation, Lidia graciously paid the bill, but nothing would have tasted good at that moment.

⌒

While standing before Michelangelo's *Pietà*, we noticed a group of youngsters in white robes filing into the church. We followed them to one of the large altars of the immense sanctuary. We sat through a mass which they sang in French. The music was sweet and I understood a good bit of what the Italian priest said. He spoke slowly and clearly. Then a cardinal in a brilliant red costume glided up to preside over part of the canonization ceremony. Joining the cardinal came three priests of an unknown rank dressed in brilliant green robes. It was as if they had never done this exercise before. They could have been the three stooges as they fumbled their papers and changed places with each other. For a solemn ceremony at one of the big altars of Saint Peter's, one would think those three fellows in green could have gotten their act together. With the cardinal standing beside them, though, their colors were nice.

It was a therapeutic experience to hear the lilting music and watch the bumbling priests. Gradually I let go of my anger and self recriminations. During the final piece of music, a wizened, old woman in a dusty black nun's habit shuffled her way through the crowd. Row by row the tiny creature worked her way among us holding out an offering plate with a trembling hand and mumbling piously. She looked authentic, but what if she weren't? What a clever scam to pull right there at the altar of the most holy church in Christendom. We left chuckling about the many ways to make a living.

⁓

The nights grew chillier and chillier and I began wearing a heavy wool sweater over my silk longjohns to bed. La Signora of our hotel calmly explained that in Rome, hotels don't turn the heat on until November 15. Provincial boards all over Italy classify and inspect hotels ranking them into a five-star system so that no one can charge more than the maximum allowed no matter what their location. That explained why this one-star hotel was so reasonable yet so close to The Spanish Steps. This "rule" about the heat seemed odd. Was it more of an unwritten code that little hotels happily followed? Certainly, the heating date of November 15 was one I'd keep in mind for future trips.

⁓

Our last dinner in Rome together was my treat. Lidia enjoyed Gran Sasso's food and the reluctant door. It was hard not to be

Rome's legendary wolf and Romulus and Remus.

jealous because she would be staying on in Italy for another nine months. The following morning, as she finished packing, she pulled out a bulky packet of letters.

"When you get to the States, you can mail these for me, okay?" she said.

"So many? Where will I put them?"

"Oh, surely you can stuff them here and there, can't you?"

Not only were there her letters but over forty others from members of her mission. By using me as a courier, they could save a lot of postage. How did they have the gall? How could I refuse her? Although my bag would be bulging already, somehow the "mail" would go through as they knew it would.

While she hurried to the American Express office, I soaked up the sight of the earth-toned buildings in Piazza di Spagna, and enjoyed the morning feel of the city without the usual hoards of young Americans draped over The Steps. When she returned, she had decided to buy that purse at Gucci's after all, and my soul screamed no, no! No more shopping.

"Do you mind if I stay here and soak up a bit more?"

"Not at all," she said. "Enjoy the sun, I won't be long."

It was a hassle handling her large luggage pieces, and she struggled to negotiate the steps and cobblestones in her pretty sling pumps. What a lot of stuff she had. Maybe she'd learn how to travel eventually, I thought. But then, who got robbed, eh?

∽

CHAPTER TWENTY-SEVEN

Alone at last. Campo dei Fiori.
WCs, important facilities.
Concrete maps on Mussolini's Way.
Fountains in the rain.
Moses' knee. The Wedding Cake.

FROM THE STATION, I CAUGHT A NUMBER SIXTY-FOUR bus toward the Campo dei Fiori area. When I spotted the open door of the church *Sant'Andrea della Valle*, Saint Andrew of the Valley, I stepped off. With its plastic wraps flapping in the air, Sant'Andrea was an easy landmark to see from a bus window. I was full of enthusiasm and felt a sense of power to be able to change my mind in a flash and have Rome to myself.

I hurried into the church before the doors closed for siesta. Sant'Andrea is a baroque building, ornate and spacious under a huge dome. The dome, designed by Carlo Maderno, is said to be the second largest in Rome, Michelangelo's at Saint Peter's being both the biggest and tallest. But, I admit, my real interest in Sant'Andrea was purely fictional because the church is Giacomo Puccini's setting for Act One of his opera, *Tosca*. In the opera, Cavaradossi sets up his palette to paint the golden-haired Magdalene which causes dark-haired Tosca such jealous anxiety. In a chapel nearby, Cavaradossi hides his friend Angelotti from the hateful Scarpia. Act Two is set in the Farnese Palace where Tosca kills the evil Scarpia, but that location is off limits to the public because it is now the French Embassy. Act Three is set in Castel Sant'Angelo where Tosca leaps to her death. I had been to the Castello, and once was enough for that grim fortress, but I never tire feeling the shiver of the Puccini drama as I enter Sant'Andrea.

It was but a short walk from the church to the market at Campo dei Fiori, a place of delight any time of day or night. In the mornings, it hosts the largest flower, vegetable and fruit market in the city, fresh fish are also on sale at the far end. In the afternoons and evenings, it is an open area for sunning or strolling past cafes and small shops that fill the ground floors of the ancient, lopsided buildings. The shops were closing for siesta and the markets were wrapping up for the day. My rumbling stomach had long forgotten its breakfast banana, yet I held off until I'd read every menu posted outside of every cafè around the Campo. Traveling alone, I can take eons searching for the perfect place with no explanations needed. In the end, I chose the handsome African man's trattoria. It was unusual to see a black entrepreneur in these parts, but it was abundantly clear the cafè was his. The Pizza Margherita was especially tasty and accompanied by a small bowl of oil with bits of hot peppers steeping in it. A mere half teaspoon dribbled sparingly over the crust gave just the right piquancy to the dish. Even so, the pizza didn't quite measure up to that of the white-haired master of Orvieto.

From my table, I had a ringside seat to watch the cleanup. What a mess it is after the market ends each day. The vendors pack up and leave mounds of trash, not just a few cabbage leaves but cardboard boxes and wooden crates with hunks of rotten veggies and fruit, and even a few fish scraps that the cats missed. A city crew dressed in green coveralls comes to the rescue.

First, they sweep with old-fashioned, but efficient, brooms that are made of bunches of strong, thin twigs tied to long handles, the kind good witches might ride on Halloween. The long, stiff straws lay flat curving up at one end; the sweeping motion uses the full length of the straws instead of only the tips. Next they scoop up the worst of the debris and toss it into dumpster trucks that crush everything—noisily, of course. Everything is noisy in Italian cities, especially in Rome. Their dumpster trucks are designed to go through narrow streets. They would look like toys in the States, but here they do their job. Then a water sweeper comes into the piazza to swish out the whole area.

When the cleanup crew leaves, the Campo is back to its quiet, antique self, and the memorial to Giordano Bruno stands clear for all to admire if any of the teenagers lounging at his feet know or care.

On this very spot, Giordano was burned at the stake for heresy on February 17, 1600. Among his many heresies was his agreement with Nicolaus Copernicus that the earth moved around the sun, a view which Galileo Galilei expanded upon later. Galileo and Copernicus, both Roman Catholics, viewed scientific discoveries as proof of God's power, not denial of it. But, Giordano Bruno further upset the church authorities because, as a monk, he taught heretical ideas including doubts about the Trinity. He had also mocked the resurrection and the virgin birth. Before his pyre was lit, another monk offered him a crucifix to kiss but he turned his head away. He was heard to say he wanted to die as a martyr so his soul would rise with the fire to paradise.

It was great to wander again in the heart of old Rome. Across Corso Vittorio Emanuele II into the Navona area and the convoluted streets around the Pantheon, I came upon an unusual church called Saint Anthony of Portugal. Inside, everything except the ceiling was of marble, everything. Green marble, grey marble, brown, cream, purple, pink and myriad patterns within the marble plus man-made patterns fabricated by cutting and matching various colored marbles. It was busy and heavy yet not as severe or cold as one might think. I found no individual masterpiece, but the strange tour de force in marble was more than enough.

I wanted to see Michelangelo's sculpture of *Moses*, but first I needed to find a WC. There were no public facilities in the area so I went into a bar. Their espresso was excellent, but the toilet was one of those ceramic holes over which one crouches by fitting one's feet in the footprints shaped there. "When in Roma . . ." It wasn't too bad and it did have plenty of paper, a basin with soap and an electric dryer that worked. A few years ago, there would have been none of these amenities. But then, I thought, what about our

Moses *by Michelangelo.*

situation back home? Some restaurants and bars are worse, and public facilities are either abominable or non existent. When they're open, department stores are usually clean at home, as well as here. In Rome, however, I can depend on the public facilities to be super—if attended.

There's a W.C. in a *piazzetta*, little piazza, behind the north end of Piazza Navona. It's a clean well-lighted place. A taxi stand dominates the concrete island in the center of the piazzetta, and the facility is unobtrusively set below street level. For 300 lire, about twenty cents, one can use all the toilet paper one wants, wash with liquid soap and electrically dry one's hands. Once I noticed a woman had washed her hair and her clothes and was using the electric dryer for them all. The attendant kindly looked the other way.

The other public WCs that I know of are also below street level: one is in the middle of Piazza San Silvestro opposite the main post office; one is at the south end of the Piazza di Spagna not far from where horses and carriages await passengers; and one is near Saint Peter's just beside the arch in the wall that connects the Vatican to Castel Sant'Angelo.

Along The Way of the Imperial Forums, or as it's sometimes called "Mussolini's Way," four concrete maps are mounted on the wall. In the 1930s, when Mussolini reorganized the streets in this area, he named this street "The Way of the Empire" and used it for flamboyant military parades. No one ever doubted his illusions of becoming a twentieth century emperor himself. When he fell, the street was quickly renamed. These plain concrete maps have become one of my sacred stops when in Rome, but if you aren't looking for them, you might pass them by. They show four different stages of the ancient Roman empire. I pulled up the hood on my raincoat against the drizzle and studied the maps. For me, it's always a place to stand and dream and wonder. Did I ever live during one of those map times? I would have felt stifled to submit to the Romans' prudish views regarding women; maybe I belonged further back with the Etruscans.

Rain was coming down harder and bringing a cold chill. What better time to peek inside the church of Saints Cosima and Damian sitting at the top of a short flight—only twenty-five steps or so. Mosaics from the sixth century were said to be in the apse although the rest of the upper church is from the seventeenth century. Roger Thynne wrote that this was the first building on the forum ever converted to Christian worship. In his fascinating book, *The Churches of Rome*, published in 1924, he said this church had started out as a small circular Temple to Romulus (not one of the famous twins) and was then converted in 516 A.D. to honor two medical doctors, Cosima and Damian, eastern Christians martyred for their belief. Back in Florence in 1389, a Medici baby was born on the saint day of one of these two martyrs. Following the tradition, still practiced today, the child Cosimo Medici was named for "his" saint and both Cosima and Damian became the family's patron saints even to the point of using six pill-shaped symbols on their coat of arms.

A delicate fountain sat in the atrium of the church. Four small kneeling horses faced outward toward the four directions. By now it was raining furiously and it warmed my spirits to see the brave little fountain shoot its spray against the heavens' onslaught. Whenever I watch Rome's fountains flowing during these downpours, they whisper to me of the city's longevity and endurance. Their spouting waters inspire the same confidence in the continuity of life that I feel walking beside the sea.

Protected by the overhang of the church, I huddled among members of a German tour group organizing itself. We all moved inside to view the mosaics. There they were in all their Byzantine glory, static and staring and other worldly. Christ was depicted with angels and twelve white sheep, similar to the scheme in Sant'Apollonare in Classe, one of the three famous Byzantine churches of Ravenna. The ancient congregation would not have had to be told the meaning of the twelve sheep as I knew the voluble guide would soon be telling her flock. Satisfied, I slipped out while her group settled down warm and dry to hear her long-winded spiel.

The rain had slackened to a gentle drizzle and the clouds were parting, but I took the Metro anyway. As I came up at the stop called Largo Cavour, there were signs pointing up to *San Pietro in*

Vincoli, Saint Peter in Chains. The church sits on a hill high above Via Cavour, a no-nonsense street that slopes from the train station to meet the wide, furiously-paced street, *Via dei Fori Imperiali* beside the Colosseum. I was glad I'd saved myself with the Metro because those steps up to the church were as steep as the side of a pitched roof. A young man in the ubiquitous brown uniform of United Parcel Service was trudging up with a package. Needless to say, with his job of delivering parcels up and down the steps of Rome, he had no weight problem. His truck, half the size of those back home, was parked in the curve of the Largo. I followed him up those thousands of steps.

By the time I huffed to the top, the UPS fellow was out of sight. After a short walk along a narrow alley beside a massive, crumbling wall on my left, which proved to be the side of the church, I came to an open space in front. Only twenty more steps up, and I was inside. Then, I gasped, "Oh no!" One interior wall and all of the ceiling were under restoration drapes. Would the infamous tomb of Pope Julius II be covered too? After reading Michelangelo's story of grief and frustration in working for Julius for so many years, I wanted to see that tomb, especially his figure of *Moses*. The vast church seemed dark and silent. It felt eerie with swathes of ghostly cloths draping the wall and ceiling.

Muffled voices came from somewhere ahead. I continued walking past heavy columns and saw a figure sitting in the shadows staring at me. No, he was looking beyond my puny self; he was looking far into his people's future. This personage could indeed persuade a multitude to follow him through the sea, across the mountains and into the desert for forty years. But, in late autumn Rome, he's almost forgotten. Only a handful of people were with him.

Michelangelo spent years designing—redesigning—starting work—stopping work—on this tomb for Pope Julius II. Julius kept withholding funds to pay for the slabs of marble that Michelangelo had personally chosen in the cold mountains of Carrara, and paid for as well as supervised their delivery by barge down to Rome. Several times Michelangelo asked for the money but the irascible pope would fly into a rage; it never seemed a good time. Because the grand scheme for the tomb fascinated Michelangelo, he went in debt several times to keep the project going.

Julius, who was involved in political and military intrigues all during his reign, was forever touting him off to do other things including the casting of a huge bronze figure of himself for the facade of a church in Bologna which took Michelangelo over two years to complete and the Sistine ceiling which took four more. When Julius later lost control of Bologna, his military enemies melted the bronze figure into cannons. Julius died before his tomb was barely begun, and Michelangelo was then forced to negotiate at least three more contracts with his heirs. In all, the project plagued him for almost forty years. Subsequent popes were jealous of his desire to continue work on a former pope's tomb, and they kept demanding his services for their own projects. Some of those projects included painting *The Last Judgment* on the wall of the Sistine Chapel and designing and carving the figures for the Medici pope's family tombs in Florence.

Julius' tomb was finally finished, but in the end, the grand plan had diminished markedly. It was placed not in the most important church in Christendom, but across the river and across town, and, after all that, the tomb is empty. Julius is buried in Saint Peter's in the same chapel as his uncle, another pope called Sixtus IV. There, however, Julius is commemorated only by a modest inscription. Now what would fiery old Julius say about that? And, would Michelangelo care that his *Moses* is neglected by the crowds? He'd be shattered.

After drawing near and walking from one side to another, I perched on a step to indulge myself. The original plan was to have included about forty carved figures placed in a huge mausoleum inside Saint Peter's which was being rebuilt at the time. Except for *Moses*, the composite substitute is dull. *Moses* is flanked by two insipid figures, *Rachel* and *Leah*, symbols of active life and contemplative life. It's hard to accept that Michelangelo made these two dull images, yet they do have a little more life than the stiff ones made by other artists on the upper level. The worst figure is the cramped effigy of the pope himself. A seated female form to

*A wet pigeon dries out on one of Neptune's cohorts
in Piazza Navona in the heart of old Rome.*

his right is hugely out of proportion to the pope, and he, the small-est of all, is sprawled awkwardly on top of his sarcophagus almost as an afterthought. I suspect by that time, Michelangelo had lost interest in the whole project.

Without moving from my position, I could watch *Moses* as he changed under the natural light coming from the upper windows or from the electric beams furnished by a few tourists inserting coins into the light meter. It was easy to understand what the expression "living marble" means. His muscular shoulders and arms are vigorous and well-shaped, not at all exaggerated as some critics suggest. This is not a young man yet he has a thick head of hair and a luxuriant beard which flows in sinewy ropes down the front of his chest. What significance did the long, ropey, twisted beard have for Michelangelo I wonder? To me, the best part of the figure is his knee. His head, his shoulders, and his beard are all fierce, but the strength is concentrated in his knee.

Much too soon a worn-out priest in a dusty cassock shuffled past and shooed everyone out; it was siesta.

"*Dieci minuti, per favore?*" Ten minutes please? I asked.

No such luck. He merely grunted, "*No. Non è possibile!*"

❧

Before tall buildings were added, I could have stood on the church porch and looked directly down on the Colosseum. Now, I had to work my way down a series of steps to the broad street far below. As I walked down toward the Colosseum, a group of gypsies appeared suddenly on a sharp turning of the steps. A number of young gypsy women with their children and babes in arms had emerged from the bushes. One beautiful breast was hanging out to nurse or maybe to distract. About five children swarmed around a man in front of me. Poor fellow, he was having a difficult time of it. He pushed and pushed but too gently, I thought. Most tourists had been warned about such a possibility, but when it happens it is still frightening. With my total financial survival in the money belt under my clothes, I should have felt secure, but the stories we'd heard made me wonder just how clever those kids really were.

While they pestered him, I slipped around the whole group and hurried down the steps. As I glanced back, I saw him giving them some money to get rid of them I supposed. Then I felt ashamed for not helping him somehow. If I had grabbed his arm, the two of us might have pushed on through. Next time I would be braver.

❧

The Colosseum sits just across the street, a blur of whizzing cars, trucks, vespas and buses. There is no traffic light. I joined several people waiting for a lull. Together we managed to make it across safely. I sat on a wall overlooking the crowd and ate a ripe, messy persimmon. It was satisfying to look at this magnificent monument once again. All those years ago with my ex-husband, I'd seen it in a haze of confusion. Other occasions spent with him had been experienced in a haze too. Looking back, I suspect he had travel anxieties. No doubt I had taken on some of his anxieties—trying to fix things for him. The result was to derail my own experience. It's no wonder I savored being here alone.

❧

Mussolini's thoroughfare enters the melee at Piazza Venezia after hurrying past the side of the *Altare della Patria*, The Nation's Altar, (also called the Vittoriana or the Wedding Cake or even Mussolini's Typewriter). The altar and its eternal flame sits at the top of this grandiose, overdone, dazzling white building made of botticino marble. Two lions stolen from Egypt guard each side of its broad, steep steps. Down at street level, on each side of this white mass are baroque fountains with large pools. Huge, heroic figures are draped over them. In the heat of summer, officials look the other way as children cavort in their waters as they do in the waters of the Trevi Fountain, but when Ursula Andress cavorted while making Fellini's film, *La Dolce Vita*, I am sure the officials paid much closer attention.

The Egyptian lions were brought to Imperial Rome, but the rest of this monument was erected in the late nineteenth century to celebrate the new king, Vittorio Emanuele II, and the new capitol of the first United Italy. Guidebooks claim that Roman citizens do not care for this building; supposedly they see it as a folly. I wonder. From a distance with its two sets of prancing horses at the top, it does look like a fanciful pastry concoction, and it's true the shape also suggests an old-fashioned typewriter, but the historic part of Rome isn't large and people pass this monument frequently while going about their business. On crowded buses, I've seen the most jaded citizens turn to look at their "wedding cake" again.

Most likely, members of Vatican City are the ones who refuse to look at it because to them it symbolizes the downfall of the papacy. In 1870, the army of Italy kicked the pope out of political power. Some say the popes locked themselves inside the Vatican for the next fifty-nine years to avoid seeing secular structures such as this one being erected. Then in 1929, the papacy came out of hiding when Mussolini and Pope Pius XI huddled to create the Vatican State. Only then did the papacy officially recognize the Kingdom of Italy!

Whenever I find myself at a good vantage point looking out over the rooftops, the Vittoriana is a conspicuous landmark riding high above the earthy glow of the rest of the city. Like the Eiffel Tower, also originally hated by traditionalists, it has become a beloved fixture.

If allowed, I'd like to climb the steps of the Nation's Altar to get a close look at the memorial for unknown soldiers. From up there I could look out onto the hectic piazza from the old king's vantage point. Astride his horse, he can stare straight down Via del Corso all the way to the Egyptian obelisk mounted in the center of Piazza del Popolo. There are twelve more Egyptian obelisks in Rome, but the only one that matters to me stands where it can be seen from each of three streets radiating like spokes on a wheel out of the piazza.

Anywhere on Via del Babuino all the way to Piazza di Spagna, I can look back over my shoulder and see the obelisk. Or, if I choose Via di Ripetta beside the river, there it is again. And, from the busiest street in town, Via del Corso, a quick glance and there it is in my direct line of sight. Since I can't whistle worth a darn, whenever a bit of trivia becomes mine, I hum. It's a smug, self-satisfied hum not unlike Pooh on one of his hummy days.

CHAPTER TWENTY-EIGHT

Albergo Pomezia: what a dump!.
Piazza Navona, Romans' favorite.
Bernini's Fountain of the Four Rivers.
Roman fountains will flow 'til the end of time.
Pensione Simonetta, a pretty name.

I NEVER STAYED AT ALBERGO FIORELLA AGAIN. THE congenial owners had gone and the prices had increased. Several small hotels in the Spanish Steps area had been busily upgrading, and their tone had changed. I wanted to try other areas anyway in the hope of staying where most Europeans did. I found Albergo Pomezia in the old medieval part of Rome just around the corner from Campo dei Fiori. A few streets from Piazza Navona and the Pantheon, Pomezia was in a choice location, but in Bette Davis' famous words, "What a dump!"

The wallpaper was a dingy, khaki color with splotches appearing at odd places, and it was peeling at the seams and along the baseboards. The room was an eyesore, and the shower down the hall strained to produce a mere dribble, but I felt cozy there my first night back in town. My inner-courtyard room was amazingly quiet for Rome.

Nearby, restoration of the church Sant'Andrea della Valle was finally completed, and it stood clean and white looking straight down Corso del Rinascimento. Another day I'd go in and imagine Tosca's scene again, for now, I was re-assuring myself that other treasured places were there. Patricia and I had used Sant'Andrea's restoration covers flapping in the breeze as a landmark to find our favorite non-smoking trattoria, L'Insalata Ricca. Pomezia was just beyond Ricca and so Andrea continued to serve as a landmark. She was in my mind as I walked past the telephone booth where she had lost her umbrella and somehow blamed it all on Rich in California who hadn't returned her calls. She had been in a glum mood and refused to go to Piazza Navona with me that night,

"What's so great about Navona?" she had said.

But this evening, Navona was dressed in full regalia. Painters, astrologers, tarot readers, and music groups were all performing around the three big fountains. The bars and gelati shops were open too. Navona is probably the most popular spot in Rome, not just for tourists, but for Romans as well. People seem to flood into the piazza year round. In the seventeenth and eighteenth centuries, it was flooded every weekend in August for the enjoyment of all. Sketches from the time show the nobility riding through the watery place in their carriages. The piazza is a narrow oblong three hundred and two yards by fifty-nine yards—big enough for three football fields. It follows the original shape of the former stadium built by Emperor Domitian in 96 A.D. Later when it was left in ruins, Romans plundered the remains for new buildings elsewhere. Now, buildings stuccoed in rusts, tans and golds stand on the ancient stadium's foundations. Most are four or five-stories tall with shops or restaurants at ground level and hotels or apartments above. Like most everyone else, I never tire of being in Navona.

Without a doubt, its centerpiece is *The Fountain of Four Rivers*. Pope Innocent X had an idea for a big fountain in Piazza Navona, then when someone showed him a large obelisk brought from Egypt in classical times that had lain forgotten near the Appian Way, he was determined it should be incorporated into his grand fountain. Gianlorenzo Bernini was given the commission for this impossible feat in 1647.

The dramatic *Fountain of the Four Rivers* draws people the moment they enter the piazza. Whether they come from the north or south end, they make a beeline to stand at the fountain. The Danube is represented by a figure raising his arms to a shield bearing Pope Innocent's emblem. The Ganges' figure holds a long oar symbolic of the length of the Asian river. The Nile's head is veiled indicating that its source was unknown, which it was in those days. The river representing the Americas is the Rio de la Plata; with its sculpted coins, it suggests the wealth found in the New World.

Bernini used slender, intersecting arches of travertine marble, strong but soft enough to carve. He then carved these arches to represent a watery grotto. Incredibly, this intricate grouping of stone bears the weight of one hundred twenty tons of granite obelisk mounted on top. The shaft appears to hover in the air because one can look through the arches that hold it. It was Innocent's idea, but by the time the obelisk was raised in 1666, it was Pope Alexander VII's emblem that was attached to its very top.

Beside the large human figures are smaller animals carved into the support. A Nile lion, a Ganges serpent, a Danube horse and a Plate armadillo. No one recognizes the armadillo. Experts suspect that Bernini and his assistants had never seen an accurate picture of the creature. Most all of Bernini's work from 1624 until he died in 1680 was executed in some part by others. The river fountain is an excellent example of the Bernini workshop approach. Supposedly, he was always in control, but all the river figures were done by others. Even though the river fountain dominates the piazza, the other two fountains are delightful. The sea creatures in the *Neptune Fountain* at the north end are grotesque; they are my favorite. The big fountain in the center is interesting yes, but I tend to hover around The Neptune. Neptune was first designed by Giacomo della Porta, and *The Fountain of the Moor* in the south end, originally done by della Porta, got its name because the dynamic figure in its center has the features of a Moor. Bernini even redesigned this fountain in 1653 but, again, the Moor was made by someone else.

People always love to be near water to see it sparkle in the sunshine or shimmer under night lights. Hearing the water splashing onto cavorting figures night and day makes Piazza Navona a constant delight. An apartment overlooking Navona would be a pleasant place to live but probably very expensive. Although it was autumn, it was as balmy as a summer night, plenty of people were about. I'd forgotten how safe it is to be out in the Italian evenings.

After checking a few favorite spots, I went back to my room where I heard drops of soft rain fall into the courtyard. As I stretched out onto the saggy bed, I re-hashed my struggle of getting in from the airport. The directions had been crystal clear, and it would have worked just fine if I'd only gotten on the bus parked *across* the street. The bus I had taken went in the wrong direction. My mistake had been to assume and not ask. It takes time to switch from country mouse to city mouse, I thought, as I drifted off.

Hoping to find a better hotel, I checked out of Pomezia leaving my bags behind the front desk, "until time to leave for Florence," I fibbed. The people were pleasant and I didn't have the heart to say I didn't like their little establishment. My guidebook recommended some inexpensive hotels just northeast of the main station. I hopped a bus to take a look. After several tries, I chose Pensione Simonetta, partly because I liked the name and partly because I was feeling anxious about getting settled.

Simonetta is on the fifth floor of one of the many blocky buildings lining drab Via Palestro. At first, the creaky, iron-caged elevator seemed romantic as it rose inch by inch, but by the time it jerked to a wobbly stop, the solid marble steps looked more appealing. The elevator opened directly into the hotel lobby. Signor Franco, a jolly man at the desk with a huge voice gave me a double room at a single price until a single became available. Obviously they operated on the bird-in-hand principle. Hoping to negotiate a better price, I stressed that I'd be staying for three weeks. He nodded and smiled. Later, I realized my negotiating ploy hadn't made a bit of difference because when I returned to Rome for four days before my plane left for home, the price was the same.

The central station, *Stazione Termini,* was just a few blocks away with its usual collection of hangers on—not exactly a savory neighborhood—but now that I had settled in, I rationalized it would give me a chance to learn about a different area of Rome. The authorities had kept the gypsies out of the station area, but the plaza in front still held clusters of beer drinkers who urinated in corners and left loads of trash.

As in any big city, the ambience can change abruptly within a few blocks. Just to the northwest lies Via Veneto, the street for embassies, expensive hotels and strutting celebrities. The Russian Embassy was around the corner from Simonetta and the Turkish one two blocks straight on up the street. Night and day there were two armed police at the Russian corner. One evening I asked the soldier about his machine gun; he joked and said something about "for sport," and then obviously thought better of it and quickly mentioned the embassy.

Directly across from the train station, immense, labyrinthine remains of the Diocletian Baths sprawl over two or three square blocks. The Baths now include a museum plus quarters for nuns connected with the church that had been redesigned by Michelangelo. After his death, however, there were numerous "adjustments" to his design. The display of these adjustments was brightly illuminated much as the restoration details of Leonardo's *Last Supper* had been in Milan. There seemed to be little left of

Michelangelo's original plan, no doubt another story of intrigue and manipulation—all part of the excitement of Rome. Rome is never static, and she certainly knows how to combine the ancient and modern. How can I pass by an open gate without peeking into someone's private courtyard? It might have a fountain with a grisly gorgon's face spitting into an ancient moss-lined sarcophagus, and the sarcophagus might hold shimmering goldfish. It might have a shiny black motorcycle parked beside an ivy covered capital fallen from an old fluted column. Cliché maybe, but Rome *is* a living museum.

Halfway between the station and Simonetta's street is Piazza Indipendenza; not only is it confusing but it's a place that feels uncomfortable. It's some sort of bus center yet countless city buses converge three blocks away at the train station so why another hub this nearby? In its center is an ugly brick structure for selling newspapers and bus tickets. Pedestrians have been completely forgotten here. No sidewalks at all. Was it a political boondoggle? Do these buses service only the northeast area? How to find the answer? Do I care? Later, however, I did learn why the place had felt all wrong; it had been the ancient site of *Campus Sceleratus* where Vestals who had forgotten their vows of chastity were buried alive!

~

My plan had been to take a bus back to Pomezia for my bags then call a cab to carry me to Simonetta, but the joy of traveling alone is the ease of changing plans abruptly. It felt so good to be walking in Rome again, and I had a spring in my step feeling settled at last. As I turned into Pomezia's street on the side of Sant'Andrea, my stomach growled. Across the way L'Insalata Ricca had *Spaghetti Integrale* written on their menu board. Seldom do you see whole wheat pasta on a menu, and with fresh tomato and basil sauce. Who could resist?

By the time I retrieved my luggage it was two o'clock. Oh no! The siesta rush hour was in full swing. There were no cabs and the buses were jammed so full they looked ready to tip over as they careened around corners. No way could a person climb aboard with luggage. It seemed a thousand blocks from one hotel to another and my forearm and shoulder ached from the weight of the bag tugging at me from behind. The wheel base of the cart holding my bag was conveniently narrow for negotiating crowded aisles of trains and planes, but it tipped easily on the uneven surfaces of cobblestones or loose paving stones. I had to grip the handle firmly to keep it steady. Muscles never heard from before screamed in pain. The cotton-mesh shopping bag I'd bought in a health-food store with the idea of showing thieves there was nothing worth grabbing, stretched and stretched and flopped awkwardly against my thighs. The holes in the net grew larger letting small items slip through. I was sweaty and feeling thoroughly embarrassed.

No more net bag, I vowed. I would carry my map and daily items in a common plastic shopping bag. I'd been rethinking my mode of dressing for next time too. Instead of the bulky, waterproof jacket with its hood and pockets and flaps worn over a long black skirt, I would find a more graceful raincoat with a wool zip-out lining. In an effort to be inconspicuous, I had overdone the frumpy look.

It was an arduous trek: first through the regional bus center at Largo Argentina; on through frenetic Piazza Venezia; up Via Nazionale's long hill; around Piazza Repubblica's circle; past the station; through Piazza Indipendenza—the one where the vestals were buried—and finally to rise slowly in the iron cage at Simonetta. The little establishment was spotlessly clean. Never had a siesta seemed such a good idea. But first, I took a long, hot bath. Late afternoon is an excellent time to bathe in small hotels because most guests are out, there's plenty of hot water, and no one knocks on the door to hurry you.

Later, feeling refreshed, I set out remembering that Bernini's *Santa Teresa* was only a few blocks away. The church was open. It is indeed glorious the way her saintly habit drapes so subtly over her body. No one could quibble over the beauty and skill found in this sculpture. The marble is meticulously polished to catch the best light, and yet, maybe one tends to focus on the "effect" more than the sculpture much as one focuses on special effects in sci-ence-fiction movies. As for Teresa, I don't believe for a moment that the glowing ecstasy she expresses is exactly spiritual. In spite of all this, she has become one of my regular stops when arriving in Rome.

Travel fatigue finally caught up with me. Let it be, I lectured myself, there was plenty of time stretching ahead to explore Rome. At the top of the broad steps of one of the two immense, curved buildings that form part of Piazza della Repubblica's grand circle, were small, round tables. From that perch I could watch the water spurting high into the Roman air from the Fountain of the Naiads in the center of whirling traffic. With the ancient Diocletian Baths as a backdrop, it wasn't a bad view. What better place to have one more cappuccino? Of course an evening cappuccino openly signals I am a foreigner, but who was I kidding anyway? No need to pretend anything else; I was a tourist although I longed to be more, a permanent resident perhaps. On the other hand, I said to myself, no one planned my itinerary, no one controlled my schedule, no one insulated me from the rough edges, and certain-ly no one had carried my luggage. In one of his books, Paul Theroux discussed this idea of when a tourist becomes a traveler.

As I took a sip, the frothy milk poised atop the freshly-ground espresso tickled my nose. Its aroma and taste blended into one delicious sensation, and I was inspired to think differently. From that moment, I began to see myself as a "traveler" like Paul Theroux. What better company could I ask for?

The tables began to fill with people and I noticed the Italians' beautiful footwear. Plain or fancy, their shoes were well made and every one I saw that evening was well polished. So were the Etruscans', I thought. Historians say one of the reasons they were successful in battle was that their warriors were so well shod. In a day or so I'd visit my favorite couple again reclining on their terra-cotta urn at Villa Giulia. Her tiny, turned-up shoes were also well polished.

~~

CHAPTER TWENTY-NINE

The Pantheon, another impossible dome.
Santa Maria della Pace, "my" piazza.
Via dei Coronari, street of antiques.
Caffè della Pace or Caffè Bramante?

THE CENTER OF THE PANTHEON'S MARBLE FLOOR WAS
wet and shiny from the huge eye above forever open to the gentle
rain. The wet area didn't look as big as I would have thought since
the opening is said to be twenty-eight feet in diameter, but then,
the entire floor of this immense antique is so much bigger. In his
book *Roman Architecture*, John B. Ward-Perkins says this building
represented a major turning point in western architecture and was
Rome's most "unique contribution to European architecture."

As much as the Pantheon looks cramped in its setting now, in
antiquity the huge mass of the rotunda was so hidden by
encroaching buildings that when a citizen approached the front
porch with its large triangular pediment held up by forty-foot
columns of Egyptian granite, it would have looked the same as
other conservative temples throughout the Roman Empire. Ward-
Perkins goes on to say that once inside, this citizen of ancient times
would have been shocked because he wouldn't find the expected
rectangular box with a flat ceiling. Instead, he would look up to a
soaring vault open to the light and the elements, just as I looked
up to enjoy the drops of rain on my face.

The deep, wine-colored porphyry on the pavement is so beautiful glistening in the rain. Anyone can sit in this stupendous space
for as long as one chooses; there's no service charge for sitting
down as there is in most coffee bars. In moments like these, I
might dream of being a visionary architect like the one who created this timeless space.

Along with my regular guidebook, I carried notes taken from a small book called *Romewalks* by Ann Shetterly. It was comforting to have a plan for the day even if it might change at any moment. As I was following one of Shetterly's convoluted routes, a sudden downpour caught me in a beautiful Piazza called *Santa Maria della Pace*, Saint Mary of Peace. I ducked into the Antico Caffè della Pace for a big pot of hot tea. It seemed strange that I'd never stumbled into this exquisite little piazza before because it's just around the corner from Navona with all its glorious spectacles.

The church of Saint Mary of Peace, seems lovely, but because of the encroaching buildings all around, its beautiful facade can hardly be seen. Still, it comes right out of a dream and sets the tone for the tiny piazza where no cars were allowed. The upper part of the front has slender, Corinthian columns which form a graceful curve, then, just below those columns, a half-oval porch curves farther out into the small space. This porch has oddly spaced Tuscan columns—those smooth, solid forms concocted by the Romans. They combined the classical Doric order with the Etruscan-temple order. The stonework is filthy, but the marble curves float above the sturdy Tuscan posts, and light or shadows move across it according to the whims of the sun or moon. Bertolucci made the most of these shadowy curves in his movie *La Luna*. Yes, the moon could work her magic here.

Most of the church was covered with restoration scaffolding and protective plastic, but just before closing time that afternoon, I was able to slip into the cloister built by Donato Bramante in 1504. The cloister was an architectural revolution for the time because he used a simple arrangement of two spaces over one space with the central pillar of the upper row of arches resting on the crown of the arch below. The dome of the church should have been visible from inside the cloister, but it too was hidden by plastic drapes. Someday it will all step out of its shrouds and when it does, I want to be there.

Caffè della Pace was an enchanting place to revive weary bones. It had a ceiling which appeared to be made of dark, polished wood timbers. There was little artificial lighting and what light came through the windows was muted. A smooth mahogany counter had a long marble top; on the marble stood a four-foot vase holding tall white lilies with rusty-red centers. Brilliant yellow mums stood on another table. My seat was far back against the wall next to where the counter was attached and my line of sight ran straight along the counter and out the open door. What a cozy, satisfied feeling I had to be dry and full of hot tea as I watched the pounding rain.

The young waiters had changed the classical music to a sensuous beat which I recognized from the old 70s movie *Shaft*. It didn't fit the setting. Then, the manager arrived and immediately she changed the music to Mozart. Perfect. I noticed a tall bronze figure holding a globe lamp on the red marble counter top. Was it bronze or merely plastic? Was it really marble? Was the ceiling really dark wood or imitation? Why was it necessary to question authenticity? Was it all too good to be true? What was this silly anxiety about? Was it fear that I might not have the fulfilling experience I should? It was as if a little demon kept warning me to enjoy every moment or else. Or else what? Doesn't everyone deserve to enjoy charming antiques in an elegant tea room in the heart of old Rome?

The tea cost 6,000 lire; at only 1250 lire to the dollar that year, it was an expensive cup of tea, about $4.80, but I rationalized it as my reward for having dragged luggage across town the day before.

Along Via dei Coronari, the annual antique fair was in full swing again. Having discovered it by chance the year before, its long, green carpet lining the length of the street seemed spread out just for me. How foolish and romantic we travelers are. A violinist and an electronic keyboard artist were playing, and their classical music sounded exactly right as it echoed along the narrow, elegant street with old-fashioned oil lamps flickering above everyone's heads. The best part of wandering aimlessly is that when I discover

Marble memories line the galleries of the Vatican Museum.

something without hired guides or guide books, it is mine forever. All the shops were open displaying dark, polished wood with not a speck of dust on them, and gleaming brass, sparkling cut glass chandeliers, marble tables, marble and ceramic figures, antique jewelry, copies of ancient Greek forms and darkened, old, oil paintings. How do they all stay in business with the economy falling apart around them? Maybe the rich do get richer.

Around four on another afternoon, the rain came again as I reached Piazza della Pace. This time my shelter was Caffè Bramante across the cobblestones from Caffè della Pace. The facade, which is the most romantic part of the church, was actually designed by Pietro di Cortona, but Donato Bramante gets all the credit. Something Michelangelo would grumble about because he had a couple of run-ins with old "bald-pate" as he called Bramante when they both served Pope Julius II.

The blond fellow who strutted around with the air of being a sophisticated cosmopolite seemed to be the manager. The female manager from Caffè della Pace across the way joined him; they seemed to be confederates as they stood in a corner conferring. Maybe the two establishments were owned by the same people?

Miles of marble hallways in the Vatican Museum of Rome.

And, maybe I would never know. Then the cosmopolite zoomed away on his motorcycle. This might be a nice area to live, I mused. I yearned to rent a tiny room with a kitchen attached. It was tiresome to eat out every meal. One day, I promised myself, I'd make it happen. At least for now, I could buy paper plates and bring food to my room from the fancy delicatessen on Via della Scrofa. Its beveled-glass windows lent the enticing meats, cheeses and cooked vegetables a tantalizing quality.

Except for copious quantities of tea and coffee, I'd had only a piece of fruit and a hunk of leftover bread all day, but it wasn't hunger that had brought on the bone-aching weariness, it was fatigue from being pressed by the hordes at the Vatican museum. What else could one expect on a free Sunday? Yet, it was interesting to see so many Italians enjoying their own treasures. My plan had been to stick to the Etruscan rooms, but museums are as distracting as dictionaries; I set out looking for one thing and end up being seduced by five others. Free is nice because the Vatican is one of the more expensive museums, but I paid by standing in long lines and battling the crowds. In the Raphael rooms, I recognized the *School of Athens* from having seen it as a backdrop for countless "Tuesday Night Concerts" at the University of Virginia in another life. Without realizing it at the time, details of that picture had been engraved in my memory. It was fun to try to identify Raphael's various contemporaries disguised as ancient philosophers. Michelangelo sits in the guise of the pessimist philosopher Heraclitus. Experts argue over this painting in their scholarly publications; the rest of us are content with speculation.

Since Patricia and I had gone to see the restored ceiling by Michelangelo two years before, and since his *The Last Judgment* was still being restored, I hadn't planned to go to the Sistine Chapel, but somehow I got caught up in the vortex of the crowd. Once inside the current, it was impossible to get out of the stifling, tortuous passageway because there were no side tributaries or escape routes. I felt almost claustrophobic.

There's too much in the Vatican; too much decoration on the walls; too much gilding on the ceilings; too much shelving loaded with ornate objects; too much cutlery locked behind glass cases; the rooms are endless and the halls go on and on. It's hoarding to the extreme. They say that when Napoleon was sent into exile, most of the loot his troops had stolen from churches all over Italy was returned *instead* to the Vatican. Surely the popes have been more acquisitive than kings or queens ever were. This overstimulation has the same numbing affect as shopping malls do, and the wealth and greed represented in both are obscene.

But, inside Caffè Bramante, I was in a dream world with the rain pouring outside and chamber music soaring inside. Because of the wavy glass in the leaded panes, people with their colorful umbrellas were strolling impressionistic figures out of a Monet or a Seurat. Some of them were closing their umbrellas, and I lazily thought about leaving, possibly when the Bach finished. The church and the other cafè across the way with its terra-cotta-colored stones and thick, strands of old ivy playing across its facade created an achingly-picturesque view.

Caffè Bramante was elegant in a different way from Caffè Pace. Chopin's soft melodies floated from a terrific sound system hidden somewhere behind the scenes. The walls were soft pastels painted

Four horsemen patrol the streets of Rome.

in a trompe-l'oeil style replicating the piazza outside. The decor didn't intrude, it was simply there if you wanted to acknowledge it. What a satisfying finish to a full day especially when the music switched to Vivaldi. One could spend one's entire holiday alternating between English tea with Mozart on one side of the piazza and Italian coffee with Vivaldi on the other.

CHAPTER THIRTY

Bar Niagara. A rehearsal.
A protest march. A free concert.
Santo Bambino: *Beautiful or ugly?*
The Campidoglio and Marcus Aurelius.

JUST TWO BLOCKS FROM PENSIONE SIMONETTA, A LIVELY morning market spreads along the middle of Via Montebello. It's not as grand as the one across town in Campo dei Fiori and geared for the people of this quarter. The vendors and customers laugh and argue with each other; tourists are politely tolerated. After taking my stash of fruit back up five flights to my room, I usually went for a cappuccino treat at a bar called Niagara. An ugly rendition of the famous falls was molded of pastel plastic and attached to the back wall. Because the barista and the cashier were such warm people, a stop at Bar Niagara became my regular morning habit.

During rush hour, the barista moved among his coffee machines with swift grace. He was a thin, dark-eyed man with black hair, a small black mustache and an unsightly, knobby mole on the side of his nose. His smile radiated good will, and I felt special when he handed me a cappuccino with the milky shape of a heart lying on top of the dark espresso. Later, I realized other baristas knew how to shape a heart onto the coffee, but it never changed my warm memory of Carlo. Once I asked him if he had been a dancer because he moved like one when he worked. He laughed and blushed, but was obviously pleased to receive the compliment. He took his work seriously and seemed proud of his chosen profession.

An attractive young woman struck up a conversation with me. Her age? Around thirty-five. She limped, either from a clubfoot or polio, and something told me that limp had affected her life in a big way here in a country where *fare una bella figura*, to cut a fine figure, is so important. I was surprised that I spoke more Italian than she did English. My perception of Italians' knowledge of English had been distorted because most people with whom a traveler speaks are shopkeepers who know enough to get by and appear to know more. It seemed that most other people knew less English than the shopkeepers. With United Europe on the move, no wonder there were so many posters touting English language schools.

She asked one question after another. Did I have children? Did I work? Why was I there? Did I like Italians? Do Americans talk to each other like this casually in a bar? I was amused that my reply sounded so typically Italian, I was saying with appropriate hand motions, *"Dipende,"* it depends. I told her that in the big cities most folks are too busy as they often are in Rome, but in small towns they take more time. A curious question was if there were mostly blonds in America. She finished her cappuccino and had to leave, but suggested we might see each other there tomorrow.

For a moment while talking with her, I feared she'd want to latch on to me for the entire day. I was ashamed that my first thought was she couldn't keep up. What a fool I was to think like that. It could have been well worth the slowdown. Another worrisome thought had been, what does she want from me? Most Italians, especially women, ignore me. Can't she make it with Italians? What's wrong with her? She was a bit odd, a bit intense and in my face. Maybe because of her limp; maybe not. I never saw her again. The encounter left me feeling incomplete, and I wished I could have atoned for my shameful thoughts somehow.

The yellow city buses are frequent and convenient especially when I need to walk up a long, sustained hill like Via Nazionale, but there are times when I can't stand the crowds another minute. Everyone is extremely polite when crammed together. There's never been a feeling of threat or inappropriate touching in spite of all the stories, but sometimes the ride feels unsafe because of overloading. On one such ride I noticed the English Church and I squeezed myself out the middle exit just in time before the doors closed on me. I hadn't come to Rome to see English churches, but for some reason I was drawn inside.

The church was in excellent repair and absolutely immaculate. A trio was rehearsing, and their music soared into the high gothic arches captivating me instantly. A pianist sat at the keyboard of a gorgeous, black, grand piano placed just below the altar. The piano was indeed special, but I suspected he knew how to bring out its best qualities. It was beautiful to look at, as was the pianist; I felt privileged. The flutist and violinist with him were excellent too, but the lush sounds the pianist drew from his instrument were heavenly. It sounds trite but he did caress the keys, and the sounds swirled up into the heavens of the church. They seemed to swirl too much, however, because at times the notes sounded a bit muddy in the lower register. The musicians were concerned too because the flutist's girlfriend was giving them feedback about it. Her long dark hair covered half her face so that she got to constantly flip her head or move it away with her hand. Young Italian women are as obsessed with their hair as young American women.

An hour and a half passed in a flash. Upon leaving, I noticed a signboard announcing their free concert that very evening—Mozart, Copland and Martinu. I made a mental note of the time. After sitting such a long time, it felt good to hustle on foot down Via Nazionale peeking into its medium-priced shops along the way. At Piazza Venezia a huge protest march had gathered; there must have been thousands idling around. It was exciting to be thrust into the thick of it. It was a happy, peaceful march; everyone was walking, laughing and chatting with each other like an oversized family reunion. One old toothless fellow took the opportunity to hold forth on his views to anyone who would listen. People congregated on the sides until they recognized their particular group and then dived into the moving crowd.

The mass moved across the Piazza toward the government offices behind the white monument to King Vittorio Emanuele II. Traffic was stymied and buses were crawling, but none of the drivers were honking. People carried signs about the minimum tax. One said Italy is founded on artisans. From what I'd deciphered from the newspapers, the minimum tax would hit small business people the hardest which in Italy includes thousands of artisans and crafts people. One sign was easy to understand, *Meno burocrazie, Piu efficienza!* Less bureaucracy, More efficiency! That sign would fit in anywhere, anytime. It was tempting to follow along, but there would be much milling around with long speeches loaded with political jargon that I wouldn't understand. A block or two away from Piazza Venezia, it was the same old Rome again with horns honking and everyone trying to be first.

At a bar, I drank a cool beer and ate a sandwich happy to pay extra for the service in order to sit at an outside table to make my plans for the rest of the day. I could visit Villa Giulia again, or

All the "me firsters" join the meleé in Rome.

climb up to the Campidoglio or attend a special exhibit at the huge art museum on Via Nazionale. I could visit Michelangelo's *Moses* again. Then there was a church with two Caravaggios near Piazza del Popolo I wanted to see, and I could try to sort out the old streets around Marcello's Theatre that were delightfully confusing. And, Trastevere was still an unsolved mystery luring me on. So many choices. This time I remembered to be a wise traveler and used the toilet before leaving the bar.

The day passed quickly. When I noticed the time, I thought I'd fooled around too long and wouldn't get to the concert by 19:00 hours. If I hurried, I might sneak in at the back of the church. They were such talented young people that I wanted to give them my support. There might not be many in their audience. Supper would have to wait. At 19:20 the church was empty except for an organist practicing from a hidden spot on high. It sounded lovely, but I was hungry and too disappointed to stay. In fact, I was so hungry I considered the huge McDonald's nearby at Piazza Repubblica.

Rome's McDonald's main attraction for me was its large, clean restroom. This was the largest McDonald's I'd ever seen. Outside, forty small tables were grouped in front, each having four chairs around them with large umbrellas attached. Inside, the counter to order hamburgers and fries looked the same as those at home, but in addition to the usual fare, there was an array of salads and desserts displayed on beds of crushed ice. Around the corner from the order counter a flight of stairs went down to another area with about sixty more smaller tables, booths *and* the restrooms. No one cares if you go in to use the toilet without buying anything; they know you'll buy eventually. All types eat at McDonald's in Rome just as in the States, but most are the young, and the women's rooms are usually crowded with primping teenage girls.

As I crossed the busy street to enter McDonald's there was a loud screech and everyone stopped to look—it was nothing, but when I looked back, I saw a familiar face. It was the violinist dressed in a tux. He had a pre-concert look on his face and was carrying his instrument. Wait a minute! I hadn't missed the concert after all. It was scheduled for 21:00 hours (9:00 p.m.) not 19:00 hours (7:00 p.m.).

Since, it was only 19:30, I could have it all. Skipping McDonald's, I hurried to a small trattoria near the church where I had a chilled glass of Frascati just dry and crisp enough to cut the smooth richness of a parmigiano-spinach omelette.

The church was packed. Here I was in a beautiful church with a full stomach, hearing gorgeous music and the price was right. The crème de la crème was the trio by Martinu. The pianist wooed his instrument and it sang and murmured sweet nothings back to him. They didn't "need" my support after all, but I needed them because suddenly I felt an intense loneliness. Was it the lush sounds? Was it the soaring arches and soft lights? Or was it simply the human need to grasp someone's arm and give it a squeeze? For that instant I wanted to be included in the joyous moment. As the crowd thinned, I spoke to the young woman from the morning hoping she would remember me. She did, and immediately I felt connected. Later, I called home for more sharing and the loneliness slipped away.

The church of Santa Maria in Aracoeli is wedged in between the Vittoriana and the Campidoglio, *the* historic center of Rome. The church can only be reached by a long flight of steep steps. *Ara Coeli* means the Altar of Heaven, and Christian legend says that when Emperor Augustus asked Apollo who his successor would be, the answer came that a Hebrew child would take Apollo's place. Legend asserts that Augustus set up an altar here to the divine child. We do know that Aracoeli was built on the former site of the Temple of Juno, the Goddess of Women. Sometimes subtly and sometimes blatantly, Paganism and Christianity continue their cohabitation in Italy. It seems especially so in Rome.

From down on the street, I can never tell whether the church door is open; if not, it's a long climb for naught. A woman was coming down and I asked,

"*E`aperta la chiesa?*" Is the church open?

"*Si, si, è aperta,* she smiled. Yes, yes, it's open.

The flat ceiling of Aracoeli is covered with carved wood entirely gilded in gold. Twenty-two columns of varying sizes and varying materials taken from various temples make up the two long aisles. I could see where the bases of some had been raised to make them even with the others; one capital had an inscription showing it came from the Palace of the Caesars. I could hum here.

Toward the front was a Byzantine Madonna and near her stood a sweeping, ultra modern sculpture of grey stone which could be a Christ figure, the contrast was startling. Many of the side chapels had names indicating which families had contributed—sometimes jointly and sometimes singly. They are familiar Roman names that keep cropping up in the history of the city.

In a corner room to the left stood *Santo Bambino*, the miraculous Christ Child said to have been carved by a sixteenth-century pilgrim from a tree on the Mount of Olives. He was a pudgy kid who looked to be about eight years old, dressed in white silk completely encrusted in gold, diamonds, rubies and other precious stones—all needing a good dusting. Into the late nineteenth, century this figure was rushed to a dying patient's bedside in a coach with liveried servants provided by the Dukes of Torlonio, one of those rich families of this parish.

Stacks of dusty letters lay around the feet and behind the figure. Letters imploring him for good health, no doubt, or asking for luck or money. John Ruskin waxed ecstatically over this Bambino, and certainly H.V. Morton, a noted travel writer, considered him a beauty, but to me he was awesome in his ugliness. From the twenty-fifth of December to January sixth they place him in a life-sized manger scene, *un presepio*, with other life-size figures. Children are brought to preach sermons or recite verses from a small pulpit set up in front of the crèche.

On a second visit to Aracoeli, I counted all 122 steps leading to the church. As I stood looking at a copy of the stolen *Santo Bambino* thinking that the Holy Copy was just as ugly as the original, a man stepped up and quietly touched the feet of the doll. When he bowed his head and touched his thick, eyeglasses, I bowed my head with him and forgot about all being a cynical art critic.

It was good to sit in the warmth and quietness of the church; I wondered about miracles. A miracle must come in response to an intense longing, I thought. It must start at a deep personal level. I can relate to personal miracles, but when masses of people accept one person's personal vision, I tend to get stuck and… At first, the sound of keys jangling didn't enter my consciousness. Evidently it had been meant as a subtle signal. When I didn't respond, a polite sacristan touched my shoulder and briskly escorted me out a side door. Standing in a cold drizzle with the locked door behind me was unsettling. I shivered partly from the cold and partly from panic. Where was I? For a few moments, I felt disoriented until I saw a short flight leading down into the center of the Campidoglio. *Un altro miracolo!* Another miracle!

The Campidoglio, The Capitol, is set on the smallest of Rome's seven hills, but symbolically it holds the most ancient and important history. On the Capitoline's two small peaks, the ancients worshiped their three main deities: Jupiter, Juno and Minerva. In their Etruscan-style temples, solemn ceremonies were conducted. Juno's temple sat on the highest of the two peaks where the Aracoeli sits. The hollow area between the two peaks is now the Piazza del Campidoglio. For centuries this hollow space was called the "Asylum" because according to the legend of Romulus, the city's founder, refugees and exiles were protected if they could get into this hollow space in time.

I stepped onto the lovely gray and white compass star in the pavement designed by Michelangelo four hundred years ago. As with so many of his designs left moldering, this one wasn't installed completely until the 1940s. Something triggered a memory and I saw again the lanterns glowing around the outer circle of the magnificent star. They had illuminated the three buildings framing the piazza during a concert on a summer evening long ago. As I stood there reminiscing in the chilly mist, I heard the sound of the fountain flowing just behind me. Had I noticed that same fountain trickling into its basin then?

A trip through the museums would wait for another day, but I made time to see again the most beautiful equestrian statue of all, *Marcus Aurelius.* The bronze horse and rider both gesture in a kind of symbiosis. The rider extends his right arm horizontally as if to point to a space beyond time. At the same time, the horse lifts his right leg as if pawing the air, and both of the riders' legs are balanced outward. He uses no stirrups, and for that, he seems more powerful, more sure. For many years, the statue had been on a pedestal designed for it by Michelangelo. It stood at the center of his compass star radiating outward in all directions—maybe to send out the noble thoughts of a great mind. Marcus Aurelius was one of the few philosophical emperors, and his writings called *Meditations* have impressed intellectuals ever since the second century A.D. He was a Stoic, a philosophy that said a person should be free of passion and should submit, without complaint, to unavoidable necessity. He never wanted to be emperor, and he became a sort of model for those who have to go against their calling. Alexander Liberman's book of exquisite photographs

Campidoglio, Michelangelo's Roman Capitol, has an essay by Joseph Brodsky entitled "Homage to Marcus Aurelius." Brodsky wrote "the Roman Empire gained a lot more from his dual loyalty to duty and philosophy than did the Stoic doctrine ... so much so, that it's been maintained, often vigorously, that this sort of inner split is a good recipe for ruling."

Yes, there he was. Stupendous. Colossal. Magnificent. Words that not only describe *Marcus Aurelius* but all of Rome.

↬

CHAPTER THIRTY-ONE

Tarquinia: Home of Roman kings.
Cerveteri: Hometown of terra-cotta lovers.
Viterbo: Etruscans were here.
Into the humanistic soup.

THE TICKET SELLER IN THE ROME STATION WOULD NOT give me one jot of information about whether the train to Civitavecchia, pronounced "Chee-veeta-VECK'-eeah," would go on to Tarquinia; it was not in his job description. Having read about buses from Civitavecchia to Tarquinia, I took a chance. It seemed odd that such a famous site was so ignored, at least it was famous in the eighth century B.C. In Southern Etruria, the area just north of Rome, there are Etruscan tombs by the hundreds, and more are discovered every year. After Orvieto, Tarquinia was next on my list of Etruscan places to visit. My dream was to reach all the major Etruscan centers, and then I'd start on the less accessible ones.

The early villages of the Tarquinii peoples were the most prosperous of the pre-urban settlements in *Etruria,* the name given to the ancient Etruscans' country. They called themselves Rasna or Rasenna, the Greeks knew them as the Tyrrhenoi from which the Tyrrhenian Sea gets its name, and the Romans called them Etrusci or Tusci. No one knows exactly where the boundaries of Etruria were, but all agree they encompassed the general area that is now modern Tuscany expanding as far as Padua with a few settlements along the Adriatic Sea. They even reached into areas south of Rome.

Michael Grant, a respected historian on the Mediterranean world, says one could go back as far as the tenth century B.C. and still call this area a Tarquinian civilization. Their skill in making bronze from the copper and iron mined in their hills was superior to others of their day, and he claims their metals and metallurgy were the main reason for their stupendous early wealth. Grant says there is evidence that they traded in southern Italy and other regions of the Mediterranean even before the eighth-century B.C. Greek colonists established themselves in southern Italy and Sicily.

Oh, to have the nerve to rent a car and meander around in Southern Etruria! Tarquinia is only about forty-five miles by car, but it takes at least three hours by train and bus. A better command of the language might give me more courage, yet being alone on the road could have its drawbacks. This is the only instance I've discovered where traveling alone is a handicap. As it was, I took a train for Civitavecchia, another word meaning old city.

A town by the sea ought to be beautiful, but Civitavecchia is not. It was bombed in World War II; the devastation must have sapped its imaginative energy because it was a dusty, derelict sort of place. After sorting out the bus problem, I had time to step over to the waterfront where a harbor fort designed by Michelangelo jutted out into the water. History books tell us he was much more than a sculptor, painter, architect and poet, but the idea didn't sink in until I saw something solid and functional like this fort to prove it.

Thank goodness for a young woman who came to my rescue in Civitavecchia because there was no help from train officials nor were there any signs showing how, when or where to catch a bus to Tarquinia. She spoke only a few words of English but took time to walk with me to a bar to ask for information, then on to the newspaper kiosk to buy the proper ticket, and finally to the bus stop. She still didn't desert me. She asked several people standing around a pole plunked into a dry, gravelly spot in the street. The pole had a torn city bus schedule stuck on it, but no one knew anything about a bus to Tarquinia. Just then a bus pulled up with the Tarquinia sign on it. When the driver opened the door, she stepped up and asked for information. Only then did she leave me. Hers was an example of genuine hospitality; she literally went the second mile. When I thanked her profusely and gave her a little hug, she laughed and seemed thoroughly pleased with herself as she hurried away.

~

The women in the Tarquinia tourist office were most helpful and handed me a timetable which included both train and connecting bus schedules; indeed a train does leave Rome going directly to Tarquinia early in the morning. The trick is to find a happy government worker in Rome who will offer complete information. The ticket seller didn't like his job, or me, or foreigners, or anyone else for that matter.

Except for the ancient wall, modern Tarquinia didn't touch me, but its museum was beautiful and everything was scrupulously labeled. From the upper balcony of this former villa, there's a sweeping view of the Tyrrhenian Sea, named after a legendary son of the first Etruscans. The sea had to be imagined my first hour there because a haze hid the entire coastline, but later, the view was gloriously revealed. Almost all Etruscan strongholds were high like this one because they wanted a good vantage point for protection from sea pirates.

Obviously their descendants found this spot agreeable for living as well, and the rooms of the villa were spacious. The entry area held several impressive sarcophagi. The indirect lighting shed a golden glow on the stone walls creating a dramatic back light for the figures stretched out on their stone coffins. What a theatrical statement they made.

In the top room of the villa the museum's prize was set apart all to itself. Two winged horses molded of golden-colored terra cotta and polished to a soft sheen were mounted on a sheet of dark gray flagstone high on the back wall. The museum director had made sure the lighting was perfectly adjusted to show off these impressive fourth-century B.C. steeds. Comfortable stone benches were provided where I could rest and dream. How fortunate to be there on a November afternoon and have them all to myself. I wasn't able to enter the tombs at the edge of town, but they were within walking distance and I promised myself there would be another time.

What a pretty part of Tuscany the Tarquinians had for a while. The tilled fields were green and the sea appeared on and off among trees and tall shrubs as the bus went back to Civitavecchia. This time, it was easy to find my way to the train station. Relaxing on the train back to Rome, I chatted with an old pensioner on his way to visit his grandchildren. His wife had died and he seemed helpless, but he knew our presidential election was coming up in a few days and asked about it. Making up Italian words as I went along, I tried hard to make it clear that I had voted by mail before leaving home. Why was it so important that he understood? Somehow I think he did.

At Cerveteri, the sun was shining and the little city of the dead was everything I hoped it would be—after I found it. "From the metro stop at Lepanto," they said at the bus information office in Rome, "take the blue bus to Cerveteri." Sounded easy, but when I came up from the underground at Lepanto, there were seven blue buses lined up along the curb. And, where to get a ticket?

The tickets were available at the corner bar—I was learning. After scurrying to the front of each of the buses, I found one that said Ladispole/Cerveteri and climbed aboard to relax. But how was I to relax when there were no road signs along the way for Cerveteri, only ones for Ladispole? Most people got off at Ladispole, pronounced La-DEES'-po-lay. I stayed on and waited; to my delight, a little farther on we came to Cerveteri, "Cher-VEH'-te-ree."

The small museum in the center of town was housed in a former palace. It was pleasant but didn't offer much of interest. Most of the local finds had been spirited away long ago by looters or into the Villa Giulia or the Vatican museums in Rome. After finding a WC and a cappuccino, I went looking for the tombs. According to my notes, they were about three kilometers away.

"*Sempre dettra,*" the old gentleman said.

Dettra? He must mean, *destra,* I thought. Always keep to the right. He was probably speaking a local dialect. With a lot of faith and by turning right at every choice, I followed the road inclining gently uphill and sure enough the tombs were waiting there, as they had waited for twenty-six centuries.

It was hot and sunny on the road and I was glad I carried water, but the tombs were in the shade of stately, dark cypress trees, and there was a drinking fountain in front of the entrance.

At last I was about to enter sixth-century B.C. Caere, hometown of the loving couple who now reside in Villa Giulia. I walked past the fenced "city" first to get a feel for the place I had read about for so long. It would be fairly easy to get inside the fences around the tomb city especially out of sight from the entrance shack. What fun it would be to play in and around those tombs. Do the town kids slip out here when the guards are gone? It would be a smashing setting for a Nancy Drew adventure.

When I requested a free entrance as a senior citizen, the ticket man wouldn't believe I qualified. At first it was a flattering game but he insisted on proof, so I reached under my sweater to pull my passport from my money belt. There were hardly any visitors and he didn't have enough to do, but it was a minor bother to save 8,000 lire. There are some compensations for being a woman of a certain age, but, I lost that advantage as Italy gradually conformed to European Union regulations; now discounts are offered only to Union citizens.

I stepped out into the beautiful mounded city and breathed in the special air of this ancient place. For a couple of hours I walked the streets of the dead and took pictures. Postcards are probably better mementoes, except for those shots that do not interest a professional's eye, but my luck with photos from Italy is abysmal.

In 1990 they were stolen, and these taken at Caere were lost by the Safeway Film Service.

In Caere, the largest tombs are of the tumulus kind similar to those in the Near East. They were from the wealthy class of the seventh century B.C. Smaller, more modest, cube-shaped tombs came later. They all crowd together now. Some have present-day steps leading down; others lead up from the road and then back down into the tomb. As in modern Italy, there are many steps to climb. Most tombs have at least two funeral biers, one for the husband and one for the wife. Hers has a triangular shape like a roof of a house at the head of the couch or bier and is always situated on the right as you enter. His, on the left, has a semicircular, flat headboard. Outside is a stone slab with niches cut into it to show how many occupants were inside, a house shape for each woman and a stylized phallic symbol for each man.

With the ticket, I received a street plan because this large complex is indeed laid out in a definite order; experts assume these necropoli resemble actual Etruscan cities. Most side streets lead straight onto the main road which someone named the Street of Hades. The Etruscans had cut a network of drainage tunnels into the soft tufa rock to draw off rain water. After all this time, the system works well. Only a little water, from the recent rain, stood in the ancient ruts, ruts worn by chariots that had carried the dead to their tombs or the living to their funeral celebrations. Small puddles also stood in a few of the tombs, but for the most part, it was possible to climb down and walk inside.

~

A glass wall kept me from walking into the most famous tomb of Caere, *The Tomb of the Reliefs*, but it was lighted and the colors were still brilliant after 2300 years. It's different from the others; it has no tumulus above it. I reached it by going down a long stairway; at the bottom was a small platform leading into a large, single rectangular chamber. Supposedly, its roof looks like an actual house did and it is supported by two square pillars which taper toward the top.

They call it "Reliefs" because the decorations are made of painted stucco attached to the walls and pillars. Helmets, shields and swords are "hanging" on the walls as if ready to go at a moment's notice. Trumpets of a type that the Romans copied for their military use are there too, and above the trumpets are two large braziers with handles. On the two central pillars is a collection of domestic objects that fool the eye. Even though one knows they are molded plaster, they look ready to be picked up and put to practical use. They include an axe, a coiled rope, a long knife, a stick hung from a leather thong, and a one-handled jug called an *oinochoe* with a shaped lip for pouring wine. It looked exactly like those in Greek and Etruscan museums. In fact, this particular jug helped the archaeologists date the tomb. There's an animal with an arched back rubbing against the base of the pillar which looked a lot like someone's favorite Tabby.

A woman's name, *Ramtha Matunai Canatne*, is written on the center of the alcove. All the objects sculpted to the right of the niche are obviously hers: a fan, some necklaces and a walking stick. As if she might be back momentarily, a pretty little pair of sandals lies sculpted on the floor beside her bench. I would have liked to meet the sensitive artist who placed her sandals just so.

When I tried to pay for the 7,200-lire ($4.35) ticket to Viterbo with a 50,000 note ($30.00), the official glared at me from under his heavy eyebrows. He said he couldn't make change. Couldn't or wouldn't? His mouth was fixed in a permanent bureaucratic sneer. This Italian penchant for not wanting to make change drives me crazy. Naturally I wouldn't expect a vendor in a market to change a large bill for a few apples, but good grief, this was the central train station in Rome.

To make matters worse, the man standing behind me reached over my shoulder and lifted notes out of my hand to show that I indeed had 7,000. He offered to pay the 200 lire to hurry things along. I tried to refuse but the pressure was fierce so I gave up my only small bills. Had I remembered to hide the small notes, the grouchy bureaucrat would have had to make change.

Then I noticed that the digital display on his ticket machine facing me seemed to indicate a change of trains between Rome and Viterbo. When I asked about it, he growled something about the information desk, but this time I insisted. He grabbed his worn timetable and looked up the times and track number for me. I thanked him, and asked again, speaking as clearly as possible,

"*Devo cambiare il treno?*" Must I change trains?

"No!"

Obviously answering that question was not in his job description, instead, I was expected to stand in a separate line for that piece of information. If he wants his cushy government job with tenure, pension, holidays, sick leave and lots of coffee breaks, he jolly well ought to answer a few simple questions even from foreigners with mangled accents. I wondered, though, how our bureaucrats would handle foreigners.

As it was, he had given me the wrong track number; was it on purpose or did he have an outdated manual? On subsequent trips, I learned to use the electronic information machines installed in some stations. When functioning, they were far superior to cranky clerks with clumsy manuals.

Since there was time, I went to a busy bar, and the woman there changed the 50,000 lire bill with a smile. This episode should seem funny given the time and distance since it happened, yet even now I feel cross thinking about it. Now that *is* funny.

It was a slow, sleepy journey to Viterbo—about fifty miles northeast of Rome. It misted and rained off and on all the way as the warm, steamy train chucked along its country route. A pleasant woman and her portly husband spoke with me; he knew bits of English but I continued replying in Italian. It was one of those times when I felt absolutely free to try the language. My antennae were becoming more sensitive as to who was willing and who wasn't.

Viterbo's Etruscan museum was entirely different from any other I'd seen. Since 1957, the Swedes had been doing excavations in the area led by their industrious King Gustav Adolf VI himself. The exhibit focused on findings at three outlying villages, Acquarosso, Luni sul Mignone and San Giovenale, where remains of huts and a few houses had been discovered. This was exciting because usually there's nothing left except tombs, and they were the first evidence I'd ever seen of ordinary Etruscans' houses.

Few artifacts were in the Viterbo museum, instead, they had built excellent displays to show how the houses were built. Great attention was paid to the tile roofs. Flat plates of terra-cotta tile were laid on top of each other, half cylinders of tile were laid over the seams, and larger half cylinders were placed where the pitch or angles of the roofs met. It seemed to be the same method used for tile roofs in Italy today. I would be looking at roofs with a more intelligent eye in the future.

The rain continued and turned bitter cold with gusty drafts pushing at me around corners of buildings. After a warming lunch, I walked up a steep, narrow street to the main piazza which sat on a former Etruscan acropolis. A twelfth century cathedral was up there with its campanile rising beside it. The top half sported the familiar black and white stripes. Also on the lofty piazza was the *Palazzo dei Papi*, Palace of the Popes. Viterbo had been a refuge for popes when Frederick Barbarossa laid siege to Rome in the twelfth century. This is where the tradition of locking cardinals away until they chose a new pope got started. The story goes that the cardinals had gathered for the election and were enjoying the pleasant air away from Rome and the good food which the citizens were forced to provide. The fat cardinals took their time. Finally, the town people grew disgusted. The mayor of the city threatened to cut off food and open the roof to their conference room to hurry their decision along. It was midwinter and the threat worked.

The popes' palace is of gray stone with one interesting balcony that has openwork and lacy archways, but on the whole, it does not offer any particular architectural joy. The crenelation is what I would expect, the square, papish, style.

The cold had seeped into my bones and I headed back to the train station. On the way, I dropped into the information center to gather brochures and maps of the numerous Etruscan sites surrounding the town. The entire area was a bonanza for Etruscan buffs. It would be good to stay in Viterbo for a few days, I thought.

Then, I would bite the bullet, rent a car, and go exploring on my own. Public transportation to out-of-the-way sites would consume hours of waiting for connections and would not take me to the remote spots.

On the train back, I wanted to get off at Ostiense in south Rome. From there I could take the Metro into the heart of the city. I began feeling nervous because the train was crowded. I worried I wouldn't be able to see the name of my station in time. Why don't they announce the stops on Italian trains? This is one more part of Italian life which adds to one's stress—at least to mine. One must always ask someone where the stops are, or how things work because instructions are seldom posted. I felt as if everyone else already knew what to do. Then I noticed that everyone didn't know and they too had to ask fellow travelers where and how. Maybe this is part of what makes up the Italian mystique. Their desire for verbal contact puts everyone into the same humanistic soup and keeps them in touch with each other. Sure enough, someone helped me watch for my stop.

∽

CHAPTER THIRTY-TWO

Yellow Denver Boots. Melancholy moods.
Fare Bella Figura. A tall tale at Bar Niagara.
Trastevere and the smallest bell tower in Rome.

ONCE AGAIN I WAS IN VILLA GIULIA AND THOROUGHLY captivated. The clownish Etruscan priests with their enlarged thighs and buttocks were still dancing around shoulders of vases. The large kraters used for mixing water with wine for banquets had figures playing flutes and dancing with odd gestures, all for the joy of being alive, it seemed to me. The reclining figures were still stretched out in leisure on top of alabaster or terra-cotta sarcophagi. Some figures hold an egg reminding us of the origin of life and its continuance into an afterlife. And, the exquisite couple of polished terra cotta were still happy to be together forever. I allowed myself plenty of time to wander leisurely, but this Etruscan museum had more rooms than I remembered, and in the end, I didn't run out of time—I ran out of museum energy.

In the garden of the villa, I had a cup of coffee and a toasted cheese sandwich at a snack bar located in a separate outbuilding of the villa. The proprietor, a tall man with a bronzed, rugged face and thick, wavy white hair, told me he was seventy-five and still worked ten hours a day. Obviously, he was proud of that. Obviously, it agreed with him. He was a handsome human being pulsing with energy, and I could imagine him dancing and grabbing at life to the last breath.

From Villa Giulia, I walked on into the Borghese Gardens. Just outside the zoo, a sweet Japanese family asked me to take their picture. Eventually I found my way out of the park onto Via Vittorio Veneto and into an unoccupied phone booth. In spite of several grand embassies, including our own, and expensive hotels displaying furs and jewelry in their boutique windows, the Veneto had a shopworn, seedy feel to it.

A well-dressed man obviously wanted the phone, but I'd waited for phones plenty of times and ignored him. Then a policeman—or was he a spiffily-dressed doorman?—knocked on the glass and said something about S.O.S. I signed off and stepped back to watch. An elegantly dressed police woman stepped up and seemed to be making the call for the gentleman because they conferred while she talked on the phone. So many official-looking costumes are confusing to outsiders; it's possible that neither the man nor the woman were connected in any way with the police. Later when I told the "doorman" I'd been talking to my husband in the United States, he made a feeble apology for interrupting me. Something told me it hadn't been an emergency at all. The "gentleman" had not wanted to wait and money may have changed hands. No doubt the emergency was nothing more than an illegally parked car, and they were pulling strings for its release.

Sometimes garish yellow trucks drive up to illegally parked vehicles and install garish yellow "Denver Boots," called *le ganasce*. While a workman was attaching one, I asked how much it would cost to retrieve a car, he replied about 150,000 lire ($100). It was reassuring to see that enforcement of parking regulations does happen, but it's a mere drop in the bucket. People park their cars on the sidewalk, sometimes so far up that pedestrians must walk around them into the street. They double and triple park, and some side streets look like parking lots. Parking spaces are so scarce that Romans take the risk until caught, then they fuss up a storm, shrug their shoulders, and start all over again.

Thoughts of how it feels to live in the USA hit me at odd moments. The radio in a small cafè played American music and a familiar singer came on; hers was a cool, jazzy voice from the 70s. For a few moments, I missed the vibrant, pulsing aspect of the States. I recalled years ago when I spent a few months in Amsterdam among all the blonds. How good it felt one day to see a couple of African Americans jiving down the street. Until that moment, I hadn't realized how much I missed the color, the mix, the zest, the exuberance of my country. Perhaps that's what is so attractive to people from other countries, our energy; it does keep the pot boiling. Maybe my warm feelings for home were kindled because my candidate had just won the presidency of the USA. His opponent with his money-grabbing, mean-spirited cronies were on their way out. Perhaps there could be some warmth and hope again. Perhaps.

Kenneth Branagh, an English actor and director, says the United States is exciting but unreal. It's like make believe to him and after awhile, he longs to go back to England to be real. Sometimes I feel torn between Italy and America and wonder where it is that I feel real.

If I stayed in Rome, I mused, I'd need to get involved with another layer of life. I must be able to converse easily in order to speculate and share ideas with others. To live here permanently, I'd need a sense of belonging. Young students make friends across cultures easily. They're out and about dancing at discos and involved in school activities. Chances are I'd never be fully accepted by the Italians, at least not by Italian women. I'd need to find English-speaking peers too. Yes, Italians are animated; yes, they are intense and emotional with each other, but in public they can be cool, even cold. They can stare without smiling and often seem withdrawn and self protective.

Are we Americans afflicted with too much of the "Have A Good Day" syndrome? We're certainly spoiled. Most of us take for granted those unnamed, implied opportunities offered to us, and we have this innate belief that any of us can go for the gold ring. The Italians seem to take themselves too seriously; could their innate sense of station in life cause that? They seem overly concerned with *fare bella figura*, making the best show—the saving of face. Yet, when a human connection *is* made with an Italian, there seems to be a humanistic response at a potentially deep level of trust and loyalty. If I send a smile to a stranger on the street, it doesn't always come back, but if I speak to them with a soft *Buon Giorno*, I get a response and a smile. Verbal acknowledgment seems to work, but, the initiation must come from me, the outsider. All these observations may be just romantic notions of a romantic traveler. Am I anywhere near the truth?

The black birds called *storni*, that normally flock amidst the orchard of trees in front of the train station, were swirling furiously by the thousands and making a terrible racket. They swooped as if they were one pulsing organism; if I were an Etruscan soothsayer, what awesome portent would I predict?

Rome seems to shrink as it becomes familiar to me. Via Veneto curves around to Piazza Barberini where Bernini's *Triton* arches up to blow into his conch shell while water splays over him. At that point, a right turn takes me onto Via Sistina and the top of the Spanish Steps in no time. A left turn takes me to Via delle Quatro Fontane (named for the four fountains on the four corners of an intersection) and from there a few more blocks brings me to Via

Nazionale. Veneto and Nazionale had always seemed so far away from each other before. They are only far apart in character. Veneto, Barberini and Spagna are elegant and upscale; Nazionale, Repubblica and Termini are workaday.

The Spanish Steps area could be said to be too touristy, yet it's strange how often I drift back to it. Certain areas attract for good reasons. From the top, the view across the city is spectacular, and the graceful steps and honey-colored buildings work their charm time and time again. The sound of a haunting violin came from the steps. Tentatively, he tried to match his melody to the symphonic accompaniment coming from a portable cassette player at his feet. He was poorly dressed, disheveled and young, but his music was oh so sweet. As usual when I hear a street violinist, I toss money remembering my eldest son, who escaped life for awhile to play his violin in the Paris Metro. A pile of one-thousand-lire notes lay in the young fellow's instrument case; in his quiet way he was doing okay.

One Sunday morning in the Bar Niagara, a man chatted with me while we drank our cappuccini. We talked about coffee here and in America, my three sons, his daughter, Italy in 1962 and Italy now. His name was Angelo. He was about fifty-five with light brown hair thinning at the top, beginning to show a bit of gray at his temples. He was an ordinary man; in detective novels he would be described as having average height, average build and last seen wearing an average brown suit. No matter how well tailored or how trim a man may be, when he wears a brown suit, he dissolves into the background. Brown just doesn't have the flair that navy or black does.

He seemed an innocuous person with whom to share a few moments over coffee. He had a nice smile and tried to teach me to pronounce my own name with a lovely rolled "R." We laughed at my efforts.

He had been a barista or perhaps an owner, it wasn't clear, but he developed heart trouble and tending bar was stressful. Certainly my barista, the dancer, had explained one day that the reason I hadn't seen women bartenders in Rome was because it was too stressful for them. Maybe not in Rome, I thought, but I'd seen women working the bars elsewhere. Could it be that a male guild kept them out of Rome? I merely smiled, knowing my comments wouldn't change his beliefs.

There was something puzzling about Angelo. He said his wife was English yet he knew no more than a couple English words. Had he learned nothing from her? Then he went on to explain that he and his wife were like sister and brother, very close, but no longer lovers. *Ah si.*

Ever since she became fifty and could not have more children, she developed rashes all over her body. He said her sole concern in life was to find the right cream for her skin. He thought it was all psychological. It was nice to be comprehending his words but disappointing to see where they were leading.

It was time to leave. My plans that day were to explore Trastevere; he offered to give me a lift.

"No grazie."

He said he knew Trastevere well.

"No Grazie."

Finally, I said I would be meeting a friend, but he insisted that there would be no trouble; he would only give me a ride. Methinks he protested too much. I walked out the door; he followed. Firmly shaking his hand, I said thanks and walked away leaving him standing beside his auto.

It was a shame; it might have been a lovely day. It might have been a chance to speak and learn more Italian. He might have shown me parts of the city that I'd never find on my own. It might have been a disaster.

⁓

That was the last time I saw my bar. The following year I dropped by; I was looking forward to being recognized by the barista and the cashier. They were superficial connections, but they felt good. When I rounded the corner, something was wrong. The glass windows and door were larger and surrounded by a wide frame of stark, polished chrome. Brassy letters announced some catchy name. Inside too, the place had been remodeled. My "friends" were gone. The ghastly, plastic mural of Niagara Falls that always amused me had vanished. The entire place was sleek and sassy. It was disappointing. It was supposed to be an improvement, but I wondered if I would have frequented this sterile place while staying at Simonetta. The cashier seemed grim and the barista didn't even look up as I entered. I was so surprised, I don't recall turning around to leave. An unseen force pushed me backward out the door; I never returned to that corner of Rome.

It was a long walk from the station area to Ponte Fabricio, the oldest bridge across the Tevere, the Tiber. Fabricio goes halfway across the river to stop in the middle of the small island called Isola Tiberina. Tiber Island is shaped like a ship with its prow facing north, and a hospital of some kind has been on the island since 154 A.D.—originally for sick slaves, now for pregnant women. A second bridge called Cestio goes on across the river to a unique section of Rome, Trastevere—Across the Tevere.

Trastevere is on the same side of the river as the Vatican. On the map, it fits inside a bump formed by a curve in the river just below Saint Peter's complex. It's a small area with a long history. It wasn't a part of Rome until the Emperor Augustus decided to incorporate it about 12 B.C. Some natives claim to be descendants of pure Roman stock which they say goes all the way back to Horatius and those who defended the city from Etruscan invasions. Some old timers even boast of never crossing the river.

Since medieval days, the area had been crumbling and pretty much forgotten, but recently, affluent Romans have noticed its possibilities. Renovations are making changes that threaten to destroy its charm. I always fret that improvements will ruin my discoveries. It's an affliction of travelers; no matter what the economic or social needs of the local citizens, once a favorite spot has been claimed, we want it to stay the same. Fighting change is impossible anywhere, of course, and especially here, because Rome *is* change.

Two great churches are in the map's curve called Trastevere. Most people find their way easily to Santa Maria in Trastevere;

with its fifth-century A.D. mosaics shimmering on the facade. An inviting fountain is in the center of the piazza surrounded by steps where people sprawl in the sun or dip handkerchiefs in the cooling water. Patricia and I enjoyed a glass of wine at an outside cafè one evening letting the mosaics dazzle us as they reflected light from cleverly placed spotlights. It's one of the most beautiful old churches in Rome. Inside gold is all over the carved ceiling. Once, just when I began to admire the thirteenth-century mosaics in the apse by Pietro Cavallini, a determined padre shooed everyone out into the sunshine. It was siesta and no arguing was allowed.

In an alley which led away from the Piazza of Santa Maria in Trastevere, I grabbed one of three tiny tables spilling out of a small cafè. Across the narrow passageway from my table, two elderly women hollered to each other. One leaned from her window three floors up and the other stood on the street. They argued a bit and then the street woman walked away shaking her head in disgust. Five minutes later the window woman shuffled down wearing worn slippers made of thick, crushed felt and a shapeless cotton house dress. She carried a plate of food for the cat loitering about. It seemed the two old women were sisters living out their lives together in that picturesque place; they kept fit by climbing their stairs and arguing over who feeds the cat.

Moving on to a nearby piazza called San Cosimato, I found a shady bench and watched boys kicking a soccer ball. The ball came uncomfortably close to my head several times. Finally, they picked up their ball and left. The idea of kids playing in the piazza is nicer than their actually being there.

Santa Cecilia, the other famous church of Trastevere, is a larger complex and more difficult to find than Santa Maria. There are endless opportunities for special experiences in Rome, and on my way to Santa Cecilia, I had a sweet one when I rang the buzzer at the tiny church of San Benedetto. It is known as the smallest Romanesque church in Rome. The year before when I'd tried this same buzzer, a cranky response had come from an old nun leaning out of an upper window, *"No, no, torna un'altra volta."* No, no, return another time, and she slammed the shutters closed. This time, a wizened little nun poked her head out of an upper window to say *"Un momento,"* and came down with a smile.

This energetic woman had a pointed little face with a small nose coming forward like a sharp beak over her thin lips. Her large squarish teeth presented an interesting composition, but she literally twinkled as she bragged that the church was one thousand years old. She was obviously proud of her church. Except for her vitality, I would have thought she too was a thousand years old.

Most of the pillars had different capitals and she explained they'd been found here and there. *"I Romani usano tutti,"* the Romans use everything, I replied, probably not using proper idiomatic Italian, but she laughed in a high fluttery voice and her eyes went all crinkly. I fell instantly in love. She spoke Italian fast and I asked her to please speak more slowly; she tried, but it just wasn't in her. She said she could speak a bit of French but English was too hard, so with nods and smiles of good will, we managed.

The frescoes were old and the mosaic marbles underfoot were beautiful, possibly done by the Cosmati brothers. When I said they were similar to the pavements in San Clemente, she said solemnly that hers were older. Then she bragged that the bell tower was the smallest in Rome, that the bells still ring at eight every weekday morning and nine on Sundays. It was time to go; both our hands overlapped each other's in a warm handshake. We parted, each feeling rewarded by the encounter.

The buildings and streets in Trastevere are fascinating and have the feel of a village. Ordinary buildings were softly prettified with ivies and flowering vines trained to flow across them. This might be the area in which to live. Trastevere is getting too expensive, I thought, but as long as I am dreaming...

Finally, I found the big church/monastery complex of Santa Cecilia. The large courtyard was pleasant, and while waiting for opening time, I strolled around a mammoth, white classical vase brought from an old pagan temple. A disgruntled nun came to open the doors at four o'clock. Was she crabby because she had to weave the wool for the pope's pallium (one of the important duties of Santa Cecilia's nuns) or because she didn't get to weave it? She bustled about setting up a table to sell tickets to see the crypt. A notice on the wall announced that Cavallini's mosaics and frescoes were only available on Tuesdays and Thursdays at ten thirty in the morning. I looked around briefly and decided to leave; surely, next time a happier nun would be in charge.

The clouds were drifting, a soft breeze lifted my spirits as I luxuriated at an outside table in Trastevere with my feet on a chair and sipped a creamy cappuccino. If it weren't for the large pots of privet hedges in front of me, I would have been sharing the narrow street with a garbage truck collecting refuse from a market across the way. Cars were trying to come through this street already constricted by parked cars on the other side. Because of the truck, there was no room to move yet they edged up at defiant angles and honked at each other impatiently. Behind a wheel, it seems every Italian forgets all the politeness learned from their Mamma and Babbo. In line at a shop or in traffic, they want to be first. It's their disease. They will smile and crash the line right in front of me at ticket windows, banks or at the post office. Once I'd had enough at the train station when I man cut in front of me. I blurted out in English, "No, no, it's my turn!" The "gentleman" understood, smiled, and politely took one minuscule step back; of course, he did not move to the end of the line. It's their way; maybe they think we Anglos are foolish to line up single file wherever we go.

Romans, more than other Italians I've seen, seem pathologically worried that someone might get the better of them. Maybe it's a need to appear invulnerable but when confronted, they usually back down with grace. Certainly, appearance is a big thing. No matter what economic strata they find themselves in, they manage to look smashing in immaculate, stylish clothes, up-to-date hairdos, flawless makeup and manicures, both men and women. It's easy to feel dumpy and intimidated about appearance here. I keep reminding myself my style was chosen on purpose in order to be as inconspicuous as possible. Moving about unnoticed is more convenient, and the older I get, the easier it is to be invisible. Occasionally, an elegant woman causes me to think I should try to be more like her. Then when I see an elegant man, I think, if I'd be more like her, he would notice me. But, my next thought is, what would I do with him? Still, one never loses the desire for approval—life's little paradox.

It was good to relax and watch the anxious drivers in front of me. Enough musing about vulnerability and elegance, I was brought up short by a teenaged whippersnapper who marched out of the bar to tell me I couldn't put my feet up. How could my stockinged feet hurt a chair? I pointed to my shoeless feet resting on top of a newspaper, but it was no go. Appearance again. Would a prospective customer pass by the bar because of my feet? Okay, it was their turf and their standards, I'd respect their rules.

↤

CHAPTER THIRTY-THREE

Rome's water system. Mrs. Stone and Me on Gianicolo Hill?
A liberating dream. My dream street.
Talking statues. Mapos. How to cross a Roman street.
Roman brawns ala carte.

WHERE *IS* THAT MARVELOUS OVERLOOK I'D SEEN YEARS and years ago? One possibility would be to take a city tour, but I want to find it on foot. A detailed map shows a route that goes through Trastevere past Santa Maria in Trastevere and then to a street called Via Glorioso. When I get there, Via Glorioso turns out not to be a street at all but a flight of steep steps—formidable ones. Only one other person is on them far up ahead. If that little nun can do it with her heavy skirts so can I.

At the top, a sign points to *Fontana Paola*, Paul's Fountain, named for the pope who restored the ancient water conduits in the seventeenth century. Pope Paul V combined some old conduits into the Acqua Paola and then ordered the creation of this overblown, baroque fountain head. His name is blazoned across its pediment. These days, the water system of the entire city is managed by Signora Luisa Cardilli Aleisi, but her name is nowhere to be seen.

For centuries, people have claimed the water in their area of town is the best water in town. Some coffee bars make grandiose claims about the water they use for making their superior coffee. Today, all water runs below the surface; half is brought by a modern system from mountains north of the city, but the other half still comes through the old aqueducts. Connoisseurs really can't be sure they are tasting their own because any part of the total inflow could be sent to any other part of the city according to its need. Signora Aleisi decides. Nevertheless, neighborhood experts cling to their beliefs.

The ancient water system was truly a marvel. Water came through cement-lined, sloping tunnels and then through conduits lifted high across the plains on top of magnificent stone-built arches. The water was protected from dust and insects and arrived as pure as when it left the hillsides. Ernest Hauser tells of the ancient water system in *Italy, A Cultural Guide.* He consulted a journal kept by Frontinus, a Roman inspector of waterworks in the first century A.D. Frontinus thought the Acqua Claudia and the Anio Novus, started by the mad Caligula and finished by his uncle Claudius in 52 A.D., brought the sweetest water. The Claudia had nine miles of arches and one can see their beautiful ruins from the train going south of Rome. The Anio Novus was the longest (59 miles) and the highest (109 feet). Around 100 A.D. these two merged just outside the city gates and formed a single bridge with one conduit on top of the other.

Rome's nine aqueducts supplied the city and suburbs with 58 million gallons a day, which is equal to the amount of water carried by a 30-foot-wide, 6-foot-deep river moving at 1.7 miles per hour. These dry statistics illustrate how serious the Romans were about guaranteeing themselves pure, refreshing water. They used huge amounts of water for public baths, for countless fountains and for mock naval battles staged in flooded arenas. For personal use, the waters were caught in cisterns and piped to tanks installed in almost every house. Truly amazing, and we think we are so modern and sophisticated.

~

The view from Pope Paul's monument is excellent, but it's not *the* view I'm looking for. Surely a bit farther will do it. I follow another winding road leading higher and higher through a shady park. A long walkway leads to a statue of Garibaldi. This is it. Yes, this is the very spot on the famous western hill called Gianicolo that I've been idealizing for thirty years, and it is just as spectacular as I remembered. My timing is perfect. The sun is at my back and the city is spread below. Hundreds of others are here too participating in Rome's golden show. It's like a big party. I could see where most people had probably driven up from the other side of the hill.

Logic tells me the glow comes from the sun's reflection off the domes and buildings, but something else whispers that it comes from past splendors locked in those old travertines and yellowed marbles.

People jostle for position along the wall to take the best pictures and laugh and point to landmarks here and there. The "wedding cake" shines brilliantly white. Cars and buses are probably still hurtling themselves at each other from those seven streams of traffic down below. Up here, coffee and snacks are for sale; pony rides are available; an Italian style Punch and Judy show is in progress—they call it *Pulcinella*. All the joys of a Sunday in the park are here for the taking.

A striking young man has been following me discreetly—so much so that at first I hardly take notice. As I approach the main piazza he is there in the background; as I walk over to look out from various vantage points on both sides of the hill, he is still there; up to the coffee shack for an espresso, he is there. Not absolutely certain he is following me, I pretend not to see him. He is well dressed, well groomed and gorgeous. Then I know. He knows I know. How interesting.

When I truly ignore him, he disappears. Good. That's what I want, isn't it?

Yes, but it is almost disappointing to have the game over so soon. It wouldn't take much to continue it: an innocent question about Garibaldi, about Rome, anything would do. Images of Tennessee Williams' *The Roman Spring of Mrs. Stone* come to mind. My bank account couldn't support him as hers did, but I have kept my dignity—something she lost in the end.

It's incredible but occasionally I have a day when I struggle with time, not worrying about the lack of it but rather how to fill it. There's more in Rome than I could ever see on a trip or a lifetime. It's as if I have to justify the trip to myself. Old voices nag about wasting time, wasting money, being selfish and self indulgent. Remembering my plan for the day usually sends the voices packing, but sometimes I have to step up to the mirror and say, "It's okay!" If only I could learn to visit Italy as they did in Forrester's *A Room with a View.* They strolled, they looked, they rested, they changed for a proper dinner and moved with measured steps, and yet here I was thinking about adding a complex self-guided walk to my day *after* I finished at Villa Giulia. Foolish woman. That immense museum was more than enough for one day, not only for the feet but for the brain. Yet, the pesky fiend on my shoulder was scolding again about making every moment "worthwhile." Freud may have been right, one does need work for fulfillment, maybe even on vacation.

If I lived here, I'd join an art support or music group; I'd volunteer my services. It would be a way to meet like-minded people. Then, at the end of the day, I could go back to my quiet apartment on Via del Governo Vecchio or in Trastevere feeling involved and justified. It's hard being a traveler—it's hard alone—and it's hard to do it right. Having some sort of goal for the day helps alleviate the need to justify my good fortune to be here. Tomorrow, I promised myself, as I turned out the light, would be done a la Forrester.

An unpleasant dream woke me just before dawn. There were many problems to solve and suddenly a dreadful creature crawled on my back, a huge tarantula. It changed from my back to someone else's. To avoid the terror, I must have distanced myself. I tried to warn the other person. *Listen carefully, trust me, this is a matter of life and death. Take your jacket off. Slowly, slowly, smoothly and when I say the word, fling it far away. Ready? Do it NOW!*

I awoke to a hot, stuffy room and felt miserable. Was it time to leave? I lay looking for an answer. The dream was telling me to throw something away. At last, I knew it had told me to throw away feelings of guilt for wasting my time by leaving my parents to come to Italy. Then I heard the sound of blessed rain. I ran to open wide the window and felt stifled no more. The air was energizing; it would be a fine day; it would be a fine trip.

Via Governo Vecchio would be the street for my dream apartment, I thought. Except for a few cyclists, it seemed to be a walking street. Some of the houses were built in the 1400s and some in the 1500s. They were in various states of repair but looked solid and graceful. They were just plain pleasing to the eye. Would our new houses look this good after five hundred years? Silly question.

One 1400 house had arched windows and doors; the travertine molding that divided the various floors was faded and chipped, yet it gave a silvery definition to the facade.

On the fourth floor of another house, there was a loggia—I go crazy for loggias. I could see iron hooks for stringing laundry. How quickly laundry dries in Rome; if I lived here and had a loggia, I could forget about installing a dryer. Live in noisy Rome? Yes indeed. In one of those thick-walled buildings with an inside courtyard open to the sky and a view of one of Rome's golden domes, why not? The courtyard would be quiet and cool with a fountain running; there would be broken pieces of pillars and statues lying about, ivy and geraniums would creep over the rough edges. Yes, I could handle that. I could withstand the red tape and bureaucracy to get it organized. It would take hours, even days, standing in lines dealing with irritated petty clerks, but in the end I would be situated in the heart of the eternal city. All roads lead to Rome, and, if I should ever want to leave, they also go out.

In the heart of Rome, hardly any houses stand alone as they once did because in 1475 Pope Sixtus IV decreed that buildings must be brought together. He said, "dark alleys harbored thieves and ruffians." Sometimes I can spot where they were patched together to close up the narrow alleys; a lot of living space was wrenched out of those joinings. Before the decree, there had been hundreds of porticos and loggias on the street level with marble columns supporting them. Now, when houses in this historic area are renovated to make luxury apartments, if a column is discovered, it's kept embedded right there to give character to the finished plain brick or stucco facade.

Number thirty-nine's windows were open and the ceilings could be seen. They were stripped of all decoration. It looked worn out and completely abandoned. According to a posted sign, thirty-nine had been held by banks for more than a year awaiting restoration. Supposedly a radical feminist group was squatting inside, but there were no signs of life. None. Directly across is number 123; the numbers on opposite sides of the street don't correspond logically. If I lived here, it could be confusing to visitors finding my apartment, but since it looks nothing like a modern subdivision, I could point out distinguishing landmarks.

The design of 123 from the early 1500s had once been attributed to Bramante because it used alternating concave and convex shapes to catch and reflect light, one of his trademarks. The Doric pilasters on the facade alternated with round-topped windows, a nice touch. That might be a nice place to live. Not far away number 118 had a plain facade and pointed windows built in the 1400s. Number 121 with square windows framed in travertine and topped with pediments was from the 1600s. I couldn't decide which I would choose. Eliminating the one from the 1600s with the square windows, it would be either the pointed windows of the 1400s or the round windows with pilasters of the 1500s. The best part of walking alone is that I don't have to worry that such details might bore my companion. The scene I envision might be something like this:

"This street is boring, why are we looking at these old buildings?"

"Why don't you go back to that cute bar we just passed? I'll join you in a jif."

"I don't remember where it is; I better stay with you," she would sigh as she leaned against the wall only to jerk forward to brush dust from her new mauve leather jacket.

I'd sigh too knowing I might as well forget about the pointed windows of the 1400s or the round ones of the 1500s.

At times it *is* lonesome traveling alone, but I converse well with myself. Italians talk to themselves too. As they walk along, they gesture as they make a point to themselves. It's not only the elderly who do it, and for the first time, I don't feel silly about my life-long habit. In Rome, there's also a tradition of "talking statues" where messages are placed on them to discuss politics or local neighborhood concerns. These comments are usually written anonymously, but the "talking statue" in Piazza Pasquino just off Piazza Navona had a notice tacked on it signed by students from a local middle school complaining that the chairs in their cafeteria were decrepit. They pleaded with the community to do something. For a few hundred years, Romans have used this third-century sculpture of Menelaus as a bulletin board. How Roman it is to attach a modern message to an ancient statue.

Menelaus had been Pietro Aretino's launching pad for his caustic remarks about the rich and famous of the sixteenth century. His wit led to his own riches and fame. He was a close friend of Titian, the great Venetian painter, who called him a *condottiere*—a gangster chief—of literature. Aretino was known internationally as the "Scourge of Princes" because he wrote scathing articles about the high and mighty. He wrote public letters to popes and kings, and they answered him! According to Thomas Caldecot Chubb who wrote *Aretino: Scourge of Princes,* "He was the first blackmailer, and the first journalist, and the first publicity man."

At Piazza Navona I bought stamps in a tiny gift shop specializing in stationery, pens, etc. One could buy cards and stamps, write them at a nearby table while sipping coffee, then drop them in the red mailbox attached to the wall outside the shop. How convenient. I can't help but wonder what favors were exchanged to get a mailbox located at the front door.

For lunch, the guidebook sent me to a pleasant restaurant called *Il Giardinetto* on my favorite street, Via del Governo Vecchio. The Little Garden was filled with flowers: huge bouquets on the serving bar; small ones on each table; and the covered patio was filled with ferns and more flowers. The prices were just as reasonable as other suggestions in the guidebook, and there was a bidet in the ladies room. The bread was superb, the house wine was fine and their Penne L'Arrabiata was spiced perfectly. Simple good taste, lots of fresh flowers, and white linens made it a triple treat. The owner's name sounded Arabic; I wondered if he were independently wealthy and simply wanted to run an elegant, inexpensive restaurant. No, no one ever operates at a loss on purpose; whatever the financial situation, I hoped he'd make a go of it.

Once again I was staring up at the beautiful houses on Governo Vecchio thinking for sure this would be the place for me, right here in Rione V. Occasionally, I saw a marble plaque embedded in a building with Rione V or Rione XVIII identifying one of twenty-two civic districts harking back to the days of the Roman Empire. During the Middle Ages, these divisions were almost fiefdoms. Then in 1143, when the modern city government was established, they were reorganized into fourteen Rioni, twelve on the east bank, one on the island and one in Trastevere. They serve as districts for postal delivery now.

Just imagine that the year 1143 marks the beginning of modern city government. This idea tickles my history bones having grown up in the middle of Nebraska where the city fathers of my hometown tore down worthless structures whose only sin was that they were fifty or sixty years old. Those "worthless" buildings happened to be the only ones in town with some notion of style: the old high school made of gorgeous red sandstone; a stately brick courthouse designed on Italianate lines; and the last to go was a red stone, turreted, Victorian charmer called the Midway Hotel.

Here they built with permanence in mind; it was as much for their souls, I think, as for practicality. There was a time when old buildings in Rome were cannibalized, and pieces were taken out to build new buildings, but, thankfully they are now preserved, not only for tourism but because their own spirits benefit from living and working among these structures. It might be more comfortable to live in a brand new building, but no, it must be here on Governo Vecchio with no new buildings in sight. A walk-up would be fine, the daily exercise would be good, and it must open onto a courtyard. If I wanted to watch the passing parade, I'd go down to the street and have a coffee.

I could take part in the evening passeggiata which sometimes leaves me feeling lonely, but if I lived here, there would be familiar faces from the neighborhood out and about. It wouldn't take long. One only has to patronize a bar or little market a few days in a row to establish a comfortable rapport. There would be no need for a car, it would be a handicap because the streets are too narrow, too crowded and offer too many confrontations. Confrontations are one thing with which I'd probably always struggle. As a traveler, it's easy to avoid them, but as a resident, I would have to face up to them if I wanted anything done. With an improved command of the language, I might even participate in a few brouhahas.

~

For the first two or three days at Pensione Simonetta I didn't unpack everything expecting to move to a single room any morning, but soon I realized I'd been living on tenterhooks for naught. It's extra work for the hotel management to make a transfer, and they don't bother unless necessary. I enjoyed a double the entire three weeks, another lesson to remember.

A nasty cold struck. At first I panicked because it is frightening to be ill away from home. After loading up on fruit from the

A possible apartment in the heart of ancient Rome?

market, I stayed in bed all the next day, and dear Maria, the house-keeper, brought me a cup of hot tea. Early in the evening I went out for hot soup and chamomile tea at the neighborhood trattoria. The proprietress recognized me and hovered a bit. With rest and sympathy, by the second day I could breathe again.

A good thing came from having a cold, the wonderful *mapo*. When I brought lemons back from the market to make a hot drink with sugar packets saved from restaurants, I discovered they weren't lemons at all, they were mapos. Mapos are a cross between a mandarin orange and a grapefruit. The name is simply a combination of the first two letters of MAndarino (mandarin) and POmpelmo (grapefruit). Their tart sweet flavor is delicious, but the best part is when I peel a mapo, it's as if all the perfumes of Arabia infuse the air. It's as if I'm walking among lemon blossoms dipped in vanilla.

~

As I lay resting, I considered the racket of auto horns and revving engines as they passed beneath my window. Roman drivers do use their horns. Once, I saw a man standing beside his car with the door open holding his hand on the horn. Someone had double parked beside him, not unusual, but he wanted out. Since he was parked legally—this time—he was terribly righteous about it all. He honked for two or three minutes, and just as his horn began to give out, a stubby-legged, bald-headed fellow came running out of the "Sexy Movie" across the street and drove his offending car away.

Certainly there are diverse feet on accelerators and perverse hands on horns, but in all seriousness, the Romans' driving skills are impressive. Drivers must dodge pedestrians, who tend to ignore *all* signs *all* the time. There are many difficult intersections without traffic lights. Americans would be petitioning city hall in droves. For all I know, the Romans may petition too, but after 2,000 years of practice, the Roman bureaucrats know how to resist.

At those difficult intersections, I must step out with authority and trust the excellent Roman drivers. My eyes negotiate with their eyes, not because they are out to get me, but because they must weave around me as well as the other pedestrians. I must walk steadily with confidence. I see them, they see me. I keep the same pace, I calculate their rate of speed as they calculate mine. Timing is all. It is a weaving, jostling, maneuvering action that everyone gets into, and it works. A sure way to cross safely is beside an elderly person. Or, one can spot someone who knows what they are doing and become their shadow. After playing shadow a few times, one soon becomes a veteran.

I've seen several minor scooter-to-scooter accidents and some near misses with autos, but nothing worthy of emergency action so why is it all day and all night one hears the whee-whah, whee-whah of the emergency *polizia* or *ambulanzia*? Are there that many emergencies or are the police merely hurrying to their favorite bar for coffee and a brioche?

Myriad cars and scooters fill the Roman air with their melodies: Vespas; big motorbikes including Suzukis and Hondas; city buses and tour buses; streetcars (which don't clang but do rumble); and a few old-fashioned Fiat 500s wheezing like lawn mowers. Add to those tunes, the whistling car alarms that everyone in the world ignores, and the cell phones chirping like birds. Up and coming young Romans have these *telefonini* glued to their ears as they wend their way in and out of the narrow streets to big deals. These walking telephones are invariably shod in beautifully made, highly-polished shoes.

When I felt better, I went to a brightly lit, working class eatery recommended by my guidebook called Luciano's. The food was good, plentiful and healthful. Healthful if the customer so chooses because, except for the occasional fixed-price tourist menus, everything in Italy is ala carte. Most customers at Luciano's were blue-color workers, and it was fascinating to see what the average laborer ordered after a hard day. Along with wine or beer and sturdy bread, but no butter, they ordered salads and veggies—lots of them. Yes, they ordered meat and dessert too, but dessert is often fruit rather than cake or pie, in fact, on many menus, *frutta* means dessert.

Beyond food choices, Italian brawns seem no different from ours. What they really want is lots of food served quickly and for little money. One, across the table from me, hunched over his plate and shoveled it in *alla grotesque*. They were curious about me but more interested in packing it in. They might use a napkin if its handy, but the back of their sleeve works too. The basic difference is that they've grown up eating fresh veggies and salads, and away from Mamma's cucina, they still do.

A fracas was going on across the dining room; the manager was trying to keep it to a low rumble. A group of young men had come in to sit at a long table, and he spent about a month or two hovering over them and another month on the telephone. Was he calling for help? Four times I asked the young waiters for my check; they kept saying, "*Si, si, un momento.*" Evidently they weren't allowed to handle money. Finally the manager came with the bill and collected my money. I would not frequent Luciano's again.

⤸

CHAPTER THIRTY-FOUR

Exclusive Via Giulia. Three Caravaggios in one chapel.
Elusive Sant'Ivo.
Back to Pomezia: A family affair.
A Benny Hill breakfast.

A STREET NAMED VIA GIULIA IS SURELY IN ONE OF THE
choicest areas of Rome. It is a long way from the Etruscan
Museum in the old Villa Giulia built by Pope Julius III. In the
1500s, another pope, Pope Julius II, the same one who forced
Michelangelo to paint the Sistine ceiling, hired Bramante to construct a long street leading toward the Vatican. It was considered a
major improvement over the dark, winding streets left from the
medieval period. Julius II was interested in opening up the city to
develop broad thoroughfares for his grand processions from one
pilgrimage church to another. Ironically, however, the medieval
streets that are left are the ones that charm us the most today.

Manicured palaces, antique stores and attractive art galleries
line Via Giulia. The best clue that this is an exclusive area is its lack
of traffic. Once, while waiting to cross the street along the Tiber, I
saw a policeman stopping some cars from taking Via Giulia which
leads to the Farnese area. A woman was heading for Via Giulia in
a snappy little black sports car. The policeman stopped her and
she tried her best to convince him of something, maybe she'd forgotten her pass. She smiled, she cocked her head coquettishly, she
talked fast with much animation. He refused to let her enter. She
then lost her composure and argued arrogantly. Still he wouldn't
give in. For a split second, I thought she was going to dart down
Giulia anyway, her body language signaled the temptation. She
resisted the urge and pulled back into the main stream heading

north. Maybe she did forget her pass. Maybe she wanted to cut through to save time. Whatever it was, he held fast, and I wanted to cheer bravo for him.

Things seem to work on special favors in Italy. If they cannot talk their way into whatever permission they desire, as in her case, they shrug their shoulders and go on to the next possible conquest. If successful, she might have bragged to friends, but in this case, I suspect she would have kept certain favors a secret hoping to cultivate them into permanent privileges. Yes, privilege seems to be how things work best. Has this developed because of bureaucratic tangles which work their way down to whether an ordinary person can get a telephone installed this year or next? Or, have these tangles developed because of the basic nature of its citizens? Traveling alone gives me more time to observe what goes on around me and speculate—a favorite pastime anywhere, and especially in Italy.

Private elegance and privilege are hidden behind old, crumbling walls along Via Giulia, and at dusk, I can see into the upper levels and into their sumptuous rooms. Some are lit by sparkling chandeliers and others seem to have indirect lighting carefully placed to reveal richly carved, wooden ceilings painted or gilded and sometimes even frescoed.

The back of Palazzo Farnese is on Via Giulia and I can peer through breaks in stone walls and iron fences protecting its lush expanse of trees and stylized gardens. Near the Farnese a graceful, vine-covered bridge crosses over Via Giulia; it was designed by Michelangelo. He had in mind more grandiose plans for the bridge, not unusual for old Michele. It was to extend above and across the river all the way to the Vatican. Power-hungry Julius loved Michelangelo's lofty ideas too; in some ways they were two of a kind. They both had more plans in their heads than could be achieved in one lifetime and both were called by the same nickname, *Il Terribilità*. It was almost a term of endearment meaning not so much the terrible one as the formidable one or the extraordinary one.

In the front of the immense Farnese Palace, French officials strut in and out and guards are ever present with submachine guns. It has been the French Embassy since 1635 when Pope Urban VIII, a Barberini, struck some kind of deal with the French allowing them to rent the palace for one lira per year for ninety-nine years. Evidently, the agreement has been renewed or re-negotiated.

Few churches in Italy label their famous art works and fewer still proclaim them from the outside, so unless you already know where to look, you will miss some spectacular masterpieces. But, a sign is in front of the French church, San Luigi dei Francesi, which announces the three Caravaggios within. They are all in one chapel. What a trove.

This trio of pictures tells the story of St. Matthew. *The Calling of St. Matthew*, is extraordinary. There are some who said Caravaggio's work was too dramatic with its intense contrasts of light and shadows; those folks probably criticize Giorgione and Rembrandt too. Others said his scenes were not noble enough, for example, in *The Calling*, Caravaggio chose the moment when Jesus and Peter found Levi in a common, rather shabby room with his assistants counting the proceeds of the day.

The beam of light coming from a window "offstage" travels along Jesus' arm directly to the face of Levi, the tax collector, who instantly becomes Matthew the Apostle. The young fellow sitting beside Levi, also receives the impact of the mystical light. We just know his life will never be the same either. Another young fellow looks up. His face is turned from us, but he's aware that something is happening because he leans forward. Peter seems to be gesturing to him to stay calm. Matthew's other two assistants never stop counting their money. Symbolically, this could mean they have rejected the chance to follow Christ for eternal life. In this dynamic moment, nothing seems to happen, but, we know that Matthew will rise and follow Jesus.

The other two paintings in this chapel are stunning as well. Opposite *The Calling* is *The Martyrdom of Saint Matthew*, and it is exactly opposite in feeling. The *Calling* is a moment frozen in time whereas *The Martyrdom* is an explosion of action. Again,

Caravaggio has picked a striking moment to snare the viewer's attention. Here, the executioner is about to pierce Matthew with a sword when an angel swoops down to hand the "Palm of Martyrdom" to Matthew. All the others pull back in fright. In the far background, a person moving away turns to look back at the scene—it is a self portrait. The light glares down on the executioner leaning over the fallen Matthew who seems to be the same model as the Matthew in *The Calling* but made to look older.

The third painting is over the altar of the chapel and faces the spectators straight on. It is *The Inspiration of Saint Matthew,* or sometimes called *Saint Matthew and the Angel.* It may represent inspiration, but Matthew is not in a contemplative pose. As if he didn't have time to sit properly, he leans over the table with his knee on a stool about to tip over. He writes in this precarious position while the angel dictates the scripture over his shoulder. Again, the same model was used for Matthew, but this time he is well aged. How fortunate to have these closely-linked paintings all together in one place.

A soft-spoken, refined German guide brought her group of tourists to see the Caravaggios, and she fed the light meter. It's an unfortunate bias I admit, but this group was well behaved for Germans. When Italians mistake me for a German, I make it clear that I'm an American and am almost always treated with more warmth. Italians like us; one reason they feel sympathetic may be because they have so many relatives living in the States. My dark bulky skirt, black wool socks and clumpy German sandals probably lead them to think I'm German. If pressed, Italians would no doubt admit that today's German women are stylish and elegantly dressed, but there must be an unconscious mind-set that says they are a dowdy lot—like me.

Two of Caravaggio's most famous paintings are violent: the *Crucifixion of Saint Peter* and the *Conversion of Saint Paul.* They are both in a chapel in the church Santa Maria del Popolo, at Piazza del Popolo. Caravaggio faced a double challenge on this commission because not only would his paintings flank an altarpiece already frescoed by Annibale Carracci, an established artist of forty years, but because Michelangelo had paired the same two subjects in a chapel at the Vatican.

In Caravaggio's painting, old man Peter has just been nailed to the cross upside down and Caravaggio catches him at the moment when workmen are hoisting the heavy cross upright. He lifts his head up in pain and disbelief. The artist used as his imaginary light source a painted burst of golden rays already on the chapel ceiling called a "glory." The "glory" sends a strong glow onto Peter's and the three workmen's bodies as they emerge from deep shadows. On the opposite wall, the same "light" is used to blind young Saul at the moment when he is struck by a heavenly force and falls from his horse. The animal is magnificent. It turns to look at Saul and lifts its front hoof in order not to crush Saul's leg. Here is another Caravaggio moment. Saul sees Christ and becomes Paul the Apostle.

Caravaggio's paintings were revolutionary then and are startling now because he had the ability to show both the action and the spiritual force behind it—usually in tumultuous ways. Caravaggio lived a turbulent, troubled life himself and died young because of it, but he left powerful religious messages in his art.

On Corso del Rinascimento, the door was open to a large palazzo; it led into a courtyard where a church sat at the back of the enclosed space. The church seemed to be built right into the rear of the building, yet I saw no entrance. I was curious. Later, when I walked around outside to the rear of the building, I grew more curious because there was no sign of a church there either. Both the church, Sant'Ivo della Sapienza and the courtyard were designed by Francesco Borromini in 1642. The entire atrium of the building is graceful; two wings of the palazzo curve around to form connections with the far wall which happens to be part of the church called Sant'Ivo. With porticoes on three sides and the church forming the fourth, it was an intriguing space.

I noticed bees decorating some friezes on the interior balconies and remembered something about the Roman family called Barberini who used bees as their heraldic device. When I asked the gate keeper if this had been a Barberini palazzo he gruffly said, "*No, no, e` Sapienza.*" No, no, it is Sapienza. Sapienza means wisdom or learning. Stupid man. Oh well, he probably thought I was stupid because there is a plaque at the outside entrance that clearly states "Palazzo della Sapienza." Later, I felt vindicated because further study confirmed that Pope Urban VIII, a Barberini, had indeed commissioned Borromini to do this work. It wasn't the guard's ignorance that bothered me; it was his rudeness. Now the bee was in my bonnet to gain access to Borromini's church.

Another year, another autumn day, and the same old energy welled up inside my chest. Unconsciously I held my breath as the train pulled to a stop in Rome. My shoulders hugged my ears, and with a huge sigh I let go.

"I'm home!"

Explain that to kin back in Nebraska.

In spite of being a dump, I returned to Hotel Pomezia because of its location. Around a corner was the market at Campo dei Fiori, and a couple of streets away were Piazza Navona, The Pantheon, and the street of my dreams, Via del Governo Vecchio. A room on an inside courtyard of Pomezia was tranquil even though the decor was just as ugly as ever.

Each morning as I stepped out into the old area of narrow streets and crumbling buildings, a soft blanket of contentment settled around my shoulders. Once, I tried another one-star hotel nearby called Albergo della Lunetta, Hotel of the Little Moon, but I had mixed feelings about Lunetta. First of all, my room was a windowless like a cell, but its door opened onto a quiet inner courtyard. When I looked up, I could see the golden dome of Sant'Andrea della Valle, "Tosca's dome." But, if I dared to look down from the narrow balcony—more like a catwalk—with its thin iron railings flaking with rust, there was a frightening drop to an atrium cluttered with potted plants and ivies. Tosca's bells were pleasant enough, but Lunetta was a strange place in other ways. The dim hallways ran off in various directions. Unlike the hallways at La Mia Casa in Florence, where I felt free to satisfy my curiosity, at Lunetta I felt uneasy and stayed strictly on one path from room to bathroom to lobby.

Maybe I was falling into a rut, but in spite of its faults I kept returning to Pomezia. Sometimes the moody young man at the front desk was friendly and well-groomed and sometimes gloomy and ill-kempt, but I was getting used to him. Once I arrived at Pomezia rather late in the day, and a different young man was at the desk. I was travel weary and his attitude was two hundred per-cent better than the sulky fellow I'd expected. He grabbed my bags and hustled them up to my room for me. That was a pleasant change. Something else had been added that year, a phone was in the room. Right away I called in comfort and privacy to report my location and to find out if all was well at home. For several years, there was a worry that one or both of my elderly parents would be in trouble. George checked on them frequently for me; this time all was well.

Before giving up for the night, I needed to inspect The Campo. My plan had been to sit at an outside table, have a cup of camomile tea and dream about the old buildings huddled around the campo, but the bar I'd had in mind was closed. The aroma of spaghetti car-bonara, rich with garlic and bits of *pancetta,* smoked ham some-what like bacon, drew me to another outside cafè. The green salad served after the pasta was a delicious mixture of piquant greens and fruity olive oil. Satisfied that good pasta and salad were still avail-able in Rome, that the Campo was indeed there with its misshapen buildings and crumbling walls, and that Giordano's dark, martyred shape was still brooding in the center, I slipped off to bed. It sagged so much that it turned up at both ends, but every bone ached from travel exhaustion and I slept like a cork.

The owners of Pomezia were stingy in furnishing their rooms. There were not enough hangars, there was no plug for the wash basin and the lowest wattage possible was in the light bulbs over the sink and beside the bed. The flat ceiling lights in the inside hallways were never all on at the same time and the elderly, worn-out maid borrowed my phone to call down to ask Riccardo to give her more light to do her cleaning. Like many older Italians, she shouted into the phone. Immediately another bulb came on, but later in the day, it was off again. The hotel was not spotless, but the old lady who cleaned must have been in her late seventies, poor, tired dear. She was a love and gave me a clean drinking glass, a couple of hangars, a large towel and a promise of a sink plug. The plug never arrived, but experienced travelers know how to find something to stop up a basin.

A dirty laundry line was strung across a miniature balcony. To the side of this balcony a door opened into a micro space barely able to hold both a shower and a toilet. It was one of those arrangements with no shower curtain so the water from the shower sprays the entire room; I needed to plan ahead. For the first time in ages, I had a room with a private bath. It was a matter of them not having a single without bath available, and I wasn't charged for it—a bargain of sorts.

At first it felt awkward stepping onto a balcony to use the bathroom, but one gets used to anything. In the evenings, there was enough ambient light so I didn't need to announce my intentions to people across the way by flipping the switch. In spite of all, I was delighted to be in Rome once again.

A friend came for a couple of days to stay in Pomezia too. It was fun being Mitch's tour guide for the weekend. As we sat in the church admiring Bernini's *Saint Theresa in Ecstasy*, we noticed a slovenly fellow rise from his kneeling bench in front of us. He shuffled behind our pews, crossed to the other side, and made a great show of piety by kneeling again at a side chapel. Mitch nudged me and I nodded, he was the concierge from our hotel, or was he? When we returned to the hotel, there was our concierge, clean shaven and neatly dressed. We told him we saw someone who looked just like him in the church. His face twisted in a grimace as he rubbed his hand down from the forehead to the chin as if trying to wipe the thought away. It was his twin, he explained; their hotel was a family business. When we asked more about his brother, he became anxious and his English became more and more fractured. Obviously, he didn't want to discuss the matter. At least now we understood why sometimes he seemed intense and sullen and other times effusive and informative. He didn't have a dual personality; there were two of him! The sunny man who had carried my bag and knapsack up the stairs revealed that he was the younger brother, so there were three; I was beginning to wonder if the cleaning woman was their *nonna*, grandmother.

⌒

Breakfast at Pomezia had never been offered before but it seemed to be a new event for the twins. They were proud of their remodeling job across the hall from the crowded reception area. The disadvantage was that their coffee machine remained in the reception area. One couple from Canada was already at a table when Mitch and I entered and soon there were five tables of patrons waiting.

Two large metal pitchers sat on a side table and remained there all the while Riccardo—or was it Claudio?—passed around cups and saucers to all. Then he walked past each table and tossed an empty straw bread basket to each table; then came the bread. With a heavy sigh, it must have been Riccardo, he reached into a big brown paper bag bumping along the floor behind him and doled out two crusty rosettes per person. Moving a little faster, he dropped foil-wrapped butter packets; on another tour, he deposited marmalade in sealed packets; and lastly some chocolate crème packets. Then and only then, did he reach for the metal pitchers, long past any hope of being hot, and poured coffee and tea. As an afterthought he brought knives, butter plates and spoons. Oh Benny Hill, I hope you were watching!

The rosettes were delicious; the huge bag had the name of the excellent bakery just across the street, but it was four feet long and about two and one-half feet wide. There were tons of rosettes; I wondered how fresh our bread would be tomorrow. The rosettes were good the following morning, but the next day was a disaster. It was Sunday. Evidently the bakery was closed and they hadn't planned ahead. They served soft, sliced bread as bad as that white bread back home with its twelve nutrients added for building good health. Why continue this breakfast farce? It wasn't worth the savings. I took Mitch to a pleasant bar two doors away where we had a fresh brioche and a piping hot cappuccino before he left to catch his train.

⌇

CHAPTER THIRTY-FIVE

Sant'Ivo's, a disappointment.
A thrift shop in old Rome. The Mouth of Truth.
Roman Centurions at the Colosseum.
Layered San Clemente. Neglected San Vitale.
A Tennessee Williams play in Italiano.
A Benny Hill supper.
Rome, I still adore you.

AFTER TRYING SEVERAL TIMES DURING TWO DIFFERENT years, I finally got inside Borromini's mysterious church Sant'Ivo, and I was disappointed. To me, the small, private chapel was dull. The focus seems to be entirely on the dome which is all undulating ribs and plaster following Borromini's ideas of integrating decoration into architecture. A noble idea, maybe, but the molded stucco reliefs of uninteresting stars, wreaths, papal insignias and angels worked into the six-sided concave dome offered no inspiration of any kind. Light comes through the six convex windows and floods the pale yellow and white walls with solar warmth, but the effect is anything but warm or spiritual.

According to Peter Gunn in *The Churches of Rome*, Borromini's architecture was considered revolutionary because he ignored the renaissance humanistic principle that a unit—usually the diameter of a column—should be multiplied in the features of a building in proportion to the human scale. Sant'Ivo's is technically elegant I suppose, but I felt nothing and took my leave.

~

Who would have expected a thrift shop on Via del Governo Vecchio? In fact, three shops were all in a row. I poked into the first two finding nothing, but in the third I walked into the middle of the shop and immediately spied my black leather jacket. It was a heavy, biker style that I'd been thinking about for a couple of years. A black biker jacket for grandma? Ridiculous? But, who's going to tell me no?

I'd seen hundreds of beautiful leather jackets, especially in Florence, but they didn't suit. They were either a longish style nipped here, tucked there, or a short military style. Often they were in flowery colors including mauve and pink. This one was a serious garment. It had four front patch pockets with brad fasteners and two more slant pockets hidden beneath the lower ones. It fit like a dream.

As I stood in front of the mirror of the crowded shop, I remembered advice given long ago by a seasoned auctioneer who said, "Always determine your top price *before* entering the heat of battle."

Okay, I thought, "How much am I willing to pay?"

My top price would be 100,000 lire, about $65. Just then, the proprietor came up and asked,

"Do you like it for 15,000 lire?"

Fifteen thousand lire? Ten dollars? He spoke English well, there was no misunderstanding. While paying for it, I told him he must have stolen it for that price. He laughed, but admitted he didn't know exactly where it came from because his "scouts" brought things in. It felt great; the leather was as soft and smooth as butter. Obviously used, the gold taffeta lining would need cleaning, but I could live with it for awhile. It had sturdy, knit collar, cuffs and waistband and would be perfect for jeans and slacks. I walked on air the rest of the day, and later that evening when a chilly breeze stirred through Piazza Navona, I felt smug and toasty in my new purchase.

~

If one counts seven bridges down the river from the flamboyant Ponte Sant'Angelo, Bridge of Saint Angelus, lined with Bernini's huge angels, there is a little no-count bridge called Ponte Palatino. Ponte Palatino comes across from Trastevere and leads directly toward the famous Palatine Hill where Roman patricians lived two thousand years ago. Julius Caesar never lived on the Palatine, but we know Cicero did. From the embankment near the Palatine Bridge, I walked down to a large fountain. It had no angels or sea monsters, just a graceful basin with water flowing over it, but a few yards from this fountain is a circular temple, called Tempio di Vesta. Workers were restoring the pretty little building with its delicate fluted Ionic columns. How many temples to the vestals were there, I wondered? I knew of at least one or two temples standing among the ruins of the Forum. Surely, I thought, this one was too small to be anything but symbolic. The vestals must have lived, studied and performed their duties elsewhere. According to Colleen McCullough in her book *Caesar's Women*, the vestal virgins served several functions for Rome other than staying chaste and tending the sacred fire. One of their crucial duties was to keep records of *all* wills made throughout the entire empire, and, to be discreet about them.

Later I learned this little temple had nothing to do with the vestals. It was built to honor Hercules at the end of the second century B.C., and it may be the oldest *marble* building left standing intact in Rome. It's truly a jewel.

Across the street *La Bocca della Verita*, The Mouth of Truth, gapes waiting to snap at liars' fingers. Originally, the Mouth was a heating apparatus or possibly the end of a canal pipe. The large, stone face with its menacing mouth probably represented the mask of a river god. There are several legends about how it was used, but surely people didn't believe their hand would be cut off or bitten by poisonous snakes if they told a lie. Of course, people were more superstitious then.

It was hard to get close to it because so many wanted to take photos of each other standing with their hand thrust into it. Finally it was my turn; I closed my eyes, stuck my hand in its mouth and whispered to myself, "I *shall* return to Roma." It didn't bite; I would be back!

⟨⁓⟩

Santa Maria in Cosmedin is an old church, I mean old. It feels old and it smells old, but because of its many external restorations, it doesn't look old. The porch, which holds the Mouth of Truth, is from the twelfth century, but inside one can almost hear ancient prayers still being murmured. No one was in the small sanctuary that day, and the quiet was like black velvet. Muffled sounds could be heard from people chattering on the porch or buying souvenirs from the shy, elderly monk in the sacristy, but in the hushed darkness lay another energy.

This sanctum had been built by Greek immigrants who came from Constantinople in the sixth century A.D. Beneath their fifteen-hundred-year-old foundation another temple to Hercules had lain dating back six hundred more years. Yes, in this space, all kinds of old prayers were whispering.

⟨⁓⟩

Standing around the Colosseum were some fellows with red satin capes emblazoned with gold and white filigreed spangles fastened across their shoulders. They wore white, short, pleated skirts showing off tanned, muscular legs. With their plumed helmets and sandals, weren't they the perfect picture of valiant Roman centurions? It might be some sort of festival, and for a moment I wished I had my camera with me. As I drew closer, it was obvious they were posing for tourists, for a fee. It was a clever scam. But, they weren't exactly begging and had gone to some trouble.

⟨⁓⟩

It was clear where my feet were taking me so I went with them and walked past the Colosseum on Via San Giovanni di Laterano toward the layered church of San Clemente. It is one of the few remaining authentic examples of an early Romanesque church in Rome and had intrigued me for a long time. It was closed but at least a sign indicated it would open soon. It seemed a good time to go all the way to the church of San Giovanni di Laterano, Saint John of the Lateran, for which the street is named. Art historians rave about the beautiful cloisters and Cosmati pavements at the

DEANNA HUNT

*One of Bernini's angels lining Ponte Sant'Angelo
as it leads into Castel Sant'Angelo.*

Laterano. When I got there, it was in restoration. This is why a person needs to live in Italy, I whined to myself. There's too much to see for short visits especially with constant restorations and skimpy visiting hours.

The wind had gone out of my sails, and I turned back heavy footed until I saw a cafè set into the front of a triangular building. Cafè tables lounged in the heavy shade cast from a building across the way, and they looked as inviting as a lush oasis must look to a discouraged bedouin. With a slice of tiramisu and a caffè Americano, I'd found an excellent spot for rejuvenation. I watched people until Clemente opened.

I had some notes taken from a nice old book found in an abbey's library set on a small hill in Oregon. Using information from Louis Nolan's book, *The Basilica of San Clemente* published in 1934, I went into the lower depths of the church trying to identify the faded, deteriorating frescoes on the walls, but it was impossible without an expert. I could see several layers as I walked down stone steps passing from the eleventh-century A.D. area at street level to a fourth-century level then to a first-century level, and just below that, a Mithraeum with a monument to Mithra, a god worshiped by Roman soldiers. In 1912 the Mithraeum with its monument and stone benches for worshipers was under about eight feet of water when an Irish priest, then in charge of San Clemente, raised funds and organized its drainage. A tunnel was cut and connected to a large drain on the far side of the Colosseum, about seven hundred yards away and nearly forty feet below the street. From there, the water was directed into the Tiber. The floors have been dry under the church ever since, yet the air felt damp and musty in the lower layers. It was eerie down there because I could see and hear the water roaring beneath the drain covers at my feet.

While below, I came upon an elderly English woman in her 80s. Immediately, I added her to my list of models of how to grow old. She stood with a younger woman in a small niche quietly talking about ritual. They had a candle and needed a match. I had none but agreed with them it was a good place for a ceremony. Were they worshipers of Mithra? It seemed unlikely since bloody Mithra was a favorite of military men.

Each layer of the old church speaks in a different voice, but it's the same story of human longings for spiritual answers.

In the upper part of the church are exquisite Cosmati marble mosaics both on the marble choir and the floor. The Cosmati family of Rome were famous for creating polychrome-marbles and mosaics. They sawed circles and squares of porphyry from classical columns found in the ruins all over Rome. The rich, red porphyry, so prized by the ancient Romans, came from quarries near the Red Sea in Egypt and was known as imperial purple. The green came from the Peloponnese in Greece. The Cosmati school used both kinds in pavements and pulpits and choirs. Other churches in Rome contain their work as well, but in Clemente, they were perfectly preserved. In fact, every inch of San Clemente was a joy to see. In the chapel of Saint Catherine, some experts claim the painting called *The Annunciation* is by Masaccio. Others say not. The truth may never be known because it has suffered from time and too much retouching.

Before leaving San Clemente, I lit a candle for my loved ones—a real one—not one of those electric abominations that had begun to appear everywhere. Smokeless electric candles may prevent damage to art work, but they have no soul.

I stepped out of San Clemente into that dusky glow that comes just before dark when objects are engraved against the Roman sky. Ordinary chimney pots are endowed with a sort of nobility. The Colosseum and the Forum ruins seem to come alive more at twilight than any other time of day. Too soon the glow went away. By the time I made it up the hill to The Campidoglio, it was already dark.

The two palaces facing each other hold the treasures of the Capitoline Museum, and the third palace, Palazzo Senatorio, is now the seat of the Mayor of Rome. It had once been an eleventh century fortress. In the sixteenth century, Michelangelo redesigned it along with the other two buildings to make this gorgeous renaissance space.

As I walked from one museum to another, it was worth the extra time to stop and really look at the facade of the Mayor's office building. The double staircase is majestic in itself, but evidently not quite enough for Michelangelo. Just in front of the split staircase are two fountains, one on each side. Giant second-century statues representing river gods, the *Nile* and the *Tiber* sit reclining in Etruscan poses with their backs to each other. In a recessed area between the two fountains, Michelangelo had intended a mighty statue of Jupiter, but instead, a delicate, porphyry statue of Minerva stands. Brought from Cori she was renamed *Dea Roma*, Goddess of Rome. Old Michelangelo would have preferred a heroic male figure, and as pretty as she is, she does seem too small for the space and easily ignored.

There's probably two months' worth of looking just to see the ancient marbles, never mind the vases, bronzes and paintings. Fragments of the *Gargantua* lie in the courtyard of one palace, and people take pictures of each other measuring themselves beside one of his fingers mounted upright beside a wall. In the courtyard of the other palace another colossal statue reclines; the river god called *Marforio*. Marforio was one of the talking statues of the sixteenth century.

Because of a special computer exhibit about Pompeii, the layout was more confusing than usual and I saw no one to ask for help. Eventually, I spied three guards huddling together. I had to interrupt their discussion of soccer scores to get directions to the permanent collection. Roman copies of Greek works included: *The Dying Gaul*, a stark figure in luminous, polished marble; *The Boy with a Thorn*, another beautiful piece of polished marble; and the Etruscan *Capitoline Wolf*, the symbol of Rome. The bronze wolf is from the sixth century B.C. possibly made by Vulca, an Etruscan sculptor of Veio, the town only fifteen miles from Rome that was one of the first Etruscan cities trampled by the Romans in 396 B.C.

There are some originals, but the majority of the marbles are Roman copies of ancient Greek bronze or marble sculptures. Oh, the little shepherd pulling a thorn from his foot is exquisite. Charming in art books but in "the flesh," he is truly touching. Intent on finding the thorn, his young face is a study in pure concentration.

The hand of Gargantua.

I circled and circled *The Dying Gaul* admiring the detailed lines of the hair, the veins in the hands, the legs and the feet. When no one else was in the room—the guards were far away—I was able

319

to look unabashedly at his penis and scrotum so perfectly detailed. If he is a mere Roman copy, one wonders how the original could have been any better. An excellent collection of Etruscan vases and naughty bronzetti kept me occupied for twenty or thirty minutes, but I needed to save energy to see the paintings as well.

At one end of a room in a prime position was a glowing painting by Caravaggio. It was a young, naked boy sprawled on an animal skin thrown on the ground over a crumple of discarded clothes. His right arm is reaching toward a ram at his left shoulder which seems ready to nuzzle the boy's neck. The youth turns back to look at us over his right shoulder with the boyish pride of having found a new pet. At the same time, there's a subtle sensuousness about his grin as well. It is intriguing. Golden light plays over his velvety body; in the shady background, one can make out a few dark tree trunks. At his feet is a lush green cluster of leaves, possibly grape leaves. It is called *Saint John the Baptist*.

One expert says the painter used the title because the ram represents a sacrificial victim, Christ, and the grape leaves represent wine, the symbol of Christ's blood, all foreshadowed by John the Baptist. One can read many meanings into a work of art, but this one tells a fine story without any explanation.

One of Caravaggio's renditions of *The Gypsy Fortune Teller* was in another room. It is a nice genre painting, but I was surprised to see no moving drama. A story told by a contemporary is more interesting than the actual painting. The story goes that in order to demonstrate that an artist need not study the past or other masters but instead, use nature and people at hand, Caravaggio asked a young gypsy woman on the street to come to his studio. There he had a friend pose in a cavalier outfit holding out his hand for her to read his future.

The museum has many other worthy paintings, but my energy and focus were gone. Before leaving, I did drag myself across that beautiful space to take one more look at Marcus Aurelius astride his mammoth horse. Some things are worth seeing over and over; then I chuckled aloud thinking of Mother who always said,

"Why are you going back to Italy? You've been there."

~

San Vitale, the poor little worn out church I'd passed so often on Via Nazionale was open at last. This small, compact church sits about forty or fifty steps below street level hard by the giant exposition hall of the nineteenth century rising forty or fifty steps *above* street level. What a vivid contrast they make. Ah Rome. It seems she seldom takes anything away. She just rearranges and adds to what is already there.

San Vitale's seventeenth-century carved wooden doors are heavy and beautiful, the ceiling is of carved wood also, but the wall frescoes of landscapes were definitely not beautiful. Some artist had attempted to make the walls appear to have columns, but the trick didn't work. It might have been the poor light or the poor condition of the frescoes. An attendant was shoving his dirty mop around to wipe up wet spots and rearranging buckets set out to catch rain as it fell through leaks in the roof.

Yellowed newspaper clippings tacked on the walls of the porch showed pictures of the pope making a visit nine months before. He was quoted as saying there was a great need to renovate this "treasured sanctuary," one of the oldest in Rome, dedicated in 416 A.D. So far, nothing had been done. I would keep watch and one of these days…

~

Plans had changed radically all day long. I changed buses on a whim and criss-crossed the town. I can't hop on and off at the last minute when I'm traveling with someone, on the other hand, it can be lonesome sometimes. Talking to myself helps and here I feel at home because Italians do it too. Since early childhood, I would clarify ideas and remember plans better if I said them aloud; maybe the same principal works with verbally oriented Italians. Sometimes they gesture to themselves as they walk. While resting on a bench, I noticed a man across the way standing at an open window talking with his phone cradled on his shoulder in order to gesture with both hands. That reminded me of a child on the train with his mother and grandmother. He was about eighteen months old and had tried to get their attention, but they were engrossed and generally ignored him. He began talking to himself in that lovely baby language which imitates grownup words and rhythms. Even more endearing was the way he imitated grownup gestures with his pudgy hands, especially that ubiquitous Italian gesture of holding one's hand palm up and touching the thumb to the tips of the other fingers in a sort of "essence-of-it-all" symbol.

Arsenic and Old Lace was playing at the National Theater; it might be fun to see it in Italian, I thought. There'd be no problem following the plot. But, it had already begun when I reached the box office. In a wild spurt of bravado, I bought a ticket to a Tennessee Williams play, *The Milk Train Doesn't Stop Here Anymore,* maybe because the title was so charming in Italian, *Il treno del latte non si fermo piu' qui.* It was probably a silly stunt on my part but the superb Italian actress, Rossella Falk, had the lead and when I saw her picture outside the theater, I just hurried in to buy a ticket before I lost my courage.

I wore beautiful new boots that evening, but they couldn't atone for my camping jacket with its many pockets. Amidst the fur coats and elegant high heels, I was no match for the fashion parade. Pushing modish thoughts away, I concentrated on the play. It wasn't a familiar one, but Williams' plays are of a type and I hoped to get the spirit of it. Rossella was marvelous and because she was such a good communicator, I understood! The ingenue was terrible and I felt sorry Rossella had to work with her, but for my own performance, I got a gold star.

Normally I avoid the fixed-price tourist menus because the food is often mediocre and I tend to eat too much. But, occasionally I weaken. On one such occasion, I was served a genuine Benny Hill Supper. The moment I ordered the tourist menu, I was hustled to a cramped corner table. Some of the tableware was removed, and my cloth napkin was exchanged for a paper one. Anger started to rise in my throat. I was on the verge of stomping out when I remembered Benny Hill's skit about an English couple in a foreign land who ordered the tourist menu. I stayed to see how this would play out.

Although the waitress almost threw the food at me, it was actually tasty. But, when she tried serving me a mealy, bruised apple for dessert, I said, *"No! Preferisco un'arancia."* No! I prefer an orange. She had not offered me the choice listed on the menu. Grudgingly she brought an orange and it almost rolled onto the floor when she slammed the plate and knife down. At the counter, when I offered my credit card to the proprietor, he asked for cash. I jabbed my finger toward his credit card sign posted in his window. He shrugged probably guessing it would be the card or nothing.

The food wasn't bad but the atmosphere was crude. Men were stuffing their cheeks full of pasta like November squirrels stuff themselves. Unlike those cute little rascals, these munchers talked loudly with their mouths full.

What a noisy city full of noisy, rude Romans. Is it arrogance? Is it to save face? Whatever it is they seem unwilling or unable to smile casually. Starting out in the mornings I vow to do the same, then I forget. Surely a person could smile when meeting you in those instances where first one person sidesteps, then the other and both end in each other's way. No doubt they get sick to death of tourists, but I suspect Romans are ornery by nature even to each other. Rome doesn't feel dangerous so what are they afraid of? No, it's not fear, it's more likely the big city mentality of not wanting to get involved or waste time. People aren't always immediately friendly in little towns either, but that comes from a different source. There, it's more of an insular wariness of outsiders. So why do I love being in Rome? In Italy? Well, besides the beauty, the art, the history, the architecture and the scrupulous attention to food and wine, there are always some nice folks.

〜

CHAPTER THIRTY-SIX

A dalliance in the rain. A political rally.
Aida *Roman Style.*
Tights, cummerbunds and batmen.
Saturday weddings. Sunday elections.
The promise stone. Fashion sense and food sense.

FOR ME, THE WEATHER WAS FANTASTIC, OVERCAST AND drizzly. During a squall, I took shelter under a building's wide overhang at Largo Magnanapoli. This is not a largo for pedestrians; it is used to slow traffic. Via Nazionale becomes broader and busier as it climbs its steepest stretch and passes Banca D'Italia, a monolithic, neoclassic building with rows of well-groomed palm trees arrayed in front. Beyond the bank, the street grows more active again with medium-priced shops and a few theaters until it reaches Piazza Repubblica. In the center of the Largo, however, a few sad palm trees protect a piece of ancient wall, said to be an extension of the same sixth-century B.C. Servian Wall near the train station. New information came out recently placing its date at only 378 A.D. That makes it about nine hundred years younger than originally thought, but it is as endearing to me as it ever was.

A young fellow waited out the rain with me under the broad eaves. His shirt was frayed around the collar, his suit was seedy and he needed a shave, or was he imitating one of our current television heroes? In spite of his rumpled clothes, with his smooth, olive skin and startling hazel eyes, he managed to look like a million. When he asked if I was in Rome alone or with friends, I replied,

"*Sono con un amico,*" I am with a friend, emphasizing the masculine ending.

He probably assumed I didn't know one ending from another and went on to ask why my friend wasn't with me. Ignoring my effort to explain we were meeting soon, he offered to show me Rome that night.

"Rome is beautiful. Tonight I will show it to you."

"*Molte grazie*," I replied, "*Ma no.*" Many thanks, but no.

The confidence of Italians in most any situation, no matter what economic or social level they come from always amazes me. Yet, when I see how parents adore their children and constantly pet them and tell them how wonderful they are, maybe it's not so surprising. He didn't ask if I wanted to go with him, he announced that tonight he would take me on a tour of the city as if it had already been arranged. For someone who grew up apologizing for every action, that sort of arrogance was seductive. Struggling in Italy alone, I hoped some confidence would rub off on me.

The rain let up, he wished me well and left. It had been a pleasant way to pass the time, nothing else. Should I be flattered? I think not. A pass to a woman alone is almost *de rigueur*, especially if she is older and foreign. Who knows, she might be insulted if one didn't try.

⁓

Near Piazza Repubblica I passed the Opera House. *Aida* was opening that very night. Without hesitating, I went in and bought a ticket for the following evening. It cost 142,000 lire, ($86), a disaster for my budget, but in the end, I was glad. I could make up the money but not the opportunity.

On the day of the opera, I knew I should take it easy because it would be a late night, but I couldn't help myself and walked miles. First to the Campo for fruits and veggies, then back up three flights to my room. Then while I read the newspaper and sipped a cappuccino in a bar facing the Farnese Palace, I watched them set up for a political rally in the spacious Piazza Farnese. Signor Rutelli was running for mayor of Rome against Signor Fini. It was a coveted position. Rutelli was my choice because he was for providing services to the ordinary people of the city. Fini was for law and order and I recognized the code words for protecting the rich and powerful. Certain themes have always run through human politics, I suppose. In ancient Rome, there were senators arguing for law and order because they wanted to protect their local property bought with "lawful" spoils won in far away lands.

Fini had close ties with Mussolini's granddaughter, a successful politician herself from Naples. They were both members of the neo-fascist party. When opponents reminded them of the fascists of the 30s, Fini and Mussolini protested there were vast differences in their organization from the Black Shirt regime. These were exciting times for the Italians because in the coming election they would try out a different voting system. It would be more like our system in that the people would choose some leaders directly rather than leave all the choices to their elected officials.

Aida is always an exciting spectacle and I looked forward to seeing it in Rome, but it was a mixed blessing. The scenery and costumes were brilliant. They had substituted four magnificent white horses for the usual elephant in the imperial parade scene. At first I was disappointed, but the horses were gorgeous. Radames strained for every high note, and he didn't care a fig for poor Aida. The rumor that Italian opera fans are hard on their stars is true. In the final tomb scene, when his voice cracked a few times, the audience was unmerciful. The first time they murmured; when it happened again, they booed and hissed. I felt embarrassed for him.

The young woman playing Aida was much more talented than he, but our own Maureen O'Flynn in Portland could have sung rings around her. Ghena Dimitrova, ordinarily a marvelous dramatic soprano, was miscast as Amneris. Her voice was weak in the contralto part and the poor dear struggled mightily with yards and yards of heavy fabric which she was compelled to wear as the royal princess. What in the world was the costume designer up to? Why all the heavy drapery in Egypt when the rest of the production kept to the desert look?

The worst was the dancing, it was absurd. The bath scene, usually delightful with graceful dancers and acrobats, was ludicrous. The opera house was overheated, the pace of the production was ponderous, and it was nearly one-thirty in the morning before I fell into bed exhausted, but delighted with myself. One day, I would attend a performance at the mecca of all grand opera, La Scala in Milan. Surely they would have better singers and dancers.

A woman on the Metro wore black tights with shiny, knee-high boots and a black leather jacket that just reached her rear. She was in her mid-fifties. Her legs were okay, her behind was all right yet somehow she looked ridiculous. Was she advertising? Her manner was certainly not provocative. She appeared rather conservative except for the tight tights and short jacket. Strange. Most mid-age Italian women are either elegantly dressed or stodgily conservative. She was an interesting anomaly.

Do the baristas wear those wide black elastic cummerbunds for back support or tradition? Certainly they all wear them at the bar on the corner of Piazza Venezia where one pays an enormous price to have a coffee and watch the traffic show.

Italy has its own Batmen, the little padres. When they walk into the wind, their large sleeves billow out, their long skirts fly up behind them, and their white socks and sandals add a certain panache.

The derelict church called, Saint Nicholas in Prison, was open only for Sunday mass or special occasions, no doubt that meant for weddings, christenings and funerals. The outside fascinated me because columns from ancient pagan shrines were used as part of its outer support and were embedded into the walls. One Saturday, the door was open while wedding preparations were in progress. Inside, those columns I'd seen on the outside seemed to grow right out of the walls. The ceiling was lovely and looked freshly restored; its carved wood was gilded and had a ground of

Pagan pillars built into the church of Saint Nicholas in Prison.

brilliant blues. The walls were disappointing; they were of fake marble that hadn't worn well. Down the center aisle, white waxy flowers were tied to the ends of every pew; at the altar two stools waited for the couple. In front of those, were two kneeling boxes covered with plush cushioning and satiny bows. I stood in the back and watched while family members made their final touches, then I slipped out before anyone really noticed me.

Saturday must be the popular day for weddings. White bridal outfits dazzled in the Roman sunshine as brides stepped out of churches or out of the city hall onto Michelangelo's piazza at the Campidoglio. What a fabulous setting that was for dramatic photos.

Sunday was election day—how practical. People are out and about with a relaxed holiday attitude rather than having to hurry to the polls on Tuesdays before going to work or forcing themselves to vote after work when all they want to do is get home and put their feet up. Here, there's a financial penalty if voters miss more than two elections in a row, while some of our states still make it difficult for voters to even register. As we do at home, the voting places were in schools and public buildings. Rome's Monday papers would be interesting; I hoped Signor Rutelli would be the next Mayor of Rome.

At Piazza Navona people were swarming around an early Christmas carnival; the temperature was about seventy-five and families were out en masse. Most of the holiday booths were tawdry and depressing. They cluttered the lovely space and hid its fountains. I left.

I'd said I wouldn't visit Saint Peter's again that year, but Santa Maria in Cosmedin was being restored. I couldn't put my hand into the Mouth of Truth to assure my return, so I had to stand on the "spot" in the center of the Piazza di San Pietro and make my promise from there. The spot is a special paving stone from which all two hundred eighty-four pillars that comprise Bernini's stone curves look exactly like one column. There are two of these promise stones, each is equidistant from the obelisk in the center of the huge piazza.

Naturally, I went inside the huge church and feasted my eyes on Michelangelo's *Pietà* again. That beautiful teenage mother holding her thirty-three-year-old son was made when Michelangelo was scarcely twenty-one himself. When I left, I looked up at the magnificent dome he had designed and supervised when he was eight-six.

On Saint Peter's side of the river and just north of the huge church is a popular shopping street for nice things at moderate prices. After walking up one side and down the other on Via Cola di Rienzo, it was clear there were no decent long skirts to be found in the entire city. If they weren't here, they wouldn't be anywhere. How was it that I wanted a long skirt when I'd purposely decided to bring only slacks? Were the fashion conscious Italians getting to me? Sometimes a skirt feels more appropriate, more powerful. After all, the pope wears one.

Because of the Italians' strong sense of conformity to current style, it made sense that stores carried only skirts that would sell. There were several styles from skinny, pencil-slim ones; short, kicky ones; full pleated ones; and ones with slits up to the groin, but no simple, gored ones. I'd been to some shops behind Via Plebiscito, one of the streets that makes its headlong rush into Piazza Venezia. Hidden around a corner on a narrow alley were a couple of discount stores. One shop had a full-length skirt covered with sequins and the other had a skirt with feathers. Obviously, I was out of touch.

Only a year before, the young Italian women had been wearing short shorts with opaque tights or regular nylons. Naturally, on slender, young women they looked fantastic. Unlike their American counterparts, most Italian women over forty do not imitate teenage fads, and they have an excellent sense about what looks good on themselves. Italian men find mature women sexy so maybe these women ignore youthful fads because they do not feel in competition with the youngsters.

For the young, however, the fashion had returned to short, girdle-tight skirts. Again, they looked good, albeit a bit ridiculous because of constantly having to pull them down. When they bent over for any reason from their spiky, clunky shoes they had to squat awkwardly to keep their bottoms covered. Those are the burdens of the fashion conscious, or I should say self conscious because they seem thoroughly involved with their apparel, how they look, and what impression they're making. Added to this is their hair fetish. They part long hair on one side then swoop it over to the other so that it must, by nature, fall back for more swooshing. I wonder how they have time to use their brains for anything else. Ah, but that's not only Italian; that's the young. How liberating to be out of that trap, almost.

My own brain was stuck on a gorgeous wool *mantella*, a graceful garment part cape and part coat. It was in my shade of red, it was well cut and of excellent cloth. I should have gone in then and there because when I went back to the shop, the mantella was gone.

~

On a side street called Via Serpenti, which does slither down the hill from Via Nazionale toward Via Cavour, was a pleasant restaurant called Due Collone. The two white columns at the entrance were poor imitations of the real thing, but inside, the ravioli stuffed with ricotta and spinach were not imitations. With a mouth-watering porcini sauce ladled over the pasta, it was delectable. Instead of meat for the second course, I requested a plate of vegetables with a half order of *cicoria* and a half order of *pepperoni*. Pepperoni are sweet red and yellow peppers found in most Italian restaurants. Usually roasted and served with olive oil drizzled over them, they are delicious. Cicoria is a member of the chicory family. With a slightly piquant flavor, it's often served as a delicious substitute for spinach.

The owner and servers were pleasant in spite of my wrinkled blouse and I was treated with every respect not like the night before at a pizzeria in a different part of town near Albergo Pomezia. There, the waitress kept trying to clear things away before I had finished. This behavior is most unusual in Italy. She was not Italian, and her manager should have trained her. She brought the pizza primavera at the same time as the *bruschetti*, grilled pieces of bread with oil and herbs. When I frowned, she explained in English it was no problem because the primavera was a cold dish anyway. Their pizza primavera had a cold salad on it instead of cooked vegetables, so naturally the crust was soggy long before I got to it. Why the rush? In Italy, even in small holes-in-the-wall, one thing I can count on is not to be rushed. It seems I'd found the exception to that rule. I didn't like it one bit and never did find out if their pizza was as good as the guidebook claimed it to be.

For salad, I had requested lemon. When she offered to squeeze it for me, I was on to her. I knew she'd squirt a drop and snatch it away; I said no, politely. Well, not too politely. Two more times she tried to remove the lemon plate. That woman had no concept of what dining is all about!

◡⁀

CHAPTER THIRTY-SEVEN

An Etruscan altar.
Tumult in Navona and calm in Trastevere.
Bramante's dirty Tempietto.
Michelangelo's ruined Redeemer.
Final Rituals.

THE POSTER OF A NEW ETRUSCAN EXHIBIT CAUGHT MY eye at the main tourist office on Via Parigi. The exhibit was at La Sapienza of the University. I knew where La Sapienza was because I'd been there to see the hidden church of Sant'Ivo—Sapienza was clearly carved on the facade. But, my building was *not* the University of Rome. It had been in olden days, but no longer. No, no, I was told, no part of the University was there anymore; it was all in the northern section of the city. Oh dear, the City University was a long way from Corso del Rinascimento, and on the map, that area looked immense, so the next day, I went back to the tourist office for help. Although the colorful poster was on their front door, no one knew a thing about the exhibition. One woman was willing to go into a back room where she found a folder containing various materials. I wondered how to say "Odds and Ends" in Italian, no doubt that was the label on her folder. She found an article about the altar and kindly copied it for me.

Armed with that scrap of information, my next stop was the bus information booth in front of the train station. Having the bus number was not exactly a magic piece of information, however, and I began to think there was no such bus. Each official asked would point 'over there,' but my bus number was not listed on any post 'over there.' Persistence finally paid off and the bus did materialize approximately where everyone had been pointing. Some things are just so hard.

The bus driver agreed to tell me where to get off, but I sat close to the front in his line of sight so he wouldn't forget me. Eventually he pulled over, nodded and pointed vaguely toward a cluster of monumental buildings in the distance. I so appreciate Italian bus drivers; there must be a special place in heaven for them. Sometimes they are vexed with traffic and seem brusque, but time and again I've gone through this same exercise of asking the driver to tell me where to get off and of feeling anxious that he didn't understand or would forget. So far, they have never let me down.

After walking a few uncertain blocks wondering whether I should have come at all, I found myself in the midst of quadrangles of blocky, institutional buildings with students lolling about a modern fountain. I was getting close. There were signs pointing toward "Sapienza." Then I noticed that several buildings carried the word carved across their facade. This must be a word used by academicians to evoke lofty ideas rather than a particular place. Sure enough, when I consulted an expanded dictionary later, I found that the word sapienza "contains the weight of perfect wisdom both intellectually and morally." All I wanted to know at that moment was which "Sapienza" contained the Etruscan exhibit. Another niggling problem was the lateness of the hour; would the doors be closed? I was weakening and about to turn back. I tried one more building and showed one more custodian my copied article. He pointed upstairs.

Eccola! There it was! The terra-cotta altar was from the temple discovered on the coast at Pyrgi just north of Rome. Pyrgi was the Etruscans' port for ancient Caere now called Cerveteri. I had been so near when I visited the mound tombs at Caere/Cerveteri. The altar stood in the middle of the room with lights focused on it from all angles. The missing materials had been painstakingly inserted in a different color of plaster and easily identifiable. The authentic bits of terra cotta stood out clearly; it was amazing how few there were. No wonder it had taken years to reconstruct this altar frieze.

Before taking time to calm down and enjoy myself, I asked a young woman how long the exhibit would be open. She replied until seven. It was only five, I could relax and take time to locate the W.C. Now that I'd found the altar, I wasn't about to worry how to get back. Somehow I would make it to a bus, to the station, to another bus, and to my hotel.

The Altar Relief of Pyrgi was intriguing. Evidently, one of the figures is Athena, recognized by her helmet, and another is Zeus. According to the archaeologists, the theme of the altar relief involves two episodes in a failed expedition against Thebes. All were to have happened a generation before the siege of Troy. I was happy to leave the mythological details to the experts; it was enough to walk all around it. The best part was having it to myself. Later it would be moved to a permanent place in the Villa Giulia. Surely on another visit to Rome, I could see it there, but bureaucrats' plans have been known to change, and, the truth is, it was great to be among the first to see it.

Since I had read translations of books by Massimo Pallottino on his discoveries, particularly on his find in 1964 at this very temple, of those three gold sheets containing writings in Etruscan and Phoenician, I had developed an imaginary personal connection to him. There were yellowed newspaper clippings as far back as the 1950s showing photos of Pallottino with his colleagues and students at the site. He died in 1995 before this restoration could be completed, but he is considered the founder of modern Etruscology and the exhibition was dedicated to him.

My struggle to find the altar was worth it, and I indulged myself for about an hour. I came away with a beautifully illustrated booklet about it and the two temples at Pyrgi. It would keep me busy for a long time because they had nothing available in English. The jargon of this branch of archaeology isn't easy to decipher and general dictionaries are no help at all. I had a good challenge for the coming year.

My immediate challenge was to find my way out of the university campus onto a bus. Every bus stop I passed seemed to go in the opposite direction, but it was a beautiful fall evening. The setting sun turned to gold the few leaves still clinging to the trees. Success had put renewed energy in my step and in no time at all I found myself at Porta Pia not far from Saint Theresa's church. I was in familiar territory again, and I breathed a sigh of relief.

⌒

Another year, at Piazza Navona, handmade posters shouted in big letters that painters and caricaturists had been allowed to work there for thirty years. Obviously a movement was afoot to ban them for some reason. A television crew was filming the uproar. It may have been in response to a new edict from Mayor Rutelli. Senegalese peddlers had been monopolizing the piazza by placing their purses, belts and jewelry all around the fountains. The day before, I'd seen a photo in the newspaper showing one of the large fountains completely surrounded by these aggressive vendors. Although the young Senegalese men were pushy in trying to make sales, they always had gorgeous smiles. It usually took two or three "No's," and then they would always leave me alone. Evidently Rutelli had suggested banning all types of entrepreneurs in the piazza.

The filming crew was rude and aggressive. They shoved microphones into people's faces asking for opinions. When I said no thank you and started to move away from a woman tele-journalist, she snarled something about wasting her time!

Navona was no fun that day so I crossed the river, walked through Piazza Santa Maria in Trastevere and on up the hill to Bramante's famous Tempietto. Legend says the Tempietto was built near the spot where Saint Peter had been crucified upside down. In 1499, King Ferdinand and Queen Isabella of Spain commissioned Bramante to build the Tempietto. The small circular building is made entirely of travertine and consists of two parts: the lower has rectangular niches and windows with a Doric frieze and is surrounded by sixteen Tuscan columns. Bramante had looked back to the simple, Tuscan forms for function as well as elegance. Who cannot be pleased by those smooth Tuscan columns? The upper part has alternating rounded and rectangular niches with a perfect little cupola above. The idea must surely have been borrowed from the Temple of Vesta in the Forum.

It was so small, so perfect in proportion and so filthy. The door was securely locked, but it looked as if it might be in use because

*Ponte Rotta, Broken Bridge, a permanent testimony
to the power of the old Tiber.*

a small altar with items for worship were visible through the grimy windows. The view over the city was almost as good as at the top of Gianicolo Hill.

Near the Tempietto was an attractive building called the Spanish Academy. A flight of steps going down beside the Academy looked like a pleasant passageway, but just as I started down, a well-dressed man stood there peeing into the corner of the steps. I held my ground and when he turned, I glared my fiercest glare. He didn't seem the least bit embarrassed. "Barbarian!" I thought. Later I wished I'd have thought to call him a barbarian to his face. But, then why? I was in *his* territory.

Another route took me down quickly and I was again in Piazza Santa Maria in Trastevere. The church was open. I never tire seeing the mosaics and the various pillars and capitals used and reused in these old beauties. Stealing from pagan temples and other shrines to build new ones has been the Roman way since its beginning. Not far from the church was a quiet restaurant where I had a glass of white Orvieto Classico, with a pasta called frutte della mare, fruits of the sea. The chunks of seafood tossed in a light garlic sauce were delicious. It was followed by a pretty plate of savory white beans seasoned lightly with more garlic and herbs. The white beans were piled beside a mound of green broccoli. Only the coffee was disappointing. I hadn't asked specifically for espresso and heard no tell-tale hiss so it was probably Nescafe, the name Italians use for all instant coffee whether sold by the Nescafe company or not.

Leaving Trastevere, I stood for some time on Ponte Palatine with its ugly iron railings looking at *Ponte Rotta*, the Broken Bridge a few yards away. A portion of an ancient, grey stone bridge stands in the middle of the river with no beginning and no end. There were tufts of grass growing from its cracks like a scraggly beard grows on a broken old man. It was a picture opportunity for a professional. For me, a couple of snaps would trigger memories of another fine day in Rome.

Not far from The Pantheon is the church Santa Maria Sopra Minerva built over yet another pagan temple, this time the Temple of Minerva. Inside is an unusual, uncelebrated sculpture by Michelangelo called *The Redeemer.* He is almost nude holding his cross upright beside him. How different this figure is from Michelangelo's other works. He is an older man; in fact, he seems older than his legendary thirty-three years. Although his body seems well proportioned, there is something about the way he stands that seems a bit off.

The sculpture had been his second attempt because after Michelangelo had started the first, he discovered a flaw in the marble which would have put a mark across the face. Evidently, he was not entirely happy with this second rendition either. Adding more injury to the project, an assistant given the task of following the sculpture from Florence to Rome to finish some details did a poor job. Michelangelo wrote a desperate apology to the patron who had commissioned it on behalf of the church and offered to make a third. Signor Metello Vari wouldn't hear of such a sacrifice, besides they had waited a few years for the sculpture already. The artist responded by giving his patron the unfinished, flawed figure of the first model. Signor Vari then responded from his own coffers by giving Signor Buonarroti a fine horse in token of his appreciation. Maybe Michelangelo kept the horse when he moved to Rome. Maybe it was the same one he rode as an old man in his eighties to Saint Peter's every day to supervise the rebuilding going on there.

The *Redeemer* is definitely a weighty body. Maybe it seems so because it represents a more mature body than the *David* who was in the bloom of firm-fleshed youth. Here, gravity has begun its inevitable pull on the sinews of the figure's arms, his legs and especially the buttocks.

It may be the first and only instance in which the Christ figure was represented entirely nude, but to Michelangelo the nudity symbolized that he was also Resurrected Man. Not long after it was placed here, some of the ecclesiastical powers decided to cover up his genitals with a wrap of a material that looks like a metallic golden cloth. A silly, half golden bow is attached at the crucial spot. Instead of being honest, the sculpture now seems obscene. Michelangelo would be horrified.

No matter how many times I visit Rome, the last couple of days begin to press on my spirit. I feel an impending sense of loss. It's always the same. There's a melancholia I cannot shake. It helps keep the depression at bay if I observe certain rituals of farewell. The burden comes from the terrifying fear of never coming back, of never feasting my eyes on the streets or feeling the breath of Rome on my skin again. Whatever it is, I become a pilgrim who is required to visit certain holy places. I feel heartsick to be leaving all of Italy, but especially Rome where her citizens are the ultimate urbanites: fashionable, arrogant, hurried, helpful, humorous, friendly, kind, sophisticated, suave, crude, and rude, and I love them all.

Of course, I wander through the market at Campo dei Fiori and have a last look at the three fountains all in a row within Piazza Navona's oval. Most of the Senegalese vendors have gone; the regular street artists are back. All is well. Through the south end of

Navona and across a street or two, the church and cloister of Santa
Maria della Pace continues to hide under restoration covers.
Patience, I murmur. Cars have angle-parked into the tiny piazza,
and a small vegetable market has been crammed onto the side of
Caffè della Pace as well. Things change. Caffè Bramante, the one
with the trompe-l'oeil murals and the wavy glass, is being torn up.
They are gutting the floor. The same officious blond fellow is
there; after a few remarks to the workers, he roars off on his
motorcycle. This area may become a hangout for the restless, and
Caffè Bramante may be transformed into a noisy disco. Too bad, I
think, but Rome is a vibrant lady and if one loves her, one accepts
her changes.

The central train station looks fabulous. At long last the construction around the new entrances to the Metro is completed and
all the debris is gone. This is what the architect originally had in
mind with the sleek, modern station functioning beside the
ancient tufa wall. It looks fine. The derelicts are gone, no more
beer bottles and trash, no more stench of stale urine, and across
the street beside the ancient Diocletian Baths no more signs of
degradation are there either.

Still moving under an impulse to observe certain rites or
"Stations of Departure," I decide to call on Santa Teresa, but her
doors are closed. Farther down her street, I feel drawn into the
territory through Porta Pia. This is the inviting boulevard with its
large leafy trees that had beckoned once before. Few tourists are
here and fewer shops, but on a side street is a small, plain bar
where I have a simple sandwich of cheese and tomatoes. With a
delicious cappuccino, all are served outside, and *il conto*, the bill,
comes to 3000 lire ($1.85). For sure, I have wandered away from
the tourist area; this same purchase and service in central Rome
would be at least 10,000 lire.

One of the last days' rituals is to put my hand into the Mouth of
Truth and make the promise. Lucky again, nothing bites me, I'll
return.

I take one more brief walk to Repubblica's fountain knowing the water will continue to spray the air long after I've gone. Then, to Piazza Barberini, where water shoots high above the *Triton's* elegant head. Before I know it there I am on Via Sistina beneath that 1962 window where it all started. With all of Rome below, I stand on the top of the Spanish Steps. Twelve flights of twelve steps and each platform offers a different last view. Slowly and heavily I descend knowing when I reach the street, it really is time to leave.

Sources and Recommended Reading

Acton, Harold & Chaney, Edward, *Florence, A Traveler's* Companion.

Alexander, Sidney, *Michelangelo The Florentine.*

_____ *The Hand of Michelangelo.*

_____ *Nicodemus, the Roman Years.*

Astronomy, *Giordano Bruno* - www.astronomy.mps.Ohio
State.edu.essays

Avery, Charles, *Florentine Renaissance Sculpture.*

Beny, Roloff, Text by Peter Gunn, *The Churches of Rome.*

Berenson, Bernard, *Italian Painters of the Renaissance.*

_____ *Looking at Pictures with Bernard Berenson.*

_____ *The Passionate Sightseer.*

Bloch, Raymond, *The Ancient Civilization of the Etruscans.*

Cambridge Ancient History, *The Augustan Empire.*

Carr-Gomm, Sarah, *The Dictionary of Symbols in Western Art.*

Chastel, Andre', *Italian Art.*

Cipolla, Carlo M., *Money, Prices & Civilization in the
Mediterranean World.*

Clark, Eleanor, *Rome and a Villa.*

Clark, Kenneth, *The Art of Humanism.*

_____ *Leonardo da Vinci.*

Clements, Robert J., ed., *Michelangelo: A Self Portrait.*

_____ *Michelangelo's Theory of Art*

Condivi, Ascanio, *The Life of Michelangelo.*

Conroy, Pat, *Beach Music.*

Cremona, Joseph and The BBC, *Buongiorno Italia!*

Dante: His Life. His times. His works. (Giants of World Literature).

DeWald, Ernest T., *Italian Painting 1200-1600.*

Dundes, Alan & Alessandro Falassi, *La Terra in Piazza—the story
of the Palio in Siena.*

Biadena, Susannah, *Titian: Prince of Painters.*

Franzero, Carlo Maria, *The Life and Times of Tarquin the Etruscan.*

Gibbons, John: *Afoot in Italy. 1932.*

Goldscheider, Ludwig, Michelangelo: *Paintings, Sculptures, Architecture.,*
Phaidon Publishers. 1953.

Gough, Michael, *The Origins of Christian Art.*

Grant, Michael, *The Roman Emperors.*

_____ *Ancient History.*

_____ *The Etruscans.*

_____ *Myths of the Greeks and Romans.*

_____ *History of Rome.*

Hellenga, Robert, *The Sixteen Pleasures.*

Hamblin, Dora Jane, *The Etruscans.*

_____ *Pots and Robbers.*

Hamilton, Edith, *The Roman Way*

Hamlyn, Paul, *Man and the Renaissance.*

Hampton, Christopher, *The Etruscan Survival.*

Harrison, Barbara Grizzuti, *Italian Days.*

Hartt, Frederick, *Italian Renaissance Art.*

Hauser, E. O., *Italy, A Cultural Guide.*

Hibbert, Christopher, *The Rise and Fall of the House of Medici.*

Higson, John W., Jr., *A Historical Guide to Florence.*

Hofman, Paul, *A Guide to the "Hundred Cities and Towns" of Italy.*

_____ *The Seasons of Rome: A Journal.*

_____ *The Sweet Tempestuous Life.*

Hollingsworth, Mary, *Patronage in Sixteenth Century Italy.*

Hooper, Finley, *Roman Realities.*

James, Henry, *Italian Hours.*

_____ *Henry James on Italy.*

_____ *Florentine Notes.*

Janson, H. W., *History of Art*

Johnson, Kevin Orlin, *Why Do Catholics Do That?*

Keates, Jonathan, *Tuscany.*

Kelen, Emery, ed., *Leonardo Da Vinci's Advice to Artists.*

Keller, Werner, *The Etruscans.*

Landon, H.C. Robbins, *Vivaldi.*

Langton, Jane, *The Dante Game.*

Lawrence, D. H., *Etruscan Places.*

Letta, Elisabetta Marchetti, *Pontormo. Rosso Fiorentino.*

Levey, Michael, *Florence, A Portrait.*

_____ *Early Renaissance.*

Lewis, Norman, *The Honored Society.*

Lewis, R. W. B., *The City of Florence.*

Lewis, R.W.B., *Dante*

Liberman, Alexander & Joseph Brodsky, *Campidoglio: Michelangelo's Roman Capitol.*

Lintner, Valerio, *A Travelers' History of Italy.*

McCarthy, Mary, *The Stones of Florence.*

McCullough, Colleen, *The First Man in Rome.*

_____ *The Grass Crown.*

_____ *Fortunes' Favorites.*

_____ *Caesar's Women.*

Macaulay, Thomas Babington, *Macaulay's Lays of Ancient Rome.* "Horatius", www.bath.ac.uk.

Manchester, William, *A World Lit Only By Fire.*

Manetti, Tuccio, *The Life of Brunelleschi.*

Massa, Aldo, *The Etruscans.*

Mate', Ferenc, *The Hills of Tuscany: A New Life in an Old Land.*

Meiss, Millard, *The Great Age of Fresco*

More, Julian & Carey, *Views From a Tuscan Vineyard.*

Morton, C. V., *A Traveler in Rome.*

_____ *Italy.*

_____ *The Fountains of Rome.*

Murray, Chris, ed., *Cultural Atlas of the World: The Renaissance.*

Murray, Peter, *The Architecture of the Italian Renaissance.*

Newby, Eric, *On the Shores of the Mediterranean.*

Nolan, Louis, *The Basilica of San Clemente in Rome.*

O'Faolain, Sean, *A Summer in Italy.*

Pallottino, Massimo, *The Meaning of Archaeology.*

_____ *The Etruscans.*

Parks, Tim, *Italian Neighbors.*

_____ *Italian Education.*

Partner, Peter, *Renaissance Rome 1500-1559: A Portrait of a Society.*

Penguin Books, *How to Recognize Renaissance Art.*

Radice, Betty, *Who's Who in the Ancient World.*

Ragghianti, Carlo Ludovico, ed., *Uffizzi: Great Museums of the World.*

Richardson, Emeline Hill, *The Etruscans: Their Art and Civilization.*

Riggs, Arthur Stanley, *Titian the Magnificent.*

Roeder, Ralph, *The Man of the Renaissance.*

Roth, Leland M., *Understanding Architecture.*

Skira, Albert, ed., *The Great Centuries of Painting: Etruscan Painting.*

Schevill, Ferdinand, *Medieval and Renaissance Florence: Vol.I- Medieval Florence. Vol.II-The coming of humanism and the age of the Medici.*

Sobel, Dava, *Galileo's Daughter.*

Spender, Matthew, *Within Tuscany.*

Sheridan, Michael, *Romans: Their Lives and Times.*

Stambaugh, John E., *The Ancient Roman City.*

Stone, Irving and Jean, *I, Michelangelo, Sculptor.*

Theroux, Paul, *The Pillars of Hercules.*

Thynne, Roger, *The Churches of Rome.*

Time-Life Books, *Etruscans: Italy's Lovers of Life.*

_____ *The World of Titian.*

Trease, Geoffrey, *The Italian Story.*

Vasari, Giorgio, *Lives of the Painters, Sculptors, and Architects.*

Wallace, Robert, *The World of Bernini: Time/Life Books.*

Wallace, William, *Michelangelo: The Complete Sculpture, Painting & Architecture.*

Ward-Perkins, John B., *Roman Architecture.*

Wellard, James, *The Search for the Etruscans.*

Wittkower, Rudolf, *Art and Architecture in Italy 1600-1750.*

Wind, Edgar, *Pagan Mysteries in the Renaissance.*

Guide Books

Let's Go, The Budget Guide to Italy. 1992 and 1996.

Macadam, Alta, Blue Guide - Rome. 1998

Macadam, Alta, Blue Guide - Florence. 1995

Michelin Tourist Guide, *Italy,* 1998.

Holler, Anne, *Florence Walks.*

Anya M. Shetterly, *Rome Walks*

Insight Cityguides, *Rome.*

Index

About the Writer

Ever since her third-grade teacher asked for a long report about Ancient Rome, Italy has fascinated Hill. When she finally visited there, it was love at first sight, sound and taste. It's where she feels best both physically and spiritually. Coming from a small town in Nebraska and with no ties to Italy, nevertheless, she has a passion for this timeless land. She suspects that she may have trod some of the same paths as her favorite Etruscans who lived in an ancient hill town called Orvieto. In present time, Marlene lives with her husband in Portland, Oregon, but no matter where she is, her heart and soul remain in Italia.

About the Artist

Deanna Hunt is a native California artist who has traveled extensively throughout Italy and Europe. She lived in Rome for eight years where she painted, taught and conducted art and cultural tours. The artist now lives and works in San Francisco, California.